FROM REBELLION
TO REFORM IN BOLIVIA

Class Struggle, Indigenous Liberation, and the Politics of Evo Morales

Jeffery R. Webber

Haymarket Books
Chicago, Illinois

© 2011 Jeffery R. Webber

Published in 2011 by Haymarket Books
PO Box 180165
Chicago, IL 60618
773-583-7884
info@haymarketbooks.org
www.haymarketbooks.org

ISBN: 978-1-60846-106-6

Trade distribution:
In the U.S. through Consortium Book Sales and Distribution, www.cbsd.com
In Canada, Publishers Group Canada, www.pgcbooks.ca
In the UK, Turnaround Publisher Services, www.turnaround-uk.com
In Australia, Palgrave Macmillan, www.palgravemacmillan.com.au
All other countries, Publishers Group Worldwide, www.pgw.com

This book was published with the generous support of Lannan Foundation
and the Wallace Global Fund.

Cover design by Eric Ruder. All interior photographs by Jeffery R. Webber.

Special discounts are available for bulk purchases by organizations and institutions.
Please contact Haymarket Books for more information at 773-583-7884 or
info@haymarketbooks.org.

Printed in Canada by union labor on recycled paper containing 100 percent
postconsumer waste in accordance with the guidelines of the Green Press Initiative,
www.greenpressinitiative.org.

Library of Congress Cataloging in Publication data is available.

10 9 8 7 6 5 4 3 2 1

For Tieneke

Contents

Acknowledgments

The research for this book was made possible through the financial support of the International Development Research Centre (IDRC) and a Sir Val Duncan Travel Award from the Munk Centre for International Studies at the University of Toronto. All translation was done by the author. Sections of Chapters One, Two, and Three are drawn from my three-part article "Rebellion to Reform in Bolivia," which appeared in *Historical Materialism*, vol. 16, nos. 2, 3, and 4, 2008. Chapter Four draws on sections of my article, "Dynamite in the Mines and Bloody Urban Clashes: Indigenous Ascendant Populism and the Limits of Reform in Bolivia's Movement Towards Socialism," in *Socialist Studies/Études Socialistes*, vol. 4, no. 1, 2008.

This book is partially the product of fieldwork conducted in Bolivia between January and September 2005 and May and June 2006. More than eighty formal interviews were conducted with leading indigenous activists, social movement leaders, trade unionists, and individuals who later became prominent officials in the Movimiento al Socialismo (Movement Toward Socialism, MAS) government. I am indebted to each of them for having shared with me their hopes, aspirations, and analyses of the conjuncture in Bolivia.

Thanks to Forrest Hylton and Luis A. Gómez for assistance with initial contacts in Bolivia and for discussing with me many of the central themes taken up in this book, to David Camfield for commentary on my dispatches from Bolivia, to Todd Gordon for repeated conversations on the Latin American scene and an ongoing writing partnership, and to Susan Spronk for insightful comments on early drafts. Sinclair Thomson provided feedback and encouragement on early versions of parts of this manuscript. David McNally has gone out of his way on several occasions to support the research that went into this book.

Silvia Escóbar de Pabón, an economist at the vitally important Centro de Estudios para el Desarrollo Laboral y Agrario (Center for Labor and Agrarian Development Studies, CEDLA) in La Paz, deserves special thanks for having shared with me her latest research on the labor market in Bolivia. Thanks to Sebastian Budgen, who encouraged me to pursue Haymarket Books as a publisher for this manuscript. At Haymarket, Anthony Arnove and Julie Fain were enthusiastic from the outset, and showed a great deal of patience as several deadlines passed. Tom Lewis read the manuscript carefully and provided crucial insights.

My family has seen me through the years involved in research and writing for this project.

Introduction

Evo Morales, of the *Movimiento al Socialismo* (Movement Toward Socialism, MAS), was elected president of Bolivia on December 18, 2005, with an historic 54 percent of the popular vote, and was reelected in December 2009 with 64 percent.[1] Morales is the first indigenous president in the republic's history, a particularly salient fact in a country where 62 percent of the population self-identified as indigenous in the last census in 2001.[2] The MAS is often associated, in popular and academic media alike, with the harder left current (Venezuela and Cuba) of a more general "pink tide" sweeping Latin America through the ballot box. How should we interpret the electoral victory of the MAS, and what is its significance for revolutionary or reformist social change in the poorest country in South America, where even official figures suggest 67 percent of the population currently lives in poverty?

Part I of this book grapples with these questions through its evaluation of the first year (January 2006 to January 2007) of the MAS government. It does so by shedding some light on the following topics: the character of the elections that brought the MAS to office; the historical trajectory of the party; the political economy of Bolivia under the first year of the administration; crucial developments in the Constituent Assembly process; the slow rearticulation of the racist autonomist right and its class and geographical bases in the eastern part of the country; and the

1

dynamics of imperialism at the international scale and weight of changes in the regional politics of Latin America in terms of how they influence the domestic balance of social forces in Bolivia. Such a wide scope has its strengths and weaknesses. It obviously sacrifices some depth for breadth. Yet, at the same time, it has the virtue of sketching broad overarching trends of a political process that has captured the imagination of the international left in the current period in a manner unparalleled except perhaps by Venezuela under Hugo Chávez. The aim is to offer an overall portrait of some of the key dynamics of the Bolivian process, something that has not yet been accomplished sufficiently in English. Such a perspective, I argue, calls into question many of the assumptions and conclusions of the existing analyses of contemporary Bolivia, whether from the right or left. Undoubtedly, some uncritical supporters of the Morales government will see the analysis offered here as little more than unctuous sectarianism. Be that as it may, it is necessary to rupture the debilitating torpor that has descended on the bulk of the left's discussions of the Bolivian process. Many analysts have heedlessly replaced careful examination of empirical reality with casual celebration of press releases issued from the presidential palace of Evo Morales. A responsible perspective, authentically in solidarity with the popular struggles for socialism and indigenous liberation in Bolivia, can ill afford such tact. That said, I offer sixteen theses in an attempt to push the debate forward.

Thesis 1: The left-indigenous insurrectionary period between 2000 and 2005 is best conceived as a *revolutionary epoch* in which mass mobilization from below and state crisis from above opened up opportunities for fundamental, transformative structural change to the state and society. The rural and urban rebellions of this period were a combined liberation struggle to end the interrelated processes of class exploitation and racial oppression of the indigenous majority.

Thesis 2: Following the second Gas War in May–June 2005, the focus of popular politics shifted temporarily from the streets and countryside to the electoral arena in the lead-up to the December 18, 2005, presidential and legislative elections. The move to the terrain of electoral politics and the victory of the MAS in the December elections dampened the immediate prospects of a socialist and indigenous-liberationist revolution growing out of the revolutionary epoch of 2000–2005. This is so because of the moderately reformist nature of the MAS party, the relative decline in the self-organization and self-activity of the popular classes and oppressed indigenous nations in the wake of the first electoral victory of Evo Morales (who seemed to represent their interests), and the common tendency for social movements to sap themselves of their transformative energy, organization, and capacity to build popular power from below in workplaces and communities when they adopt a preeminently electoral focus.

Thesis 3: The December elections were characterized by the fundamental breakdown of the traditional neoliberal parties in Bolivia, which had reigned supreme through various coalitional governments since 1985. The electoral results exemplified the popular disgust in Bolivia for neoliberalism as an economic and political model.

Thesis 4: The trajectory of the MAS as a party needs to be understood in the context of its shifting class composition, ideology, and political strategy over time. The party originated as the political arm of an indigenous-peasant movement in the department of Cochabamba in the mid-1990s. It was anti-imperialist and anti-neoliberal. It was modeled on the assembly-style, rank-and-file democracy of the peasant unions in the region. Its primary social base was the *cocaleros* (coca growers) who were fighting against the machinations of the militarized, U.S.-led "drug war" against their livelihoods. Extra-parliamentary activism was the essential strategy of the party from the late 1990s until 2002. Since 2002, however, the MAS has emphasized electoral politics and distanced itself from radical activism in the streets. The highest echelons of the party's decision-making structures came increasingly under the influence of an urban, mestizo (mixed race) intelligentsia of the middle class. The party's ideology became increasingly reformist as a consequence of this shift in the class composition of its upper leadership layers, as well as through the party's effort to court the urban middle class in electoral contests. The ascendancy of Álvaro García Linera to the vice presidency is a major indication of this trend.

Thesis 5: The Morales victory was a democratic gain in race relations in Bolivia in the sense that indigenous rights fully entered the national political agenda in an unprecedented manner after decades of in-digenous movement struggle.[3] The rise of a party with a largely indige-nous social base and an agenda prioritizing indigenous issues has been an important step toward bringing an end to white-mestizo minority control of the state and an apartheid-like culture of race relations in the country. However, there are also disturbing parallels with the 1994 elec-toral victory of the African National Congress (ANC) in South Africa and the ANC's subsequent political trajectory. Indigenous liberation has been disassociated from the project of revolutionary socialist trans-formation within the MAS. The combined liberation struggle for in-digenous liberation and socialist transformation of 2000 to 2005 has been altered into a struggle of distinct stages. The MAS emphasizes in-digenous liberation today, with socialist transformation only a remote possibility, fifty to one hundred years in the future.

Thesis 6: In many ways, MAS government policy and the class in-terests it serves represents a significant degree of continuity with the in-herited neoliberal model. Possible exceptions to this general continuity over the first year in office were discernable in hydrocarbon (natural gas and oil) policy, foreign relations with Venezuela and Cuba, and re-lations with the International Monetary Fund (IMF).

Thesis 7: Popular social movements, beginning especially with the Cochabamba Water War in 2000, put forward the demand for a revolu-tionary Constituent Assembly that would fundamentally transform the Bolivian economy, state, and society in the interests of the poor indige-nous majority. This vision included the organic participation of the main social movement organizations in the formation and execution of the assembly. The Constituent Assembly actually introduced by the MAS government in 2006 precluded all such revolutionary and partici-patory components. Instead, it resembled the traditional politics of the Congress because the MAS made overt efforts to appease the bour-geoisie of the eastern part of the country concerning the rules defining the assembly's conduct and content. The failure to institute a revolu-tionary Constituent Assembly provided room for the rearticulation of right-wing forces. While the Bolivian right was perhaps at its weakest politically in the winter of 2005, because of the room afforded to it by the MAS it began to rearticulate a political project in the form of right-wing autonomism in the departments of Pando, Beni, Santa Cruz, and Tarija.[4] The autonomists obstructed the functioning of the Constituent Assembly process introduced by the MAS and increased the threat of civil war at various junctures in 2006.

Thesis 8: The domestic instability and social polarization within Bolivia, in conjunction with weaker-than-usual imperial threats, and a favorable regional dynamic elsewhere in South America, may yet lead to a renewal of racialized class struggle from below and to deeper, perhaps even structural, reforms on the part of the MAS government. For this to transpire the *combined liberation struggle* of the revolutionary epoch witnessed in the first five years of the twenty-first century would need to express itself with new life, in dramatic form, from below. The most important allies in the regional context are Venezuela and Cuba. New ties with these countries have afforded Bolivia more autonomy from imperialist forces than would have been possible otherwise. Also, the relative decline in the power of the International Monetary Fund (IMF) in Latin America as a whole, and the choice by the Bolivian government not to renew its Stand-By Agreement with the IMF when it expired in March 2006 were positive developments during the first year of the Morales government.[5] At the same time, Bolivia's foreign policy was rife with contradictions. The Bolivian state maintained troops in occupied Haiti even as MAS officials spoke of Latin American liberation from imperialism. The Bolivian government also continued to seek a bilateral trade agreement with the United States. The United States, for its part, carried on with its attempts to influence the Bolivian process by way of the "drug war" and "democracy promotion." The trajectory of the Bolivian process therefore remained uncertain after the first year, even if discernible patterns were available to those who looked closely.

Thesis 9: Much of the existing literature, both academic and otherwise, tends to pit conflicts arising over Morales's first year in office as those of a homogeneous left, embodied in the MAS, against an equally coherent right, represented by the bourgeois-autonomist opposition of the *media luna*, or eastern lowland departments. The scene on the ground during the first year was substantially more complex. There were different occasions where popular social forces to the left of the MAS sought to express their dissatisfaction with the limited reforms of the government through direct actions of their own, even while defending the government against the reactionary far right and threats of imperialism. Two obvious examples are the violent confrontations between unionized, state-employed miners and cooperative miners at the Huanuni mine in October 2006, and the urban insurrection against a hated, right-wing prefect in the department of Cochabamba in January 2007.

If Part I of this book documents the trajectory of rebellion in the streets and countryside between 2000 and 2005 to reform in the presidential palace in the opening year of the Morales administration, Part II tracks the consolidation of that shift in popular politics toward a reconstituted neoliberalism. Another set of theses is advanced to address this later period.

Thesis 10: When Evo Morales won a second term in office in the December 6, 2009, elections, a new pivotal phase in contemporary Bolivian politics was introduced. Morales won 64 percent of the vote, and control of both houses of the Congress, on a turnout of close to 90 percent.[6] These results came on the heels of victories for the MAS in the recall referendum of 2008 and the popular referendum for the approval of the new constitution in January 2009. Moreover, the December elections were followed by MAS victories in six of nine governorship races in the departmental elections of April 2010.[7] This level of institutional consolidation of political power within the apparatuses of the state is unprecedented in recent Bolivian history.

Thesis 11: The reelection of Morales in December 2009 ignited a wave of veritable euphoria in leftist circles throughout Latin America and internationally. Much of this celebatory response relies heavily on the regime's image-promotion and Morales's supposed commitment to communitarian socialism. Within Bolivia, the theoretical debates on the origins and character of the MAS are more firmly rooted in reality. Getting a handle on these competing intellectual currents can be enlightening when this understanding is related to the historical conditions out of which they arose.

It is argued that three principal intellectual camps have emerged that in many ways reflect the contradictory and complex social and political forces at work in the country. There are, first, those intellectuals who rally to the defense of the social hierarchies and political-economic structures of capitalist development ensconced in the neoliberal model constructed in the country since 1985. Within this camp, there are conservatives who exaggerate the radicalism of the MAS, and who favor regime change as a means of neoliberal restoration. Alongside the conservatives are liberals who share a reverence for the basic foundations of the neoliberal order, but understand the Morales government to be an effective dam against the flood of radical left-indigenous revolt that might otherwise erupt in the context of an extreme legitimacy crisis of neoliberalism. The liberals have a more or less realistic analysis of the limited scope and depth of socioeconomic reform actually carried out by the Morales regime in its first term in office but are, at the same time, interested in circumventing any moves toward further, more structural, changes to the development model.

A second intellectual current brings together divergent streams behind a singular loyalty to the MAS government: moderate promoters of indigenous rights who advocate the advance of multiculturalism dissociated from, or at least unconcerned with, any socioeconomic transformations of the country's class structure and development model; social democratic and populist moderates who overlap ideologically with the liberals but who are more faithful to the MAS as a project; and an eclectic array of anticapitalists, some of whom believe Morales has planted the seeds for radical transformative change just over the horizon, and others who acknowledge the modesty of the encroachments on neoliberalism, but see in those subtle moves the only realistic change possible given the structural constraints of global capitalism.

A third group, a critical left-indigenous collection of thinkers, is congealed around a politics of revolutionary indigenous liberation and anticapitalist transformation of the Bolivian state, society, and economy. While committed to the defense of the Morales administration against destabilization campaigns from the domestic right and various imperialist forces, this current also believes that the break with neoliberalism actually introduced in recent years has been exaggerated by the

Morales administration. Rather than waiting for transformative change to come from on high in the form of state officials aligned with the MAS, this group views agency rooted in the struggles and capacities of the exploited and oppressed themselves, working independently from the MAS.

Thesis 12: The development model that gradually unfolded over the entire four years of the first MAS administration (2006–2010) is best understood by locating it within wider debates that have exploded throughout the Global South since the mid-1990s. A crisis of neoliberal legitimacy has made itself increasingly visible, however unevenly, across large swaths of the Global South over the last fifteen years. The latest crisis in global capitalism, beginning in 2008, has accelerated this trend. The response of ruling classes and their organic intellectuals has been adaptation, not transformation, of the neoliberal project. A new consensus in mainstream political economy circles, international financial institutions, and state managers in the Global South suggests that unbridled market fundamentalism has been insufficient and is unsustainable in light of the intense social conflicts it tends to produce. The best way to facilitate the full flourishing of the market, the new consensus argues, is to embed the market in a coherent set of institutions, with a more active state that engineers subtle movements in Adam Smith's famous "invisible hand." The state might even need to take control, directly or indirectly, of the means of production and allocation in order for the market to perform.

Internationally, the latest development approach is most commonly known as "neoinstitutionalism," but in Latin America it is more frequently called "neostructuralism," and has been associated with the United Nations Economic Commission for Latin America and the Caribbean (ECLAC) since roughly the mid-1990s. While neostructuralism signifies an advance from neoliberal orthodoxies, it continues to obfuscate key components of class relations under capitalism and mischaracterizes the state as a neutral actor, fairly arbitrating between perennially conflicting interest groups. The state's role in reproducing the conditions for accumulation and enabling the generation of profits for private capital is concealed, as is its repressive role in policing the inevitable class conflicts, struggles, and explosions of resistance that occur in response to the exploitation, alienation, and dispossession inherent to capitalist society. In reality, the state maintains capitalist order and seeks to regulate its social contradictions, and it does so in the economic and political interests of the ruling class. Class exploitation and the state repression it frequently necessitates are constituent elements of capitalism as a system, not episodic or anomalous phenomena as neostructuralists like to imagine.

Thesis 13: Latin American neostructuralism as a theory of development has sanitized ECLAC's classical conceptualizations of Latin American political economy by excluding the thematic foci of conflict and power relations from its analytical lens and policy prescriptions. Indeed the new theory is better described as a reconstituted neoliberalism. This theoretical and practical shift across large parts of Latin America, from neoliberal orthodoxy to a reconstituted neoliberalism under the guise of neostructuralism, has played itself out in the Bolivian context in ways specific to the country.

We suggested earlier that the first year of the administration showed deep continuities with the inherited neoliberal model. Alone, the record of the first year might be dismissed as too early to detect any coherent pattern. However, an examination of the political economy of the Morales government over the next three years (2007–2010) reveals the deepening and consolidation of the initial trend toward a reconstituted neoliberalism. This is a tendency, not a law, and the trajectory of the Bolivian economy clearly continues to be subject to the changing dynamics of domestic and regional class struggles, formations, and alliances, as well as the changing character of global capitalism and geopolitical strategies of large imperial powers in the hierarchical world system of states. That said, it is still important to record the observable and structural trend toward the consolidation of reconstituted neoliberalism in the first term of the Morales government.

Thesis 14: Most of Morales's first four years can be described, from an economic perspective, as high growth and low spending. Prior to the fallout of the worldwide economic crisis, which really started to impact the Bolivian economy in late 2008 and early 2009, the country's gross domestic product (GDP) had grown at an average of 4.8 percent under Morales. It peaked at 6.1 percent in 2008, and dropped to an estimated 3.5 percent in 2009, which was still the highest projected growth rate in the region. This growth was based principally on high international prices in hydrocarbons (especially natural gas) and various mining minerals common in Bolivia.

Government revenue increased dramatically because of changes to the hydrocarbons tax regime in 2006. But fiscal policy remained austere until the global crisis struck. Morales ran budget surpluses, tightly reigned in inflation, and accumulated massive international reserves by Bolivian standards. Public investment in infrastructure, particularly road building, increased significantly, but social spending rose only modestly in absolute terms, and actually declined as a percentage of GDP under Morales. Fiscal policy changed in 2008 and 2009, as a consequence of a sharp stimulus package designed to prevent recession in the face of the global crisis.[8]

Thesis 15: The social consequences of reconstituted neoliberalism have been almost no change in poverty rates under Morales, and deep continuities in social inequality. Both of these axes persist as monumental obstacles standing in the way of social justice in the country.

Thesis 16: One of the dominant theoretical and practical innovations of Latin American neostructural economic theory has been *proactive labor flexibility,* or the prioritization of state efforts to build consensus among workers around submission to the imperatives of export-led capitalist development in a fiercely competitive world system. States attempt to co-opt and reengineer labor movements so that they abandon class struggle in favor of cross-class cooperation and stability in labor-state relations. This synergistic relationship is thought to make all social classes winners under the development model, and advance "systemic competitiveness" of the country as it inserts itself ever more deeply into international markets. In Bolivia under the MAS, this framework has taken the form of strategic co-optation and division of labor and peasant movements on the part of state managers, while capital simultaneously seeks to deepen the flexibility and precariousness of the workforce to its advantage. While the rate of exploitation has risen under the MAS, the strategy of the state and capital has not unfolded seamlessly. Class contradictions inherent to the development model are slowly generating cracks and conflict, expressed in episodic strikes and other social movements such as those in the Colquiri mining district in 2009, and the teacher, factory worker, miner, and health care worker strikes of May 2010. These may signal the renewal of collective action from the left of the MAS, something that could very well grow in the near future so long as the Morales administration continues to pursue an economic model based in reconstituted neoliberalism.

Structure of the Book

Chapter One aims to introduce the basic class structure of Bolivia, set the country's political economic process into the context of changes in Latin America more broadly, and delineate the current threats and opportunities posed by the contemporary state of capitalist imperialism for the advance of transformative change. Subsequent chapters in Part I will assess the theoretical debates on revolution in the country, chart the revolutionary epoch of 2000 to 2005, examine the results of the December 18, 2005, general elections, and explore the origins, ideology, changing class composition, and leadership of the MAS party. They will also provide a sweeping bird's-eye view of a number of characteristics defining the political economy and indigenous politics of the MAS government's first months in office and examine some of the specificities of the supposed nationalization of hydrocarbons (natural gas and oil) announced through a presidential decree on May 1, 2006. Additionally, they will analyze the contours of the Constituent Assembly process in 2006, and the rise of the autonomist right of the media luna departments. Finally, Part I closes with a focused examination of the Huanuni mining conflicts of 2006, the leftist uprisings against a right-wing prefect in the department of Cochabamba in January 2007, the presidential and vice-presidential recall referendums of August 2008, and the subsequent right-wing destabilization campaigns of late August and early September that year.

Part II of the book shifts gears, broadening the scope of investigation to include the last three years of the Morales administration (2007–2010). Chapter Five investigates the December 2009 elections and sees them as a new stage in contemporary Bolivian politics. It also maps intellectual currents in Bolivia under Morales, and connects these currents to the concrete historical, material, and ideological realities of the period out of which they emerged. Chapter Six explores the political economy of the entire first term of the MAS government (2006–2010). It concludes that the development model of this period can be accurately described as reconstituted neoliberalism, and compares this phenomena with three major traditions in Latin American political economy of the twentieth century: classical structuralism, orthodox neoliberalism, and neostructuralism.

This book does not attempt to provide a synopsis of every important cultural, political, ideological, and social trend in Bolivia today.[9] Its overarching purpose is to understand the Bolivian political economy in the contemporary period through the lens of Marxism in an effort to make a modest contribution to anti-imperialist, revolutionary-socialist, and indigenous-liberationist aims of fundamental transformation.

PART I

From Rebellion to Reform, 2000–2007

One

Domestic Class Structure, Latin American Trends, and Capitalist Imperialism

Bolivia's Social Formation and Its Place in the World

There has recently been a healthy renewal of interest in Leon Trotsky's associated concepts of combined and uneven development and permanent revolution, redirecting our attention to the interactions between global capitalism and the specificities of particular geographical spaces and social formations in precise historical periods.[1] While here I have focused on the domestic balance of racialized class forces in Bolivia, it is imperative, following Trotsky, that we situate the unfolding process in this country within the wider regional and international context of global capitalism and imperialism. What we find is that there are considerable openings for transformative change in Bolivia within the current world order that were not available only a decade ago. At the same time, "democracy promotion" by the U.S. state and economic imperialism by various international actors remain formidable foes. In terms of the interrelated political, military, and economic components of imperialism, Bolivia is quite obviously vulnerable to their worst manifestations. Being the poorest country in South America, Bolivia's social indicators reflect the depth of its underdevelopment (see Table 1.1). In the United Nations Human Development Program's (UNDP) Human Development index of countries, Bolivia is ranked 113.[2] As late as 1975, only 41.3 percent of the population lived in urban areas. As is the case elsewhere in the third world, the country experienced rapid urbanization during the neoliberal period.[3] By 2003, 69 percent of the population was urbanized (UNDP 2005).[4] In the public health system there are only 6.8 qualified doctors per 10,000 inhabitants, which is nonetheless double the number of doctors only a few years ago. There are only three main highway arteries in the country, with the vast majority of the road systems outside of urban areas still unpaved. Landlocked, transportation costs for the country's main exports are much higher than if it enjoyed access to the sea. Agriculture's share of the GDP was 15.9 percent in 2004. Mining was 4.9 percent of GDP the same year.[5] Manufacturing, if the measure includes processed agricultural commodities, contributed 18 percent of GDP and 35.9 percent of total export earnings in 2005. Manufacturing, however, is mostly "labour-intensive, small-scale and directed largely at regional markets." Financial services accounted for only 13 percent of GDP in 2004. As in most other areas of Latin America, the size of the informal economy is formidable: "By far the largest share of the workforce—around 66%—is engaged in the informal sector, including thousands of micro-businesses, small-scale and often contraband commerce and the illicit coca trade."[6] With a GDP per capita of only US$974—compared to US$6,121 in neighboring Chile, for example—Bolivia is an impoverished and weak country in the hierarchical configuration of nation-states within the global capitalist system.

TABLE 1.1: MAIN SOCIAL INDICATORS

Total population living in poverty (%) (2003)		67.3
Rural population living in poverty (%) (2003)		79.5
Infant mortality (no. of deaths per 1,000 births) (2003)		53.0
Life expectancy at birth (years; avg.) (2003)		64.1
Schooling (avg. years of attendance; population ages 19 and over)		7.4
Male	8.4	
Female	6.7	
Adult literacy rate (%; avg.)* (2001)		13.3
Male	6.9	
Female	19.3	

* Proportion of the population over the age of fifteen who cannot with understanding compose and read a short simple statement about their everyday life.

Source: EIU, Bolivia: Country Profile 2006 *(London: Economist Intelligence Unit, 2006). Derived from data compiled in* UN Human Development Report *and by the Instituto Nacional de Estadística.*

Urban and Rural Class Structures

If we think of social classes as social-historical processes and relation-ships rather than static entities, "capturing a precise and complete pic-ture of classes at any specific moment is difficult if not impossible."[7] Setting many complexities aside, however, the following description of Mexico's basic dynamic of class struggle by the middle of the twentieth century captures just as accurately the contemporary Bolivian reality: "…a very clear dividing line polarizing the classes emerged. On one side of the line stood the triad of imperialism/state/domestic and for-eign bourgeoisies; on the other side gathered much of the lower-paid intermediate classes, and the masses of workers, peasants, and under-paid, underemployed, or unemployed people."[8]

Urban Class Structure

Regarding urban class structure, it is useful to frame our discussion in terms of sociologist Lorgio Orellana Aillón's categorization of three gen-eral regimes of accumulation in the history of Bolivian capitalism.[9] All three distinct accumulation regimes fall within the general unity of Bo-livia's incorporation into global capitalism as a producer of primary ma-terials.[10] The first regime of accumulation was the cycle of the "mining superstate" led by a small group of tin barons combining British, Chilean, and Bolivian capital. This regime solidified itself in the late nineteenth century with the expansion of silver capitalism, reached its apogee with the rise of the Liberal Party to power after the 1899 Federal War and the shift to tin capitalism, began its decline in the 1930s during the Chaco War with Paraguay, and reached its terminus with the National Revolu-tion of 1952. This era was characterized by the promotion of liberal capi-talism, the consolidation of a tiny white-mestizo elite in power, the ex-pansion of large landholdings and dispossession of indigenous land, and the repression when necessary of worker and indigenous rebellions.[11]

The second accumulation regime, nationalist populism, was born in the wake of the 1952 revolution. The state in this cycle controlled and led the productive process through the establishment of various state enterprises. Most important among these were the state mining company, COMIBOL, and oil and gas company, YPFB. The state-led capitalist development model established in this period was characterized by centralized state administration, state ownership of natural resources, extensive state employment, considerable state direction in economic development and production, and a host of limited yet real social citizenship and welfare rights. The state established its legitimacy through the nationalization of the mines and agrarian reform, among other measures. Finance, agriculture, and mining were the major areas of activity for capitalists in this period, with manufacturing industries only employing 3 percent of the economically active population in the 1970s.[12] Under the dictatorship of Hugo Bánzer (1971–1978) millions of dollars of cheap credit subsidized agro-capitalists in Santa Cruz who subsequently expanded into finance, industry, and the service sector.[13]

The cycle of populist accumulation began to decline after the right-wing military coup of 1964 and ground to an abrupt halt in the mid-1980s in the midst of an acute economic crisis and growing worker and peasant radicalism.[14] The nationalist populist accumulation regime was displaced by a "neoliberal oligarchic" regime beginning in 1985 with the introduction of an orthodox neoliberal structural adjustment program called the New Economic Policy (NEP).[15] This cycle was defined by the rise of domestic financial capital subordinated to transnational companies and international financial capital, the dramatic liberalization of trade, the penetration by foreign capital of the Bolivian economy, and the wholesale privatization of the country's natural resources, strategic state-owned enterprises, and public services. In the 1990s water was privatized in various cities and the government sold the state-owned oil and gas, telecommunications, airlines, smelter, power generation, and railroad enterprises to a series of multinational corporations.[16]

The underpinnings for the shift to this neoliberal regime of accumulation began as early as the 1964 coup, but really took off in the

1980s and 1990s. Between 1978 and 1982 Bolivia was plagued with an incredible succession of military coups producing intense uncertainty for Bolivian capitalists and foreign investors alike. In addition, peasant and worker radicalism was expressing itself with renewed vigor, continuing to mobilize in the streets after the rise of the center-left government of the Democratic Popular Unity (1982–1985) in an effort to provoke a transition to socialism. The Bolivian bourgeoisie organized itself through the Confederación de Empresarios Privados de Bolivia (Confederation of Private Entrepreneurs of Bolivia, CEPB) and began advocating electoral democracy and neoliberalism by the end of the 1970s, "as a means of avoiding a further degeneration of the military and a transition controlled by the radical left."[17] Finance and mining segments of the capitalist class dominated the CEPB and played an instrumental role in the implementation of the neoliberal model.[18] Juan Cariaga, an executive at the Banco de Santa Cruz, and Gonzalo Sánchez de Lozada, a millionaire and large stockholder in one of the biggest Bolivian mining companies, COMSUR, were the most important ministers (finance and planning) in the cabinet of the first neoliberal government in the mid-1980s.[19] Because industrial capitalists dependent on the development model of import substitution constituted a smaller part of the economy than in neighboring Latin American countries, there was significantly less intra-class dispute between fractions of capital concerning the introduction of neoliberalism.

The unprecedented unity of the Bolivian bourgeoisie in the mid-1980s was made more powerful by the threat the radical left constituted at the end of the 1970s and early 1980s. As anthropologist Harry Sanabria observes, "While not all dominant class factions gained or lost equally in the short run, neoliberalism *has* enhanced the viability of the existing social order."[20] At the end of the 1990s the neoliberal oligarchic regime of accumulation entered into crisis opening up a period of massive left-indigenous rebellion that sought to resign neoliberalism to the dustbin of history.[21] But while the political project of the Bolivian capitalist class has suffered resounding setbacks, the economic power of the regional bourgeoisie in the eastern lowlands remains intact today. The Santa Cruz bourgeoisie, in particular, maintains its base in agriculture (particularly soy), hydrocarbons, and finance, with intimate ties to foreign capital. The department attracts more foreign direct investment (FDI) than any other department in the country and leads all other regions in export and tax revenue.

The structure of the urban working class forms the other side of this story. First forged between 1880 and the 1952 national-populist revolution, the Bolivian workers' movement has been defined by powerful ideologies of revolutionary Marxism, anarcho-syndicalism, and anti-imperialism.[22] For much of the twentieth century the Bolivian labor movement was unique in Latin America for its militant independence, radical consciousness, and its relative freedom from the shackles of state corporatism. Led overwhelmingly by the tin miners, the workers attempted unsuccessfully to steer the 1952 revolution toward revolutionary socialism, fought against a string of military dictatorships between 1964 and the early 1980s, and played a leading role in the recovery of electoral democracy in 1982, even as they sought to transcend liberal democracy and achieve a transition to socialism.[23]

Parallel to the onset of neoliberalism, the international price of tin crashed in the mid-1980s, destroying the material basis for the tin miners' vanguard role in the labor movement. The tin mines were privatized and just under thirty thousand miners lost their jobs. This marked the beginning of critical changes in the structure of the working class over the next fifteen years. On top of the layoffs in the state mining sector, the first two years of the NEP (1985–1987) witnessed the addition of hundreds of thousands of workers to the growing reserve army of unemployed, including six thousand from the private mining sector, ten thousand from public administration, and two thousand from banking. In addition, more than 110 factories were shut down in this period.[24] As the neoliberal project advanced and consolidated itself throughout the 1990s, the decomposition of the traditional working class continued to accelerate.

In the Bolivian context, as elsewhere, the restructuring of the world of work was not simply capital's attempt to exercise the best technical tools to reduce labor costs in the economic sphere. It was also an explicitly political project to restructure work in such a way as to make the objective obstacles to worker resistance as onerous as possible and to reduce the collective capacities of the working class to act on its interests.[25]

TABLE 1.2: ESTIMATES OF BOLIVIAN LABOR FORCE, 2006–2007

Economic Activity	2006	2007
Agriculture	1,777,288	1,804,569
Hydrocarbons	13,980	14,813
Mining	64,006	70,021
Manufacturing	547,593	575,829
Electricity, Gas, Water	17,178	17,972
Construction	159,685	185,509
Commerce	649,127	672,366
Transport	197,390	205,338
Communications	19,248	20,019
Financial Services	33,593	36,792
Public Administration	145,945	151,941
Other Services	479,197	495,450
Total Bolivia	4,104,231	4,250,618
Total Urban	2,312,963	2,431,236

Table shows actual numbers of people formally employed in the various sectors. Despite the small changes between 2006 and 2007, I think it is nonetheless a useful panorama.

Source: CEDLA, "Bajará el desempleo, pero…261 mil personas no encontrarán trabajo en las ciudades," Alerta Laboral (mayo 2007), 4. (Centro de estudios para el desarrollo laboral y agrario, CEDLA, www.cedla.org).

The most dramatic change to the structure of production on a national level was clearly the process of accumulation by dispossession of the main state-owned enterprises.[26] With the privatization of these companies, there was a general process of "rationalizing" and "flexibilizing" their labor forces. This meant the restructuring of the enterprises in ways that maintained or reduced the number of employees, subcontracted out certain activities to non-union labor, and created obstacles to the unionization of these new sectors.[27] At a slightly lower tier of the economy, just below the peak state enterprises that were privatized, the largest one hundred foreign and local enterprises in industry, mining, commercial agriculture, and banking also saw an augmentation of subcontracting and the "informalization" of production processes. This level of the economy is increasingly integrated into the informal economy by way of utilizing small, non-unionized production units that contribute various small parts to the final product during the production process. This almost invariably means the increasing use of non-unionized female, teenage, and child labor.[28] Below the key privatized state enterprises and the one hundred main firms of the next tier, there were an estimated half million microenterprises by the late 1990s in agriculture, commerce, and artisan activities. Table 1.2 provides an estimate of the various sectors of the current Bolivian workforce. Table 1.3 indicates estimates of urban unemployment.

TABLE 1.3: ESTIMATES OF UNEMPLOYMENT IN URBAN BOLIVIA

	2004	2005	2006	2007
Total Population	5,875,679	6,055,392	6,129,586	6,388,232
Working Age	4,659,349	4,831,745	5,010,519	5,195,909
Economically Active	2,563,173	2,625,714	2,695,558	2,769,955
Employed	2,262,035	2,308,397	2,389,753	2,508,026
Unemployed	301,138	317,317	305,805	261,930
Economically Inactive	2,096,176	2,206,031	2,314,961	2,425,953
Global Level Participation	55.0%	54.3%	53.8%	53.3%
Open Unemployment	11.7%	12.1%	11.3%	9.5%
Growth of EAP*	4.7%	5.2%	4.9%	4.8%

* The percentage of people technically defined as "economically active population" (EAP) out of the total number of people of working age.

Source: CEDLA, "Bajará el desempleo, pero… 261 mil personas no encontrarán trabajo en las ciudades," Alerta Laboral (mayo 2007), 5. (Centro de estudios para el desarrollo laboral y agrario, CEDLA, www.cedla.org).

In the decade between 1985 and 1995, public sector employment in urban areas shrunk quite dramatically from 25 percent of the workforce to 13 percent. Neoliberal theory held that these job losses would be compensated with new formal jobs in expanding private businesses. However, the formal private sector accounted for only 18.4 percent of the workforce in 1995, up barely more than two points from 16 per-

cent in 1985. The real growth as a proportion of the workforce occurred in the informal sector, which expanded from 60 percent in 1985
to 68 percent in 1995 (see Table 1.4). One of the key benefits for employers in the expansion of the informal sector is that this is non-
union work, and that unionization is actually illegal in enterprises that
employ under twenty individuals.[29] The obstacles to forming new
unions are consequently extremely difficult in the informal sector.

Advocates of the neoliberal model point to official unemployment rates below 5 percent during the late 1980s and into the late
1990s, with the exception of a level of 10.4 percent in 1989. However,
by some estimates *underemployment* reached 53 percent of the economically active population (EAP) in 1997.[30] Work was dramatically
more precarious with the proliferation of the informal economy: the
employment of more and more young workers between the ages of
ten to twenty-four with no union experience or knowledge of their
rights; increasing numbers of female workers who also had less union
experience and were more vulnerable to intimidation and sexual ha-
rassment on the worksite; and the decline of permanent contracts and
the increase of short-term contracts, day laborers, and part-time work
with no benefits.[31] A good deal of new hiring was made through temporary contracts. Only 14 percent of the formal private-sector contracts registered with the government in 1994 were "indefinite" contracts, as compared to 68 percent fixed-term contracts, and 18 percent
short-term specific job projects.[32] Increasingly, workers could obtain
only part-time jobs of under forty hours a week, making them ineligi-
ble for better social benefits that come with full-time employment. At
the same time, across different sectors of the economy, the neoliberal
period witnessed the amplification of the number of hours worked
per individual at lower rates of pay, as people were increasingly forced
to take on second jobs.[33] The number of workers taking home salaries
without any complementary benefits increased significantly between
1982 and 1992 in various sectors: from 40 to 55 percent in industrial
manufacturing, 71 to 82 percent in construction, 49 to 55 percent in
transportation, 42 to 61 percent in commerce, and in services, 22 to
38 percent.[34]

TABLE 1.4: EMPLOYMENT BY SEGMENT OF THE LABOR MARKET

Year	Public	Private Business	Informal Private
1985	24%	16%	60%
1995	13%	19%	68%

Source: Tom Kruse, "Transición política y recomposición sindical: Reflexiones desde Bolivia," in Marco A. Calderón Mólgora, Willem Assies, Ton Salman, eds., Ciudadanía, cultura política y reforma del estado en América Latina *(IFE Michoacán: El Colegio de Michoacán, 2002), 232.*

The fragmentation of the production process into smaller and smaller units means that workers are no longer concentrated in large groups, as factories are displaced by smaller workshops. The material conditions of the Bolivian working class under neoliberalism have been fundamentally rearranged through this dynamic. A central paradox has emerged as a result: the number of workers constituting the urban working class—defined expansively as those who do not live off the labor of others—continued to expand in the 1980s and 1990s, while the visibility and social power of this working class deteriorated.[35] The external subcontracting by large enterprises of various tasks that contribute to the overall production process meant that a growing sector of subcontracted workers labored in small workplaces with worse working conditions and environments, no unions, lower wages, and worse quotas than the older, formal employees of the main firms. In other cases, different production stages were subcontracted to "one-person" firms or "family enterprises" the employees of which are sometimes referred to as "micro-entrepreneurs" in the economics literature. They are better thought of as informal proletarians frequently working under awful conditions without protection, doing the tasks "once done by a regular worker enjoying social security, health benefits, and bonuses."[36]

By the late 1990s, full-time unionized workers represented a meager 20 percent of the Bolivian workforce, while the other 80 percent were atomized and fragmented, lacking job security and social benefits.[37] With this shift in organizational class power, to the benefit of capital and the detriment of labor, employers in various parts of the public and private sectors used a series of illegal and legal mechanisms to encroach even further on the rights of workers in an effort to extract more value while reducing labor costs. Some of the most obvious and egregious examples include the plain rejection by formal (public and private) and informal sector firms of the basic right to unionize, threats and firing of individuals suspected of trying to organize workers, and the prohibition at some unionized work places of union dues collection, making union sustainability virtually impossible.[38]

Oscar Olivera, a former shoe-factory worker who attained national and international notoriety for his leadership role in the Cochabamba Water War of 2000, described succinctly the aims and consequences of the reorganization of the world of Bolivian work under neoliberalism: "The forms of hiring and subcontracting are extremely varied but they all have the same goals: atomizing workers and dividing us against ourselves, taming our resistance and unity, inciting competition among us, and forcing greater productivity per worker at lower wages. This problem of the fragmentation of the Bolivian working class—our dispersion and the variety of working conditions we endure—is the principal problem that Bolivian workers must face up to if we really want to resist, to challenge, and to overcome neoliberalism."[39]

The combined consequences of the new precariousness of work, the disarticulation of the Central Obrera Boliviana (Bolivian Workers Central, COB) as an effective organizing body of the working class, the structural heterogeneity of the work experiences of the new urban working class, and the boldness of a capitalist class relatively unified behind the project of political and economic neoliberal transformation, together worked against the collective capacities of working-class resistance in the late 1980s and throughout the bulk of the 1990s.

Union strategies and the strategies of rank-and-file workers tended to be more improvisational, defensive and reactive, and less political, than they had been in the past. As some analysts have suggested, this was more out of basic necessity given the balance of social forces and dramatic changes in the material world of work than the result of changing political choices and ideologies.[40] Much of the theoretical literature on the obstacles to collective action on the part of the popular classes in Latin America suggests that social formations with large and stable industrial labor forces tend to provide the conditions for a certain commonality of interests among workers and are consequently more favorable to the organization of unions and class-based collective action than social formations with more segmented and differentiated labor markets.[41] Bolivia's social formation certainly turned toward the more segmented and differentiated wing of this dichotomy after the structural transformations of neoliberalism were enacted. And for much of the period between the mid-1980s and the late 1990s, the structural difficulties to mounting class-based collective resistance predicted in theories of Latin American popular sector collective action were accurate to a large degree. However, there were also notable exceptions as the Bolivian rural and urban working classes began to experiment with new forms of organizing and doing politics by the end of the 1990s. Most important was the growing success of the *cocalero* movement in the Chapare. There also emerged sectors of the urban union movement that began to forge novel ties with informal proletarian organizations and social movements and the growing rural indigenous-peasant movements. This sort of social-movement unionism was especially evident in the cities of Cochabamba and El Alto–La Paz, the two epicenters of urban insurrection in the 2000–2005 period. Thus a complex process began in the late 1990s through which the urban and rural *infrastructures of dissent* began to recompose themselves after fifteen years of neoliberal onslaught.[42] The result was the most important surge in left-indigenous popular mobilization in the continent between 2000 and 2005.

Rural Class Structure

At the outset of the twenty-first century the rural class structure in Bolivia is characterized by a dramatic concentration of land in the hands of a few, on the one hand, and a sea of poor—often landless—peasants on the other. Haciendas (large landholdings) dominate 90 percent of Bolivia's productive land, leaving only 10 percent divided between mostly indigenous peasant communities and small-holding peasants.[43]

In a country with a total population of nine million, while roughly four hundred individuals own 70 percent of productive land, there are 2.5 million landless peasants.[44] Most of the peasants are indigenous, with 77 percent of rural inhabitants self-identifying as such in the 2001 census.[45]

Bolivia's rural structure prior to the 1952 National Revolution was dominated by large landholdings in which "neo-feudal" social relations predominated, "based on established modes of colonial extraction and exploitation in the countryside."[46] Pre-revolutionary Bolivia had the highest inequality of land concentration in all of Latin America, with 82 percent of land in the possession of 4 percent of landowners.[47] As the nationalist-populist revolutionary process of 1952 unfolded, mass direct-action tactics and independent land occupations orchestrated by radicalized peasants in Cochabamba, La Paz, and Oruro, and to a lesser extent in northern Potosí and Chuquisaca, challenged this rural class structure profoundly.[48] The new revolutionary government of the Movimiento Nacionalista Revolucionario (Revolutionary Nationalist Movement, MNR) was forced to enact the Agrarian Reform Law of 1953 in response to the pressure from below. Forced labor was made illegal and haciendas in the altiplano (La Paz, Oruro, Potosí) and the valleys (Cochabamba, Chuquisaca, Tarija) were divided and the land redistributed, creating a new small-holding peasantry in large sections of these departments.

The MNR, though, was never a socialist party. Its interests coincided with the radical peasants only insofar as the MNR saw the breakup of semi-feudal agrarian modes of production as a prerequisite for establishing and developing a dynamic capitalist agricultural sector with ample state support. The geographic fulcrum for capitalist agriculture in Bolivia became the eastern department of Santa Cruz, beginning shortly after the revolution. Santa Cruz was relatively uninhabited at the time of the revolution and was largely unaffected by the agrarian reform. Over the next several decades it became the most dynamic center of capitalist agriculture in the country, producing cotton, coffee, sugar, and timber for export; the department also spearheaded the reconcentration of land in the hands of a few that eventually spread again throughout much of the rest of the country, reversing, through complex legal and market mechanisms, many of the reforms achieved in the 1952 National Revolution.

With the onset of neoliberalism in the mid-1980s, the agro-industrial dominance of Santa Cruz was solidified. Bolivian neoliberalism emphasized the orientation of agriculture toward exports for external markets. Transnational corporations and large domestic agricultural enterprises based in Santa Cruz led this intensified insertion into the global economy. The traditional peasant economy was increasingly displaced in various parts of the country as large agro-industrial enterprises solidified control and focused increasingly on a few select commodities, soy in particular. In 1986, 77 percent of the total land area under cultivation was devoted to the production of cereals, fruit, vegetables, and tubers in which small-peasant production predominated. By 2004, this area had been reduced to 48.2 percent. By one estimate, in 1963 peasant production represented 82.2 percent of the total value of agricultural production in the country, whereas by 2002 peasant production accounted for only 39.7 percent of total production, and agro-industrial capitalist production accounted for 60.3 percent of the total.[49]

Of the approximately 446,000 peasant production units remaining in the country today, 225,000 are located in the altiplano departments of La Paz, Oruro, and Potosí, 164,000 in the valley departments of Cochabamba, Chuquisaca, and Tarija, and only 57,000 in the eastern lowland departments of Santa Cruz, Beni, and Pando. Capitalist relations of production now predominate in the eastern lowlands and are increasingly displacing small-scale peasant production in the valleys and altiplano although the latter continues to be the most important form of production in the altiplano.[50] Of the 2,118,988 hectares of land cultivated in Bolivia in 2004, 59 percent were in the eastern lowland departments. These departments were home to 96 percent of industrial crop production (cotton, sugarcane, sunflowers, peanuts, and soy), 42 percent of production of vegetables (beans and tomatoes), and 27 percent of fruit production (mainly bananas and oranges). These eastern departments furthermore accounted for 73.3 percent of national cattle ranching, 36.3 percent of pig farming, and 37.8 percent of poultry production. Finally, 60.1 percent of the timber extracted from Bolivian forests came from Santa Cruz, Beni, and Pando.[51] Large agro-industrial capitalists dominate in this part of the country.

In the valley departments, small and medium capitalist enterprises account for most of the agricultural sector. These departments play a significant role in ranching. They account for 60.3 percent of poultry production, 48 percent of pig farming, and 18.5 percent of Bolivian cattle ranching. The rural altiplano, on the other hand, is still dominated by small peasant producers and indigenous communities. This region accounts for only 19 percent of total cultivated land in Bolivia, and its contribution to national ranching is circumscribed to the sheep and llama sectors.[52]

The rural population is diminishing throughout the country as processes of semi-proletarianization and proletarianization accelerate with the gradual extension of capitalist relations of production into all corners of the country. Beginning in the early 1970s, migrant semi-proletarians provided the workforce for sugarcane and cotton harvests while for the rest of the year they maintained small plots of their own land in the departments from which they primarily traveled— Cochabamba, Potosí, and Chuquisaca. Between 1976 and 1996, the rural population as a proportion of the total population fell from 59 percent to 39 percent.[53]

This exodus has to do with two interrelated developments in the agricultural sector. On the one side, peasant production has been going through a prolonged crisis. Peasant families are increasingly unable to reproduce themselves and must supplement their farming income by selling their labor power, whether in the countryside or in the cities. In the altiplano, small-scale peasant producers and indigenous communities are experiencing diminishing productive capacities of their soil, the division of land into smaller and smaller plots (*minifundios*) as families grow in size from generation to generation, the migration of young people to cities, and an acute absence of new technologies, making competition with foreign suppliers to the domestic Bolivian markets impossible.[54] Meanwhile, in the dynamic center of agro-capitalism in the eastern lowlands, technical innovation and modernization has led to more capital-intensive forms of agricultural production and consequently a paucity of employment opportunities even as industries expand.[55]

As capitalist social relations increase their reach, the differentiation of the peasantry into rich, middle, and poor peasants also intensifies. Survey data from 1988 suggested that 76 percent of the peasantry were poor peasants, meaning they did not have the means to reproduce their family labor power based on the income generated from their land and were obligated to sell their labor elsewhere on a temporary basis. Medium peasants constituted 11 percent of the peasantry when defined as peasant family units fundamentally based on family labor with the ability to reproduce that labor without selling their labor power elsewhere. Rich peasants—those who regularly made a profit after reproducing their family and their means of production, purchased the labor of poorer peasants, and utilized modern technology—constituted 13 percent of the peasantry.[56] This process of differentiation within the peasantry has only accelerated since that time, with the transformation of some rich peasants into commercial farmers in specific regions of the altiplano and valley departments.[57]

Such have been the changing urban and rural class compositions of Bolivian society up to the current period. Having set out these basic patterns it is important to situate them within the broader dynamics of global capitalism and the imperialist system it generates.

Contradictions of Capitalist Imperialism in Bolivia

Beginning with the debt crisis of the 1980s, the influence of the IMF, World Bank, the Inter-American Development Bank (IDB), various imperialist members states of the European Union, and the U.S. state in setting the domestic economic agenda in Bolivia was amplified dramatically.[58] As has been the case elsewhere in Latin America, the U.S. "drug war" has also supplied a useful pretext for the American state's intervention in Bolivia's domestic political and military affairs.[59] U.S. intervention in Bolivian matters has undergone other ideological shifts as well, such as the intensification of "democracy promotion," or as William I. Robinson suggests, "polyarchy promotion."[60] Polyarchy, is "a system in which a small group actually rules, on behalf of capital, and participation in decision making by the majority is confined to choosing among competing elites in tightly controlled electoral processes."[61] With the decline of the traditionally neoliberal parties, the rise of left-indigenous forces in the early 2000s, the perceived threat of Evo Morales and the MAS, and the overthrow of two neoliberal presidents in 2003 and 2005, U.S. "democracy promotion" intensified in Bolivia. According to Reed Lindsay, "Publicly available information, documents obtained through the Freedom of Information Act (FOIA) and interviews with recipients of U.S. aid in Bolivia reveal that the U.S. government has spent millions of dollars to rebuild discredited political parties, to undercut independent grassroots movements, to bolster malleable indigenous leaders with little popular support and to dissuade Bolivians from talking about whether they should have greater ownership rights over their natural resources."[62]

In a 2002 cable from the U.S. embassy in La Paz to the State Department, accessed through the Freedom of Information Act, it was stated that a planned USAID project would "help build moderate, pro-democracy political parties that can serve as a counterweight to the radical MAS or its successors."[63] Along these lines, between 2002 and 2004, the U.S. National Democratic Institute for International Affairs (NDI), with funding from the U.S. National Endowment for Democracy, sponsored trips to Washington of emerging political leaders of the traditional neoliberal parties—Movimiento Nacionalista Revolucionario (Revolutionary Nationalist Movement, MNR), Acción Democrática Nacionalista (Nationalist Democratic Action, ADN), Movimiento de la Izquierda Revolucionaria (Revolutionary Left Movement, MIR), and Nueva Fuerza Republicana (New Republican Force, NFR)—for political training. These funds were also used to support "party-strengthening" initiatives in Bolivia of these same parties.

The NDI, with funding from USAID, opened an office in La Paz in January 2004. Likewise, USAID funded the activities of the U.S. International Republican Institution (IRI) in Bolivia, allowing the IRI to open an office of its own in the capital in March 2004. The IRI focused on "democracy promotion" within "civil society" domains, teaching "democratic culture" and "authority and responsibility" to tens of thousands of kids in high schools through the mass distribution of pamphlets, for example. Finally, USAID financed the opening of the Office of Transitions Initiative (OTI) in La Paz in the same month as the new IRI office was established. OTI's 2004–2005 budget was $11.8 million, with which it focused on the rebellious countryside of the altiplano and the massive urban shantytown of El Alto in an explicit effort to depoliticize popular movements rising up around the nationalization of natural gas and water. It has also been reported that 40 percent of the Bolivian government's public relations budget under President Carlos Mesa was financed by OTI. Following the failure of these initiatives to save Mesa's administration from massive insurrections in May and June 2005, USAID cut funding from the NDI and IRI projects.[64] All this is simply to note the dynamics and depth of U.S. imperial intervention in Bolivia's political processes and economic policy making.

However, if we left it at that we would miss the crucial opportunities for the radicalization of the Bolivian process offered up by the present conjuncture of imperialist strategies and regional political dynamics elsewhere in Latin America. Militarily, the United States is experiencing a crisis of imperial overreach in Iraq, Afghanistan, and Pakistan, with its eyes set next on Iran. Despite the Americans' new military bases in Paraguay and Colombia, which will enhance their military capabilities in the region over the longer term, there is no evidence thus far of imminent threats of overt military intervention in Bolivia.[65] Politically and ideologically neoliberalism has been completely discredited in Latin America, with political parties of various ideological hues finding rhetorical rejection of the model a prerequisite for serious political contestation in elections. The widely held association of the U.S. state with the imposition of the neoliberal model in Latin America has shed the American state of any credible leverage through persuasion in good chunks of the region, even with the passing of the torch from Bush to Obama.[66] Beginning in the 1990s the American state began pursuing a dual strategy in Latin America of "free trade" promotion and the installation of military bases in multiple locales. However, the most important project of the last two decades, the Free Trade Area of the Americas

(FTAA), failed due to "conflicts between globalized and dependent corporations in internal markets [of Latin America], clashes between exporters and industrialists, and extensive popular rejection of the project."[67] While the United States has brandished bilateral trade agreements as their alternative weapon of choice, the collapse of the FTAA was clearly a prodigious blow to American imperialism in its own backyard.

The Economics of Imperialism

We must still account for the subtler economics of imperialism, however. In a world in which imperialist domination no longer relies on permanent colonies, "Capitalist imperialism has become almost entirely a matter of economic domination, in which market imperatives, manipulated by the dominant capitalist powers, are made to do the work no longer done by imperial states or colonial settlers."[68] In this area as well, a confluence of conjunctural factors has enabled the Bolivian state with more room for maneuver than a cursory glance at its economic indicators would imply. Economic domination of the Global North over the Global South is typically exercised through the overlapping media of multilateral lending institutions (IMF, World Bank, IDB), international financial markets, and core capitalist states. Specific mechanisms include the manipulation of trade, aid, and debt, as well as a myriad of other political and military threats and actions. As Table 1.5 indicates, the largest part of Bolivia's debt is external (70.2 percent), more than 90 percent of which is owed to multilateral lending institutions.[69] The table shows $243.8 million owing to the IMF, of which $232.5 million was canceled in 2006 following the July 8, 2005, decision by G-8 countries to cancel the IMF debt for Highly Indebted Poor Countries (HIPC). At the same time, a process was initiated through which $1.53 billion of the $1.62 billion owed by Bolivia to the World Bank will be canceled: "So this debt ($1.53 billion) can be seen as canceled in the near future."[70] In mid-March 2007, the IDB also announced that it would cancel $1 billion of Bolivia's outstanding debt to that institution.[71] While the IMF cancelation only represents 4.7

TABLE 1.5: BOLIVIA: TOTAL PUBLIC DEBT, 2000–05

	2000		2001		2002	
External						
Multilateral	3077.3	36.60%	3261.1	40%	3637.2	45.80%
IMF	220.2	2.60%	207	2.50%	194.6	2.50%
IDB	1392.8	16.60%	1373.7	16.80%	1450.2	18.30%
World Bank	1096.3	13.00%	1146.8	14.10%	1323.5	16.70%
CAF	255.4	3.00%	420.7	5.20%	577.4	7.30%
Other	112.6	1.30%	112.9	1.40%	91.5	1.20%
Bilateral	1371.8	16.30%	1227.2	15.10%	757	9.50%
Japan	523.4	6.20%	464.1	5.70%	513.5	6.50%
Germany	325.4	3.90%	306.1	3.80%	6.9	0.10%
Belgium	57.7	0.70%	54.8	0.70%	0	0.00%
Spain	142.3	1.70%	137.8	1.70%	134.9	1.70%
France	40.7	0.50%	37.9	0.50%	16.1	0.20%
USA	60.1	0.70%	59.3	0.70%	0	0.00%
UK	18.1	0.20%	17.9	0.20%	0	0.00%
Brazil	21.9	0.30%	33.5	0.40%	56.2	0.70%
Other	182.2	2.20%	115.8	1.40%	29.4	0.40%
Private	11.2	0.10%	8.4	0.10%	5.5	0.10%
Total External	4460.3	53.00%	4496.7	55.10%	4399.7	55.40%
Domestic						
Public Sector*	55	0.70%	68.5	0.80%	64.5	0.80%
Private Sector	780.6	9.30%	1192.9	19.60%	1267	16.00%
OMAs (Market Auctions)	263.6	3.10%	538.9	6.60%	460.5	5.80%
AFPs (Pensions)	517	6.10%	654	8.00%	786	9.90%
Other	0	0.00%	0	0.00%	20.5	0.30%
Total Domestic*	835.6	9.90%	1261.4	15.50%	1331.4	16.80%
Grand Total	5295.9	63.00%	5758.1	70.60%	5731.1	72.20%

percent of Bolivia's total external debt it nonetheless represents 2.5 percent of the country's GDP, and meant that the Bolivian state would pay the IMF $16.5 million between 2006 and 2009 rather than the hitherto scheduled $236 million.[72] Significantly, the Morales government chose not to renew a Stand-By Arrangement with the IMF, which expired on March 31, 2006, releasing the country from some of

2003		2004		2005*		2005†	
4318.4	53.30%	4662	53.10%	4519.9	48.40%	4290	45.90%
276.5	3.40%	306	3.50%	243.8	2.60%	13.9**	0.10%
1626.5	20.10%	1658.2	18.90%	1622.8	17.40%	1622.8	17.40%
1571.2	19.40%	1748.6	19.90%	1666.6	17.80%	1666.6	17.80%
740.6	9.10%	836.9	9.50%	871.3	9.30%	871.3	9.30%
103.6	1.30%	112.3	1.30%	115.4	1.20%	115.4	1.20%
820.6	10.10%	382.9	4.40%	420.7	4.50%	420.7	4.50%
567.6	7.00%	71.6	0.80%	63	0.70%	63	0.70%
9.5	0.10%	39.1	0.40%	34	0.40%	34	0.40%
0	0.00%	0	0.00%	0	0.00%	0	0.00%
130.9	1.60%	142.8	1.60%	139.3	1.50%	139.3	1.50%
17.2	0.20%	17.2	0.20%	13.3	0.10%	13.3	0.10%
0	0.00%	0	0.00%	0	0.00%	0	0.00%
0	0.00%	0	0.00%	0	0.00%	0	0.00%
73.5	0.90%	87.4	1.00%	121.5	1.30%	121.5	1.30%
21.9	0.30%	24.8	0.30%	49.6	0.50%	49.6	0.50%
2.8	0.00%	0.4	0.00%	0.2	0.00%	0.2	0.00%
5141.8	63.50%	5045.3	57.40%	4940.8	52.90%	4710.9	50.40%
55.3	0.70%	38.9	0.40%	44.6	0.50%	44.6	0.50%
1463.6	18.10%	1729.5	19.70%	1953.3	20.90%	1953.3	20.90%
531.7	6.60%	660.5	7.50%	726.3	7.80%	726.3	7.80%
913.1	11.30%	1049	11.90%	1207	12.90%	1207	12.90%
18.8	0.20%	20	0.20%	20	0.20%	20	0.20%
1518.9	18.80%	1768.4	20.10%	1997.8	21.40%	1997.8	21.40%
6660.7	**82.20%**	**6813.7**	**77.60%**	**6938.6**	**74.30%**	**6708.7**	**71.80%**

(before IMF cancelations), †(after IMF cancelations)

Source: Weisbrot and Sandoval, Bolivia's Challenges, 16.

the rigid conditionalities typically attached to IMF loans. Historically, the IMF has played a "gatekeeper" role in lending to Latin American governments such that even though proportionally its loans have been small, without approval from the IMF it has been difficult for poor countries to get loans from the much bigger stockpiles of the World Bank, IDB, and bilateral lenders.[73]

However, since the 1990s, the IMF's influence in middle-income countries worldwide has been diminishing, constituting, in the words of one analyst, "the biggest change in the international financial system since the breakdown of the Bretton Woods system in 1973."[74] The portfolio of the IMF internationally has been reduced from $96 billion in 2004 to $20 billion today, with only 3 percent of its outstanding loans owed by Latin America:

> The power of the IMF has declined drastically since the late 1990s. After the East Asian economic crisis the middle-income countries of that region began to accumulate large amounts of foreign exchange reserves, partly to avoid ever having to borrow from the IMF again. The experience of Argentina since 2002, in which the country rejected key policy recommendations of the IMF and received no net funding from the Fund or allied multilateral lenders, and experienced a robust economic recovery, also had the effect of greatly reducing the IMF's influence over middle-income countries. Most recently, there has been a sharply reduced demand for IMF loans. In the past few months two of its biggest borrowers—Argentina and Brazil, paid in full their remaining debt to the IMF.[75]

Indeed, as the *Economist* reported, "The IMF's natural clients in emerging Asia and Latin America have repaid their loans and amassed their own defences against financial crises. This has left the fund all suited up with nowhere to go."[76] Compounding the decline of the IMF's influence, moreover, has been the availability of alternative financing from the oil-rich Venezuelan state under the Hugo Chávez government. Recently, Venezuela has committed $3 billion to Argentina, and hundreds of millions to Bolivia, Nicaragua, and Ecuador, among other countries.[77]

U.S. influence also appears to be eroding in relation to aid. Current levels of Bolivia's net borrowing from multilateral lending institutions remain significant, but are not overwhelming. Furthermore, they are diminishing over time through debt cancelations, alternative means of financing from the Venezuelan state, and increased domestic hydrocarbon revenues under the new arrangements negotiated by the Morales government with the transnational petroleum companies in 2006. Table 1.6 indicates that a majority of the grants and donations going to Bolivia come from Europe. It is true that the "United States does supply other funding through its 'Bureau of International Narcotics and Law Enforcement Affairs'—$90.3 million for 2005. Washington also contributed $48.2 million for other projects. However, other than the $8.4 million from USAID noted [in Table 1.6] this money does not fund the central government."[78] Finally, as can be seen in Table 1.7 the U.S. state tentatively projected an 11 percent reduction in total economic and social assistance to Bolivia in 2008 relative to 2006 levels.[79]

TABLE 1.6: BOLIVIA, GRANTS AND DONATIONS 2006

Government/Organization	US$ millions	% of GDP
European Union	24.64	0.24%
Basket Funding*	16.94	0.16%
Netherlands	12.99	0.12%
Spain	10.32	0.10%
USAID	8.46	0.08%
German Bank for Reconstruction	5.64	0.05%
International Development Agency (IDA)	5.17	0.05%
Denmark	5.13	0.05%
World Food Program	3.57	0.03%
Japan International Cooperation Agency	2.90	0.03%
Belgian Technical Cooperation	2.14	0.02%
UN Global Environment Facility	1.99	0.02%
Inter-American Development Bank	1.10	0.01%
Swiss Agency for Development and Cooperation	1.05	0.01%
UNICEF	0.81	0.01%
Other	6.90	0.07%
Total†	**109.75**	**1.05%**

*Source: (Weisbrot and Sandoval, Bolivia's Challenges, 16); derived from data of Presupuesto General de la Nación, Ministerio de Hacienda, Viceministerio de Presupuest y Contaducia.

†Dollar amounts and percentages are based on a projected exchange rate of Bs. 8.12 per U.S. dollar and a nominal GDP of Bs. 85,029 millions by the Ministry of Finance of Bolivia.

TABLE 1.7: ECONOMIC AND MILITARY AID REQUESTED FOR BOLIVIA
(ALL NUMBERS IN THOUSANDS OF U.S. DOLLARS)

Program	2006	2008	Change
Andean Counterdrug Initiative—			
Alternative Development	36,630	0	-100%
Child Survival and Health	17,233	11,500	-33%
Development Assistance	10,091	39,000	286%
Economic Support Fund	5,940	17,000	186%
Public Law 480 (Food Aid)	15,953	13,000	-19%
Transition Initiatives	5,373	0	-100%
Peace Corps	2888	2858	-1%
Total Economic and			
Social Assistance	**94,108**	**83,358**	**-11%**

Source: AIN, The Shifting Weight of U.S. Funding in Bolivia (Cochabamba: Andean Information Network/Red Andina de Información, March 20, 2007). Derived from the Bush administration's Foreign Operations Congressional Budget Justification for Fiscal Year 2008. That document is available at http://www.state.gov/documents/ organization/80701.pdf.

Unfortunately, the MAS government continues to solicit funds from the U.S. state through the Millennium Challenge Account (MCA), established by George W. Bush in 2001 as part of what his administration refers to as the "new global development compact." The MCA, according to one analyst, "seeks to gain more control over Third World governments through the practice of extending grants as opposed to loans."[80] She writes:

The changing *form* of the MCA is best described by what I call "preemptive development." This term describes a set of coercive strategies aimed at seizing upon assets to the exclusion of other claimants. Unlike the traditional strategy of imposing conditionality, in which recipient countries were required to meet after loans were dispensed by the IMF and the World Bank, pre-emptive development entails the reverse: by using grants, as opposed to loans, creditor countries can withhold funds until all demands are made by the donor country are met, largely through quantitative measurement. Despite the presence of pre-emptive forms of development, the *content* of the MCA reflects the same goals and interests that have been propagated by the Washington consensus over the past two decades: that the path to increased growth and prosperity lies in countries' willingness and ability to adopt policies that promote economic freedom and the rule of bourgeois law, such as private property, the commodification and privatization of land, and so on.[81]

The extent to which the American state can leverage its power in Bolivian affairs through aid is contingent on various processes that are still in flux, but overall we can conclude that this leverage is in decline. In terms of bilateral trade, imperialist countries can make access to their markets conditional on a series of free market reforms in the weaker country. However, U.S. leverage on this score is also more tenuous than it once was in the Bolivian case, for two fundamental reasons. First, between 2000 and 2004, the United States already declined from first to third position in the ranking of Bolivia's trading partners in terms of both imports and exports, primarily because of the surge in demand from Brazil for Bolivia's natural gas (see Table 1.8). Second, the U.S. market is likely to enter into further decline and saturation making it even more difficult to penetrate—and therefore less attractive and less important as a bargaining chip—for countries such as Bolivia:

> …in coming years the market for imports in the U.S. is not going to grow as it has in the past. It is widely recognized by the vast majority of economists that the U.S. trade and current account deficit is not sustainable. As a result, the dollar will have to fall, and the U.S. trade deficit will adjust. The result of this adjustment is that the market for imports (measured in non-dollar terms) in the U.S. will have to shrink over the next decade. This means that developing countries that want to increase their exports to the U.S. market will have to displace other exporters (e.g. Mexico or China) that are already there. To sum up the situation regarding trade, it seems unlikely that the threat of cancelling trade preferences could be used to alter the new government's course with regard to either trade or other policy issues.[82]

In each of these components of economic imperialism, then, we have shown that Bolivia enjoys more autonomy to advance a radical, transformative politics in the current world order than many presume, even while tremendous obstacles clearly persist. Turning from these international dimensions, the most important regional development has been the relationship with Venezuela and Cuba.

TABLE 1.8: BOLIVIA'S MAIN TRADING PARTNERS (% OF TOTAL)

	2000	2001	2002	2003	2004
Exports to:					
Brazil	11.3	22.1	24.3	35.7	34.0
Venezuela	3.5	7.3	12.8	13.3	12.6
United States	24.0	13.9	14.1	12.0	12.4
Colombia	13.3	14.2	10.2	12.4	11.8
Imports from:					
Brazil	15.5	16.2	22.0	24.5	28.2
Argentina	17.3	18.0	17.4	16.4	18.9
United States	24.8	18.4	15.6	12.4	11.5
Chile	9.3	8.3	7.0	9.6	8.3

Source: EIU, Bolivia: Country Profile 2006 *(London: Economist Intelligence Unit, 2006), 45. Derived from IMF,* Direction of Trade Statistics.

Counterhegemonic Bloc? Bolivia, Venezuela, and Cuba

Without a doubt, the relationship between Evo Morales, Fidel Castro, and Hugo Chávez is increasingly important at the domestic, regional, and international levels. The specter of a covert Venezuelan takeover of Bolivian domestic politics through the machinations of Chávez is a bogeyman scenario frequently invoked by the far right in Bolivia.[83] Exaggerated claims concerning the influence of Chávez in directing radical politics in Bolivia plainly obscures the role of the formation of massive popular movements in Bolivia over the last seven years. At the same time, the new regional alliance is, in very real ways, opening up new space and potential for deeper anti-imperialist politics within Latin America generally, and Bolivia, in particular. As we noted, U.S. economic imperialism within Latin America in recent years has in part focused on the promotion of the North American Free Trade Agreement (Canada-Mexico-U.S.), the Central American Free Trade Agreement (CAFTA), bilateral trade agreements with a number of Latin American countries, and, always its most important long-term goal, the FTAA.

Bucking these imperial efforts, Venezuela, Cuba, and Bolivia agreed, on April 29, 2006, to work toward building the Alternativa Bolivariana para los Pueblos de Nuestra América (Bolivarian Alternative for the Peoples of Our America, ALBA), starting with the Tratado Comercio de los Pueblos (Peoples' Trade Agreement, TCP) between the three countries.[84] The latter strategic agreement seeks to build binational public enterprises, and to put in place subsidiaries of state-owned banks in partner countries, as well as collective agreements for reciprocal lines of credit. In recognition of the unequal political and economic status of the countries involved, Venezuela has made available to Bolivia its air and sea transport infrastructure, as well as guaranteeing a market for Bolivian agricultural products shut out of Colombia in 2006 after Colombia signed a bilateral trade agreement with the United States.[85] Cuba has set up Cuban-Bolivian ophthalmological medical centers within Bolivia with the capacity to treat more than one hundred thousand patients free of charge each year. The Caribbean island state has also provided to Bolivia a number of other medical services, equipment, and doctors, and increased to five thousand the number of scholarships that will be granted to Bolivians by 2007 to study medicine free of charge in Cuba.[86] All these measures are extraordinary examples of what reciprocal agreements based on solidarity can look like. This space is critically important for increasing the possibility that the Bolivian working classes and oppressed indigenous nations will realize their own future. Elsewhere in Latin America's so-called pink tide of governments shifting to the left, the potential for cooperation in building a counterhegemonic bloc against the interests of U.S. imperialism is more ambiguous, to say the least. Nonetheless, over the long term, constructing popular power from below in a socialist direction throughout the region is a necessity for the survival of any transformative change within Bolivia.

The most important facet of contemporary Latin America providing a basis for reasoned optimism on this score is the proliferation of what Argentine economist Claudio Katz calls the "combative impulse."[87] The level of popular movement activity was certainly uneven in 2006, when Morales assumed office, with receding momentum in countries such as Brazil and Uruguay, for example. At the same time, though,

popular protagonism had surged since the late 1990s in Bolivia, Venezuela, Argentina, and Ecuador. Closer to the time of Morales's inaugura-
tion, the relatively quiescent Chilean and Mexican lefts exploded with
intermittent popular uprisings and workers' revolts.[88] Developing the
widespread combative impulse and anti-neoliberal and anti-imperialist
sentiments into a continent-wide socialist consciousness with organizational capacities to contest the ruling classes of each country leaps out
as the immense outstanding challenge. Meaningful socialist and indigenous liberation in Bolivia is tethered to the outcome of current struggles across Latin America just as it is a constituent part of and leading
contributing force in these struggles.

Conclusion

This chapter has situated Bolivia in the international and regional
contexts in at least a cursory fashion. It has also attempted to outline
some of the core features of the country's rural and urban class structures. I built a preliminary foundation for understanding the set of
nine theses advanced for the first part of this book, all of which challenge many of the existing interpretations of the current conjuncture in
Bolivia. I hope to further substantiate these theses as the book proceeds. From the basis of my international and regional synopsis I am in
a position to move to a much more detailed, fine-grained analysis of
the domestic situation in Chapters Two, Three, and Four. Our first task
will be to tackle the question of revolution.

Two

Revolutionary Epoch, Combined Liberation, and the December 2005 Elections

The introduction to this volume introduced several theses that challenge many of the underlying premises and conclusions of the existing scholarly and journalistic literature on the current social and political situation in Bolivia under the Evo Morales government. Chapter One then offered an analysis of the country's rural and urban class structures after more than twenty years of neoliberal economic restructuring. It also sought to contextualize the domestic scene within the wider trends of the regional and international political economy.

This chapter builds on these foundations. It begins by briefly surveying some of the literature that has been grappling with the question of revolution in contemporary Bolivia. The suggestion is made that we ought to distinguish between the concepts of *revolutionary epoch* and *social revolution*. The second section then shows how the left-indigenous insurrectionary period between 2000 and 2005 meets the criteria of a revolutionary epoch. During this five-year cycle of urban and rural revolt, sustained mass mobilization from below and a multifaceted state crisis from above created opportunities for transformative structural change to the Bolivian state and society. The mass movements of this period were engaged in a combined liberation struggle to overcome the interrelated processes of class exploitation and racial oppression of the indigenous majority. The revolutionary epoch of 2000 to

2005 did not conclude with a social revolution, however.

The third section provides a detailed analysis of the December 2005 elections that brought Evo Morales, leader of the MAS, into office. It is argued that these elections were defined by the utter exhaustion of the traditional neoliberal parties in Bolivia that had ruled the country through various coalitional governments since 1985. The electoral results were symptomatic of the widespread rejection of neoliberalism as an economic and political model.

Fourth, and finally, we review the trajectory of the MAS party, in terms of its shifting class composition, ideology, and political strategies. The party originated as the anti-imperialist and anti-neoliberal political arm of an indigenous-peasant movement in the department of Cochabamba in the mid-1990s. In this period it was structured along the lines of the assembly-style, rank-and-file democracy of the peasant unions in the region. Its primary social base was the cocaleros, a militant peasant population in direct confrontation with the American Empire vis-à-vis the local machinations of the militarized, U.S.-led "drug war" against their livelihoods. From its founding years until roughly 2002, the party focused strategically on extra-parliamentary activism and mass mobilization in the countryside and cityscapes of the Cochabamba department. Since 2002, the MAS began to change course, stressing electoral politics and distancing itself from direct action in the streets. The highest layers of the party were increasingly composed of a mestizo, middle-class, and urban intelligentsia. The consequences of this shift in class composition, combined with the party's new tactic of courting the small urban middle class in electoral contests, led to substantial ideological changes. Anti-imperialism and anti-neoliberalism faded from view as reformist electoralism moved to the fore.

Revolution

Trotsky wrote approximately one hundred years ago that, "Revolution is an open measurement of strength between social forces in a struggle for power."[1] Such a naked measuring is widely believed to have been in the offing in the Bolivian context since the beginning of the current century. A brief overview of select interventions in the discussion on revolution that has been reverberating around the current Bolivian process will provide at least a taste of the relevant debates. One of the most important proponents of the revolutionary thesis from outside of Bolivia is the Mexican historian Adolfo Gilly. Here he is referring to the October 2003 Gas War:

> A revolution is not something that happens in the State, in its institutions, and among its politicians. It comes *from below and from outside*. It happens when centerstage is taken over—with the violence of their bodies and the rage of their souls—precisely by those who come from *below and outside*: those who are always shunted aside, those who take orders, those whom the rulers look down on as a mass of voters, electoral clientele, beasts of burden, survey-fodder. It happens when these erupt, give themselves a political goal, organize themselves in accordance with their own decisions and awareness and, with lucidity, reflection, and violence, insert their world into the world of those who rule, and obtain, as in the present [Bolivian] case, what they were demanding [the resignation of President Sánchez de Lozada].[2]

Gilly maintains that "what we are witnessing is a revolution, whose moment of triumph was the taking of the city of La Paz and the flight of the government of Sánchez de Lozada on October 17, 2003. I do not know what will come after. I know that revolution is once again alive in these Latin American lands, even if to conservative eyes it appears as 'a confused, amorphous and bloody conflict.'"[3] Historians Forrest Hylton and Sinclair Thomson are in one sense more cautious, employing "revolutionary" only as an adjective. Writing in 2005, prior to the electoral victory of the MAS, they argue, "The current cycle…constitutes the third major *revolutionary moment* in Bolivian history," the first being the anti-colonial indigenous rebellion led by Túpaj Katari in 1781, the second being the 1952 National Revolution, which they posit as "the first national-popular revolution in postwar Latin America."[4] The endgame of the revolutionary moment was still in play at the time their piece was written, and for Hylton and Thomson there were no predetermined outcomes: "The twin volcanoes of 2003/2005 have shifted Bolivia's political landscape; yet their outcomes remain highly uncertain."[5] James Dunkerley, long an incisive analyst of Bolivia, is somewhat reticent to speak firmly of a Third Bolivian Revolution, though, in the final instance, he is willing to go along with proponents of this view. His reticence flows from the fact that he remains concerned about long-term consequences and not simply the process of rebellion: "Is it, then, at all sensible to talk of a 'revolution' that was at least six years in the making and that had yet to deliver, in the form of materially implemented public policy, striking changes in the human condition? This may, indeed, be tantamount to a promotion of rhetoric and popular ambition over substantive and lasting change. Yet the first years of the 21st century have continually upheld the images, expectations, and behavioural patterns associated with the urgency and emergency of revolution. It is plain that a revolution is widely *felt* to be under way."[6]

Nonetheless, while advising we "should take care" about using the term "revolution," Dunkerley suggests that we ought not to be too preoccupied in our usage, given that the usual "social science criteria" for defining revolution "are simply unmeetable in the present or foreseeable future."[7] We can, on this view, call what is happening in Bolivia a revolution in spite of the fact that it does not meet the traditional criteria.

I argue, conversely, that social revolution has not been unmeetable in recent years in Bolivia, nor should it be seen as impossible in the foreseeable future, and that, furthermore, we ought to retain the strict "social science criteria" for defining revolution. One way out of the quandaries of process and consequence that arise in defining revolution is to separate the notion of *revolutionary epoch* from *social revolution*. The concept of revolutionary epoch provides us with a way of understanding that revolutionary transformative change is possible but not predetermined in a certain period, stressing the uncertainty—and yet not wide openness—of alternative outcomes. The concept of social revolution, on the other hand, while it still connotes process and uncertainty, nonetheless is more decisively concerned with accounting for and measuring the *depths and consequences* of lasting structural change that have been successfully won through the popular struggle of a revolutionary epoch.

I will employ the useful definition of revolutionary epoch developed by Bolivian intellectual and current Vice President Álvaro García Linera, following Karl Marx:

It was Marx who proposed the concept of the "revolutionary epoch" in order to understand extraordinary historical periods of dizzying political change—abrupt shifts in the position and power of social forces, repeated state crises, recomposition of collective identities, repeated waves of social rebellion—separated by periods of relative stability during which the modification, partial or total, of the general structures of political domination nevertheless remains in question...A revolutionary epoch is a relatively long period, of several months or years, of intense political activity in which: (a) social sectors, blocs or classes previously apathetic or tolerant of those in power openly challenge authority and claim rights or make collective petitions through direct mobilizations...; (b) some or all of these mobilized sectors actively posit the necessity of taking state power...; (c) there is a surge of adherence to these proposals from large sections of the population; the distinction between governors and governed begins to dissolve, due to the growing participation of the masses in political affairs; and (d) the ruling classes are unable to neutralize these political aspirations, resulting in a polarization of the country into several "multiple sovereignties" that fragment the social order.[8]

Finally, the standard social science criteria of social revolution that I propose we retain, and to which Dunkerley refers, are famously outlined in the work of Theda Skocpol:

Social revolutions are rapid, basic transformations of a society's state and class structures; and they are accompanied and in part carried through by class-based revolts from below. Social revolutions are set apart from other sorts of conflicts and transformative processes above all by the combination of two coincidences: the coincidence of societal structural change with class upheaval; and the coincidence of political with social transformation. In contrast, rebellions, even when successful, may involve the revolt of subordinate classes—but they do not eventuate in structural change. Political revolutions transform state structures but not social structures, and they are not necessarily accomplished through class conflict. And processes such as industrialization can transform social structures without necessarily bringing about, or resulting from, sudden political upheavals or basic political structural change. What is unique to social revolution is that basic changes in social structure and in political structure occur together in a mutually reinforcing fashion. And these changes occur through intense sociopolitical conflicts in which class struggles play a key role.[9]

The Revolutionary Epoch

Following fifteen years (1985–2000) of right-wing neoliberal assault, elitist "pacted democracy" between ideologically indistinguishable political parties, and the concomitant decomposition of popular movements, left-indigenous struggle in Bolivia was reborn with a vengeance in the 2000 Cochabamba Water War against the World Bank–driven privatization of water in that city.[10] This monumental uprising initiated a five-year cycle of rural and urban reawakening of the exploited classes and oppressed indigenous nations that gradually spread throughout most of the country.[11] The rebellions reached their apogee in the removal of two neoliberal presidents, Gonzalo Sánchez de Lozada in October 2003, and Carlos Mesa Gisbert in June 2005.[12] These two moments were dubbed the "Gas Wars" because of the centrality of the demand to renationalize the oil and gas industry in Bolivia—the country has South America's second largest natural gas deposits after Venezuela.

The social forces behind the rebellions were multifarious, but the Aymara indigenous peasants of the western altiplano (high plateau), and the 80-percent-indigenous, informal proletarian city of El Alto—with its rich insurrectionary traditions of revolutionary Marxism from "relocated" ex-miners, and indigenous radicalism from the Aymara, Quechua, and other indigenous rural-to-urban migrants—played the most important role at the height of sometimes bloody confrontations with the state. While the popular forces were overwhelmingly unarmed, the state responded with repression at various intervals, most viciously in October 2003, when Sánchez de Lozada ("Goni") sent in the military to crush the slum revolt in El Alto, leaving at least sixty-seven dead and hundreds injured and maimed by bullet wounds.

Guiding demands of this wave of protest were the nationalization of, and social control over, natural resources such as water, natural gas and oil, mining minerals, land, and indigenous territory. A plethora of popular organizations and movements rekindled an historic fight to refound Bolivia through a revolutionary Constituent Assembly that would see the organic participation of representatives of all the popular sectors in the country, and reverse the internally colonial racial domination by the white-mestizo (mixed race) elite over the majority indigenous population, a system of oppression petrified in state institutions at the founding of the republic in 1825 and resistant to change even in the wake of reforms carried out during the 1952 nationalist-populist revolution. Anti-imperialist resistance to the multileveled interventions of the United States and other core capitalist states, and international financial institutions such as the World Bank, the IMF, and the IDB, were entrenched in the common sense of these movements.

Radical visions of anticapitalism and indigenous liberation were readily visible in leading sectors of the left-indigenous forces, even if they were not universally ascribed to by all participants in the movements. Left-indigenous forces from 2000 to 2005 represented a *combined liberation struggle* that clarified the overlapping of racial oppression and class exploitation and was rooted in the experience of the traditional Bolivian working class, the urban informal proletariat, and poor and/or landless indigenous peasants. It was a combined struggle that registered the necessity of overcoming both sides of racial and capitalist class exploitation and oppression simultaneously because of the deeply intertwined bases of these phenomena in the Bolivian context. The rebellions, in their best moments, were characterized by assembly-style, democratic, and mass-based mobilization from below, drawing from the organizational patterns of the Trotskyist and anarco-syndicalist tin miners—the vanguard of the Bolivian left for much of the twentieth century—and variations of the indigenous *ayllus*—traditional communitarian structures—adapted to new rural and urban contexts. The movements were rooted in the everyday necessities of the popular classes while at the same time—at least at points of greatest intensity and mass mobilization—effectively linked these issues to the broader quest for political power and fundamental structural transformation of the state and economy. Notably absent from the scene, however, was a revolutionary party with roots in the key movements and a broad, cross-regional social base capable of unifying the multiplicity of popular struggles on the rise. Rather, the

MAS, led by cocalero union leader Evo Morales, was the only popular party able to articulate some of the sentiments of the organized masses beyond a local or regional basis.

While the MAS played an important role in the Cochabamba Water War of 2000 and anti-imperialist cocalero peasant movement, it was largely absent from the streets in the defining moments of October 2003, and played a moderating, reformist role in the May–June 2005 uprising. In the first case, the MAS opted for a constitutional exit to the state crisis, aligning itself initially with the neoliberal successor government of Carlos Mesa. In May–June 2005, the MAS distanced itself from the massively popular demand for a real nationalization of natural gas and oil, and steered the political conjuncture away from the radicalism of the streets toward the tamer terrain of electoral politics. It is against this backdrop that we need to situate our discussion of the current government in office in La Paz. History did not begin on January 22, 2006, when the MAS took office and Evo Morales gave his historic inaugural speech.

The December Elections

The results of the December 18, 2005, presidential, legislative, and prefectural elections in Bolivia were trailblazing in a variety of ways (see Tables 2.1 and 2.2). Most astonishing, of course, was the 53.7 percent of the popular vote garnered by Evo Morales. Not even the "most optimistic [MAS] militants had imagined such a result."[13] This was the first time in over forty years that a presidential candidate in Bolivia won an absolute majority. The percentage of votes obtained by the MAS exceeded by almost fifteen points the top showing of any party in any of the elections since the return of electoral democracy in 1982.[14] The MAS won over 30 percent more of the popular vote than it did in the preceding presidential elections of 2002, a gargantuan climb without precedent in Bolivian history. Moreover, the overall electoral turnout was an impressive 84.5 percent of eligible voters, up 12.5 percent from the 2002 elections.

TABLE 2.1

Party	Presidential and Vice-Presidential Candidates	Number of Votes	Percentage of Valid Votes Obtained	Change Since 2002 Elections (Percentage)
MAS	Evo Morales Ayma Alvaro Garcia Linera	1,544,374	53.7	30.3
PODEMOS	Jorge Quiroga Ramirez Maria Rene Duchen	821,745	28.5	
UN	Samuel Doria Medina Auza Carlos Dabdoub Arrien	224,090	7.8	
MNR	Michiaki Nagatani Guillermo Bedregal	185,859	6.4	-14.9
MIP	Felipe Quispe Huanca Camila Choquetijlla	61,948	2.1	-4
NFR	Gildo Angulo Gonzalo Quiroga	19,667	0.6	-18.8
FREPAB	Eliseo Rodriguez Adolfo Flores Morelli	8,737	0.3	
USTB	Nestor Garcia Rojas Julio Antonio Uzquiano	7,381	0.2	
Blank		124,046		-0.3
Invalid		104,570		0.5
Participation		3,102,417 (84.5%)		12.5

Source: Derived from Salvador Romero Ballivián, El Tablero Reordenado: Análisis de la Elección Presidencial de 2005 (La Paz: Corte Nacional Electoral, 2005), 41.

TABLE 2.2: MAIN POLITICAL PARTY PARTICIPATION IN 2005 PRESIDENTIAL ELECTIONS

MAS	Movimiento Al Socialismo
PODEMOS	Poder Democrático y Social
UN	Unidad Nacional
MNR	Movimiento Nacionalista Revolucionaria
MIP	Movimiento Indígena Pachakuti
NFR	Nueva Fuerza Republicana
FREPAB	Frente Patriótico Agropecuario de Bolivia
USTB	Unión Socialista de Trabajadores de Bolivia

Geographically, the elections broadly sliced the country into eastern and western parts. The MAS won in the departments of La Paz,
Oruro, Potosí, Cochabamba, and Chuquisaca, while the neoliberal
coalition, PODEMOS (We Can), finished second overall, and first in
Pando, Beni, Santa Cruz, and Tarija. As was expected, the MAS had its
best results in the countryside. In particular, the party continued to
dominate the rural parts of the department of Cochabamba, where the
cocaleros' peasant unions remain the party's *columna vertebral* (spinal
column), even if their influence in directing the MAS's overall agenda
has subsided. The MAS also did well in the northern sector of the department of Potosí, the southeast of the department of La Paz, and the
east and south of the department of Oruro, extending in this way its
dominance in the vast majority of rural areas in the western and central parts of the country, where the party maintains important influence in rural union and indigenous community networks at the local
levels.[15] The strong showing by the MAS was also contingent on concentrated peasant support from various rural agricultural zones of the
department of Santa Cruz, such as San Julián, Cuatro Cañadas,
Mineros, and Yapacaní, colonized by Aymara and Quechua indigenous
migrants from the western highlands. In addition, the MAS attracted
the votes of both organized sectors of the mining industry—the *cooperativistas* (cooperative miners) and the state-employed miners—who
are otherwise perennially in conflict. These and other alliances helped
secure an absolute majority of the votes in the north and center of the
department of Chuquisaca, the center and east of the department of
Potosí, the eastern part of the department of Oruro, and the western
region of the department of Santa Cruz.[16]

But the MAS also took the cities. Appealing in part to the informal
urban proletariat of the suburban slums and older working-class barrios of the major urban centers, the MAS was able to win in all cities, except the reactionary heartland of Santa Cruz. The MAS's vice presidential candidate Álvaro García Linera was instrumental in the party taking
"33 per cent to the Right's 42 percent in Santa Cruz Department," where
he engaged in "months of campaigning."[17] Likewise, García Linera's emphasis on the moderate features of the party's electoral platform and the

reformism of its ultimate aims helped win over sufficient middle- and upper-class urban voters in the wealthy neighborhoods of La Paz and Cochabamba to secure victory. Analysts have pointed out that for some sectors of the Bolivian middle and upper classes ensuring a victory for the reformist MAS was perceived as a realistic strategy for a potential end to the left-indigenous insurrections and road blockades of the preceding five years, which they despised, whereas allowing a victory for the far-right PODEMOS was thought a suicidal tactic that would most assuredly result in a rebirth of those movements.[18] In other words, the smooth reproduction of the capitalist system in the Bolivian context was more probable under the MAS than PODEMOS. Undoubtedly, the fact that García Linera is a light-skinned, mestizo intellectual from a middle-class *Cochabambino* family, made support for the MAS more palatable among the "comfortable" urban populations. The "chronically racist mentality" of the middle and upper urban classes accounts for them seeing in the bibliophile García Linera a "complement" to the supposed intellectual limitations of Evo Morales.[19]

PODEMOS, while ostensibly a new party formation, is in fact a reconfigured coalition of major sectors of the so-called traditional parties—the Movimiento Nacional Revolucionario (National Revolutionary Movement, MNR), the Acción Democrática y Nacionalista (Democratic and Nationalist Action, ADN), and the Movimiento de la Izquierda Revolucionario (Revolutionary Movement of the Left, MIR)—which, because of their association with neoliberalism, suffered considerable decline in the 2002 elections, followed by an even worse fate over the next few years. Jorge "Tuto" Quiroga, the presidential candidate of PODEMOS, was vice president in the ADN government, which was began its rule in 1997 under the leadership of ex-dictator Hugo Banzer Suárez. When Banzer was diagnosed with lung cancer and vacated the presidency prematurely in August 2001, Quiroga became president and served out the remainder of the five-year term. PODEMOS, then, is properly understood as an attempt by the old-guard neoliberals to reinvent themselves under a new electoral banner, and their primary social base remains those sectors that benefited during the neoliberal era—primarily the internationally oriented fractions of capital in the eastern department of Santa Cruz, including those in natural gas, agro-industry, banking, and illegal narcotics. The party's distant second-place finish to the MAS—with a mere 28.5 percent of the vote—highlights the extent to which the neoliberal model had been discredited by December 2005.

Another remarkable component of the 2005 elections, and an additional signifier of the collapse of neoliberal ideological hegemony in the country, was the dismal showing of the MNR, certainly the most powerful party of the last two decades in the country, and the most visceral proponent of neoliberalism in Bolivia. The MNR won only 5.9 percent of the vote, and placed fourth overall. Similar conclusions can be drawn from the results of the other "new" contender in the electoral scene, the *Unidad Nacional* (National Unity, UN), led by Samuel Doria Medina. Doria, a multimillionaire whose wealth is based in the cement industry as well as in his proprietorship of the Burger King franchise within Bolivia, attempted to position the UN as somewhere in the murky middle between the "extremes" of Morales and Quiroga. However, Doria, like Quiroga, has a neoliberal personal history. Most importantly, he was minister of government under the Jaime Paz Zamora (MIR) government between 1989 and 1993.[20] The Bolivian populace was unmoved by his reincarnation and the UN finished in third place with 7.8 percent of the popular vote.

Everything said thus far rightly indicates the triumph of anti-neoliberal ideas and the expression of indigenous pride through the ballot box in the elections of 2005. However, there were two important wrenches thrown into the MAS's electoral finish that deserve mention. First, results of the legislative elections were less positive than in the presidential election (see Table 2.3). While the MAS won a majority in the Chamber of Deputies, with 72 out of 130 seats, the party achieved only a minority in the Senate. The MAS occupies twelve Senate seats to PODEMOS's thirteen, the UN's one, and the MNR's one. Negotiations with—or, as right-wing opposition senators claim, the "buying of"—dissidents from within these opposition parties was therefore a feature of the MAS administration in its opening year. At the outset the MAS was able to secure opposition support to appoint a *masista* president of the Senate. A second obstacle to emerge for the MAS within the electoral domain was the right's dominant performance in the first departmental prefecture elections in Bolivian history, which occurred simultaneously with the presidential elections. The MAS won only three of the nine prefectures (Chuquisaca, Potosí, and Oruro), with the other six (La Paz, Beni, Santa Cruz, Tarija, Pando, and Cochabamba) going to the right (see Table 2.4). The deepening of the already well-developed attempts by the bourgeoisie to destabilize the MAS government through departmental politics was therefore a foreseeable component of the political scene in the immediate aftermath of the December 2005 elections. In order to understand the polarizing class, race, and regional dynamics of the first year of the MAS government, however, we need to delve much more deeply into society than would be possible in an exclusively institutional examination of electoral outcomes. We can begin such a reflection by considering the origins and trajectory of today's ruling party.

TABLE 2.3: DISTRIBUTION OF SEATS IN CONGRESS, 2006

Party	Senate	Chamber of Deputies	Total
MAS	12	72	84
PODEMOS	13	43	56
UN	1	8	9
MNR	1	7	8
Total	27	130	157

Source: Corte Nacional Electoral

TABLE 2.4: 2005 ELECTIONS FOR DEPARTMENTAL PREFECTS

Party	Number of Votes	Percentage of Votes
Beni		
PODEMOS	46,842	44.6
MNR	31,290	29.8
AC*	19,755	18.8
MAS	7,054	6.7

Prefect Elected: Ernesto Suarez Sattori (PODEMOS)

*Autonomía Vecinal

Party	Number of Votes	Percentage of Votes
Cochabamba		
AUC	246,522	47.6
MAS	222,974	43.1
FUN*	27,757	5.4
MIP	20,314	4.0

Prefect Elected: Manfred Reyes Villa (AUC)

*Frente de Unidad Nacional

Party	Number of Votes	Percentage of Votes
Chuquisaca		
MAS	66,999	42.3
PODEMOS	57,552	36.3
FUN	15,127	9.6
MIR*	9,621	6.1
MNR	9,069	5.7

Prefect Elected: David Sanchez Heredia (MAS)

*Movimiento Izquierda Revolucionaria

Party	Number of Votes	Percentage of Votes
La Paz		
PODEMOS	361,049	37.9
MAS	321,369	33.8
FREPAB	113,856	11.9
MIP	51,101	5.4
FUN	46,021	4.8
MNR	23,464	2.5
NFR	17,456	1.8
MIR	16,096	1.7

Prefect Elected: José Luis Paredes (PODEMOS)

Party	Number of Votes	Percentage of Votes
Oruro		
MAS	63,630	40.9
PODEMOS	43,912	28.3
MOR*	12,898	8.3
FUN	12,791	8.2
MNR	7,525	4.8
MIR	6,019	3.9
MIP	3,614	2.3
USTB	3,184	2.0
NFR	1,833	1.2

Prefect Elected: Alberto Luis Aguilar Calle (MAS)

*Movimiento Autónomo Regional

Party	Number of Votes	Percentage of Votes
Pando		
PODEMOS	9,958	48.0
UN-MAR*	9,530	46.0
MAS	1,244	6.0

Prefect Elected: Leopoldo Fernandez Ferreira (PODEMOS)

*Unidad Nacional—Movimiento Amazónico de Renovación

Potosí		
MAS	79,710	40.7
PODEMOS	58,392	29.8
MOR*	24,907	12.7
MNR	13,528	6.9
IP[†]	10,105	5.2
FUN	9,253	4.7

Prefect Elected: Mario Vierreira Iporre (MAS)

*Movimiento Originario Popular
† Integración Potosina

Santa Cruz		
APB*	299,730	47.9
TRES-MNR[†]	175,010	28.0
MAS	151,306	24.2

Prefect Elected: Ruben Dario Costas Aguilera (APB)

*Autonomía Para Bolivia
† Trabajo Responsabilidad Eficiencia y Seguridad—
Movimiento Nacionalista Revolucionaria

Tarija		
ER-CC*	64,074	45.6
CR[†]	47,637	33.9
MAS	28,690	20.4

Prefect Elected: Mario Adel Cossio Cortez (ER-CC)

* Encuentro Regional: Camino Al Cambio
† Convergencia Regional

Source: Derived from Elecciones generales, prefecturales 2005, www.bolivia.com
(accessed on February 13, 2007).

The MAS: Origins, Ideology, Class Composition, and Leadership

Where did the MAS come from? What is the party's class composition and how has it changed over time? What have been the key components of its ideology and how have these altered with each new circumstance? What tactics—extra-parliamentary and parliamentary—has the MAS employed as its basic collective action repertoire in different periods? Exploring these questions will bring us to a fuller understanding of the complexities of the party and its evolution than would a string of citations from the contemporary presidential speeches of Evo Morales—important as these are in the construction of the new government's popular image.

The historic roots of the MAS are in the coca-growing zone of Chapare, in the department of Cochabamba. After the crash of the international price of tin and the corresponding privatization of the bulk of the state mining industry in the mid-1980s, tens of thousands of jobless miners were "relocated" throughout the country, searching for new means of survival. While many migrated to major urban centers, thousands of others migrated to Chapare to begin a new life as smallholding cocalero peasants. Responding to the country's comparative advantage, as neoliberal doctrine demands, the coca leaf became a central source of foreign exchange and a basic means of livelihood during the debt crisis of the 1980s and the deepening of neoliberal restructuring in the 1990s. Demand for cocaine was accelerating on the world market and therefore prices were high for much of this period. In the closing years of the 1980s, the Bolivian government, under pressure from a U.S. administration that was launching its "War on Drugs," began to eradicate "illegal" coca crops in Chapare, quickly militarizing the area and threatening the means of subsistence of the cocaleros and their families.[21] Ideological convergence and mutual transformation quickly congealed a coalition of social forces in the newly volatile, semitropical setting of Chapare, where the Marxist ideas and organizational strategies brought to the area by the migrant miners melded with those visions and tactics of the preexisting networks of indigenous and peasant union and community structures.[22] Through hunger strikes, road blockades, grand protests, and historic marches tracing long stretches of Bolivian countryside and cityscapes, the cocaleros—throughout the late 1980s and 1990s—became the leading light of left-indigenous forces otherwise in retreat and disarray throughout the country.[23] The *hoja sagrada*, the sacred coca leaf, became a symbol of national dignity in the face of the imperial hubris of the U.S. state, and its brutal counter-narcotics policies and support for neoliberal restructuring in Bolivia.[24] The cocaleros began constructing a thoroughgoing anti-imperialist, anti-neoliberal, and eclectically indigenous-nationalist critique of the status quo. They demanded the reassertion of popular collective control over privatized natural resources then in the hands of transnational capital, the recognition of indigenous land and territory, the free trade and industrialization of the coca leaf, democracy and social justice, human rights for the indigenous population, popular sovereignty for the Bolivian state (meaning both Bolivian independence from imperial impositions and the popular sovereignty of indigenous nations within the Bolivian state as against elite domination by a white-mestizo ruling class), the renationalization of privatized state enterprises, and a general rejection of the neoliberal economic model.[25]

However, as early as 1992, the cocaleros and indigenous peasant organizations in the altiplano were together articulating what they perceived as the limitations of community and peasant union mobilization in confronting the tremendous obstacles facing the popular movement. At the Asamblea de los Pueblos Originarios (Assembly of Indigenous Peoples), held on October 12, 1992, under the umbrella of the Central Sindical de Trabajadores Campesinos de Bolivia (CSUTCB), the necessity of a *brazo político*, a political arm, for the peasant union movement was put on the table. The diverse currents and organizations attending the assembly were too internally fractious, however, to determine anything about the shape and content of that political arm.[26] Gradual steps toward the formation of an *instrumento político*, or political instrument, nonetheless proceeded over the next few years. In the First Land and Territory Congress in Santa Cruz in 1995, the main peasant and indigenous organizations of the country met and reaffirmed the necessity of a political instrument.[27] This set the stage for the Seventh Ordinary Congress of the CSUTCB in March and April 1996 in Santa Cruz, where the move to consolidate the construction of a political instrument was ratified.

Thus was born the Asamblea por la Soberanía de los Pueblos (Assembly for the Sovereignty of the Peoples, ASP). Peasant leader Alejo Véliz was elected as head of the party. Due to technicalities, the ASP was unable to gain recognition as a registered party in the 1995 municipal elections, but through a tactical electoral agreement, the new party ran jointly with the *Izquierda Unida* (United Left, IU), and won forty-nine town council seats and ten mayoralties, all in the department of Cochabamba.[28] The ASP described its basis in 1995 as a struggle for a communitarian, multinational, socialist Bolivia, in which the class struggle and the national struggle would be combined.[29] In the 1997 presidential elections, the ASP candidates again ran under the IU banner with Alejo Véliz as their presidential contender.

However, by 1998 disputes between the three main indigenous leaders in the country—Felipe Quispe, Alejo Véliz, and Evo Morales—characterized in equal parts by ideological disagreement and personalist *caudillismo* (big man politics), led to the eventual disintegration of the ASP. In its place two new parties eventually emerged, the Movimiento Indígena Pachakuti (Pachakuti Indigenous Movement, MIP), led by Felipe Quispe and primarily appealing to the Aymara indigenous radicalism of the altiplano, and the Instrumento Político por la Soberanía de los Pueblos (Political Instrument for the Sovereignty of the Peoples, IPSP), led by Evo Morales and appealing to a much broader, inter-ethnic, and cross-regional social base. Again, due to technicalities, the IPSP was unable to establish status as an official party in the electoral arena and therefore assumed the name of an officially registered but defunct political party, the Movimiento al Socialismo. Under this banner, in the 1999 municipal elections, the IPSP-MAS ticket garnered 3.27 percent of the national vote, ten mayoralties, and seventy-nine municipal council seats.[30]

To be clear, municipal electoral politics was only one component of the MAS strategy in the late 1990s, a period, it should be remembered, of relatively weak popular resistance to the neoliberal model through-out the country. The cocaleros and the MAS continued to engage in the extra-parliamentary actions highlighted earlier. Moreover, when the so-cial movement tide turned in 2000 with the Cochabamba Water War, and shortly thereafter with the Aymara indigenous uprisings of 2001 in the altiplano, the MAS continued to focus on extra-parliamentary, mass action. Indeed, Morales was expelled from Congress in 2001 for his "il-legal" participation in cocalero street actions, and was famously de-nounced by then-U.S. ambassador to Bolivia, Manuel Rocha.

In addition to recognizing the extra-parliamentary radicalism of the party in these years, it is also important to note that the MAS was consciously formed as a *political instrument*, rather than a *political party*, because of the deep and broad disgust with the Bolivian political class throughout society, but also, and more importantly, so that the MAS would act as a federating body of diverse social movement organ-izations deeply rooted in urban and rural union and community net-works, rather than as a crude overseer in the Stalinist style, or a clien-telist machine in the manner of the "traditional" neoliberal, or old populist, parties. At least from the late 1990s until 2002 these principles closely approximated the real functioning of the party, with a great deal of its power residing in the grassroots. Hence, anthropologist Robert Albro can write the following passage, based on field research carried out in 2001 and 2002, with a certain credibility:

> Morales and other *masistas* emphasise that the MAS 'does not have its own separate structures'. MAS legislators claim not to be politicians or political representatives. They are, rather, "messengers" to congress, "spokespeople" for a base-driven consensus, emergent from face-to-face rank-and-file union meetings, at which they are expected to report...The mid-level MAS hierarchy functions as a variable number of "cabinets," created on an ad hoc basis to define key issues. These cabinets have tried to institutionalize the "public assemblies" used so successfully during the Water War. At the most local level, the MAS can be hard to distinguish from the local union structure of the Six Federations of the Chapare, and where it has won elections, from the provincial municipal bureaucracy. This is what MAS militants mean with their talk of "refounding the country based upon an authentic participatory democracy" or of "recu-perating a democracy kidnapped by neoliberalism" (*Prensa Obrera*,

2002). They are referring to the politics of face-to-face assembly that is so ingrained in both indigenous community and local union politics.[31]

Therefore, during this period we can establish that the MAS was rooted in extra-parliamentary political action, deeply responsive to its *columna vertebral*, the cocaleros of Chapare, and functioned as a radically anti-neoliberal and anti-imperialist party. Regarding this era in the MAS's development, the common descriptions of the party as a radical and left-wing movement hold considerable weight. During this period the MAS was a messy amalgamation of a new left nationalism in which the national-popular contradistinctions of the early 1950s—between the "people" and the "oligarchy," and the "nation" and "imperialism"—were maintained, but in an altered form. The MAS helped to "indianize" that nationalism, bringing indigenous issues to the center of political life by drawing on the legacy of the *katarista* indigenous movement of the 1970s, and, at the same time, reflecting the basic cultural tenor of the popular cycle begun in 2000.[32] Hylton and Thomson capture this new cultural orientation when they write, "The mingling of these symbols [the *wiphala* indigenous chequered flag and the Bolivian flag] reflects the degree of overlap between Indian and Bolivian identities, and between Indian and national-popular struggles today."[33] The new Bolivian left, which the MAS helped to define in the late 1990s and early 2000s, was led by indigenous rural poor, an unprecedented trait of party politics across the political spectrum in the country's history. The calls for indigenous solidarity of the MAS in those years "acquire[d] their potency as an invitation to the recognition of an indigenous heritage shared by all of Bolivia's popular sectors that is in explicit contrast to the perceived 'individualism' of the neoliberal market."[34]

It was out of this milieu that Evo Morales arose to become a national political figure. He was born Juan Evo Morales Ayma on October 26, 1959, in the province of Sud Carangas in the department of Oruro. Four of his seven Aymara indigenous siblings died from illnesses related to poverty and the absence of sufficient health infrastructure in the region. His family, like many others, migrated to northern Argentina in search of work. In Argentina, Morales dropped out of school because of difficulties with the Spanish language after having being raised exclusively in Aymara. He would eventually return to school in Oruro, working at various points as a baker and a trumpeter in the well-known Banda Real Imperial. At the outset of the 1980s, his family was forced to migrate to Chapare due to a massive drought in the altiplano.[35] Today, his primary language is Spanish, and while he is also relatively fluent in Quechua (from his time spent in the Chapare), he no longer speaks confidently in Aymara. In Chapare, Morales began his gradual ascent through the ranks of cocalero peasant unions, becoming secretary general of the Six Federations in 1988. Ten years later, he was elected leader of the MAS and has maintained this post ever since. By 2002 he was a serious candidate in presidential elections.

This is the year when the trajectory of the party takes a rather sharp turn, the depth of which passes unnoticed in many sympathetic accounts of the party's history. In the 2002 elections, Evo Morales and the MAS placed second with 20.9 percent of the popular vote to Gonzalo Sánchez de Lozada and the MNR's 22.5. This unexpected triumph spurred changes in party tactics. The sights were set on contesting the 2007 presidential elections. Parliamentary strategies were privileged over protest politics, as witnessed most dramatically in the relative absence of the MAS in the October 2003 rebellions.[36] The party began moderating its economic demands in an effort to attract urban middle-class voters, a moderation captured in party officials' constant refrain: "*de la protesta a la propuesta*" (from protest to proposal). There was an explicit effort made to extend from the cocalero regional and corporatist base to a wider, cross-regional, and cross-class constituency that would incorporate other indigenous movements, peasant movements, the urban poor, and the urban working class; however, the thrust of the new trajectory was to win over urban intellectuals and the urban middle class.[37]

The shift in the party's ideology toward moderate reformism after 2002 cannot be explained as fallout from the whims of a few important leaders, nor as a consequence of changes in the outlook of Morales himself; rather, the shift is indicative of an alteration in strategic orientation toward electoral politics and of the changing class composition of the party over time. The weight of the anti-imperialist, anti-neoliberal cocalero peasantry diminished, while an urban middle-class intelligentsia played an increasingly important role. The character of the first MAS cabinet in 2006, and the slightly broader peripheries around the cabinet (such as vice-ministerial portfolios), reflects these developments. It is evident that the *origins* of many of the individuals selected to fill these positions are in the popular classes (peasants, miners); however, they *currently* make up part of the relatively privileged, middle-class sectors of the rural and urban economies.[38] One indication of this is the fact that, on average, the ministers in the first MAS cabinet each had declared net assets of over US$50,000.[39] In Bolivia, such an accumulation of wealth places them squarely in the middle layers of the urban and rural economies.

Some of the rationale behind the party's decision to ask Álvaro García Linera to run as the MAS vice presidential candidate in the December 2005 elections has been rehearsed above: a light-skinned mestizo intellectual with calming, moderate rhetoric was thought to appeal to the middle and even upper-middle-class sectors, while Morales was expected to continue to bring out the popular indigenous vote.[40] While Morales continued to invoke many of the symbols that conjured up the radical past of the MAS, García Linera became the primary public voice of the MAS's new economic development program during the 2005 campaign. As part of this trajectory he began publishing and speaking in various forums about the impossibility of establishing socialism in Bolivia for at least fifty to one hundred years. Instead, García Linera posited that Bolivia must first build an industrial capitalist base. The capitalist model he envisions—Andean-Amazonian Capitalism—projects a greater role for state intervention in the market. The formula essentially means capitalist development with a stronger state to support a petty-bourgeoisie that will eventually become a powerful national bourgeoisie to drive Bolivia into successful capitalist development. That national bourgeoisie will be indigenous, or "Andean-Amazonian." Only after this long intermediary phase of industrial capitalism has matured will the fulfillment of socialism be materially plausible.[41] Fernando Molina, a neoliberal critic of the MAS, has correctly pointed out that in many respects Andean-Amazonian Capitalism closely resembles the old line of the Stalinist Partido Comunista Boliviana (Bolivian Communist Party, PCB), which stressed the necessity of a "revolution by stages": feudalism to capitalism (bourgeois), and, *eventually*, capitalism to communism (communist).[42]

García Linera expounded further on the character of the MAS after the party formed the government in 2006, attempting to define the ideology of "Evismo." The indigenous, democratic, and cultural "revolution," he reminds us, does not imply "radical" economic change, or even transformative restructuring of political institutions. Rather, "modifications" in the existing political structures of power and elite rule are all that is promised in the current context: "In the case of Evismo, we are before a political revolution that has its impact in the economic realm but not in a strictly radical manner. Evo Morales has himself conceptualized the process that he is leading as a democratic cultural revolution, or a decolonizing democratic revolution, which modifies the structures of power, modifies the composition of the elite, of power and rights, and with this the institutions of the state. It has an effect on the economic structure because all expansion of rights means the distribution of wealth."[43]

Having thus charted in some depth the trajectory of the MAS we are now in a better position to begin our evaluation of its first year as government in the following chapter.

Conclusion

In this chapter, I explored four major themes. I showed, first, that the left-indigenous cycle of rebellion between 2000 and 2005 and the subsequent election of Evo Morales have provoked renewed theoretical discussion regarding revolution in Bolivia. It was argued that distinguishing between revolutionary epochs and social revolutions should help to clarify the terms of debate. From here, the mass mobilizations between 2000 and 2005 and the parallel state crisis were shown to have precipitated the opening of an authentically revolutionary epoch in the country. It was also claimed, however, that this epoch has not led to a social revolution.

A third objective of this chapter was an extensive analysis of the December 2005 elections. The results show the unambiguous trounc-

ing of the traditional neoliberal parties and the exhaustion of neoliberal ideological hegemony in the country. Finally, I examined the shifting trajectory of the MAS from an anti-neoliberal, anti-imperialist, and
mass-mobilization party to an increasingly reformist one focused on
winning elections by moderating its platform. It was determined that a
principal cause of this shift was the changing class composition of the
higher layers of the party structure over time.

In the next chapter, I shift my attention to central features of the
MAS government's first year in office. I examine some of the complexities of the politics of indigenous liberation, trends in macro-economic
policies, reforms in the hydrocarbon (natural gas and oil) sector, the
constituent assembly process, and the incipient rearticulation of the political right through a politics of "autonomism" in the eastern lowlands.

Three

Neoliberal Continuities, the Autonomist Right, and the Political Economy of Indigenous Struggle

In Chapter One, the political and economic dynamics of contemporary Bolivia were discussed in connection with changes in capitalist imperialism at the international level, and foreign relations with Venezuela and Cuba at the regional level. The principal features of Bolivia's rural and urban class structures in the neoliberal age were outlined. Chapter Two reviewed distinct perspectives on revolution in contemporary Bolivia, and argued that we ought to distinguish between *revolutionary epochs* and *social revolutions* in order to better understand the peculiarities of both phenomena. It then shifted away from this theoretical terrain and showed in detail how the left-indigenous insurrectionary period, between 2000 and 2005, constituted a proper revolutionary epoch. Urban and rural revolt from below coincided with a multidimensional state crisis from above, creating opportunities for fundamental structural change to the Bolivian state and society. This revolutionary epoch, moreover, was characterized by a combined liberation struggle in which mass movements of indigenous proletarians and peasants fought to overcome inextricably intertwined processes of class exploitation and racial oppression. This was an anticapitalist and indigenous-liberationist insurrectionary cycle. The revolutionary epoch of 2000 and 2005 did not, however, develop into a social revolution.

Rather, as Chapter Two also explained, revolutionary energies were redirected into the moderately reformist politics of the presidential campaign of Evo Morales in late 2005. The electoral results revealed clearly just how deeply and broadly the neoliberal project had been rejected by the popular majority. But in order to understand why the election of Morales, as leader of the MAS, did not portend a profound rupture with neoliberalism as many had expected, it was argued that we must examine the trajectory of the party's formation, and its shifting class composition, ideology, and political strategies over time. With this as a framework, Chapter Two traced the MAS's origins as an anti-imperialist and anti-neoliberal political instrument of the indigenous-peasant movement in the Chapare region of the department of Cochabamba. Militant cocaleros were the party's principal social base between the mid-1990s and early 2000s. The politics of the party were characterized by assembly-style democracy, which mirrored the practices of the peasant unions in the region. The cocaleros of the party were in near-constant confrontation with American imperialism vis-à-vis the "war on drugs." They developed militant tactics of direct action to counter the militarization of the Chapare, the destruction of their livelihoods, and the neoliberalization of Bolivia's economic and political structures. During this era, the MAS was consequently driven by extra-parliamentary politics and mass mobilization in the city streets and countryside. The party's evolving platform called for an end to neoliberalism and denounced imperialism in all its nefarious forms.

However, beginning in 2002—after Morales narrowly lost the presidential election—the party's politics began to shift away from radical critiques of neoliberalism and imperialism. The party began also to turn its back on strategies of popular class mobilization and direct confrontations with state authorities and capital. The highest layers of the party's infrastructure were increasingly populated with urban middle-class and mestizo intellectuals who emphasized the need to moderate the party's radical public profile. Accompanying this change in class composition at the top of the party was a turn toward electoral politics as the definitive domain of party praxis. The challenge for the party was increasingly seen as courting the urban middle-class voters in electoral contests and assuring foreign and domestic capital that their fundamental interests would not be encroached upon if Morales were to become president. Anti-imperialism and anti-neoliberalism were pushed to the background as reformist electoralism was given pride of place. The consequences of these changes were most evident in the explosive Gas Wars of 2003 and 2005, in which two neoliberal presidents were overthrown by hundreds of thousands of largely indigenous urban working-class and peasant protesters, mostly concentrated in the cities of El Alto and La Paz. The MAS failed to provide revolutionary leadership in these two opportunities. Worse, to the extent that the MAS was present in 2003 and 2005, it acted to steer incredibly powerful mass demonstrations into constitutional exits, in which elite negotiations between established neoliberal politicians took precedence.

With all this as a backdrop, this chapter proceeds in three parts. First, we examine the complex relationship between indigenous liberation and political economy during the first year of the MAS government (January 2006–January 2007). Second, we explore reform in the hydrocarbons (natural gas and oil) sector. This deserves particular attention both because Bolivia has South America's second largest natural gas deposits after Venezuela, and because the demand for the nationalization of hydrocarbons figured very prominently in the popular protests of 2003 and 2005 as well as in Morales's presidential campaign. A third topic addressed is the Constituent Assembly (CA). Demands to convene a revolutionary CA to remake Bolivia with the direct participation of the indigenous proletarian and peasant majority was a central motif in numerous rebellions, marches, and strikes between 2000 and 2005. Here we show how the CA organized by the Morales government differed quite dramatically from the type of assembly envisioned by left-indigenous movements. Also discussed is the formation of a right-wing autonomist movement in the media luna departments of the eastern lowlands—Beni, Pando, Santa Cruz, and Tarija. This new Right, representing agro-industrial, petroleum, and finance capitalists, used the CA as a fulcrum in its strategy to destabilize the Morales regime and set back even the most modest of social and economic reforms proposed by the government.

This chapter argues that the Morales victory in December 2005 was a democratic gain in race relations in Bolivia. Indigenous rights were thrust to the center of the national political agenda to an unprecedented degree, following decades—indeed centuries—of indigenous liberation struggle against Spanish colonialism and then internally colonial race relations throughout the republican era. This is an important conquest for popular forces, a measurable blow to white-mestizo minority control of the state and race relations long-rooted in informal apartheid. This victory has been dampened, however, by disconcerting parallels with the 1994 electoral victory of the African National Congress (ANC) in South Africa and that party-regime's trajectory since. While the MAS has not become an enthusiastic protagonist of unbridled neoliberalism—as the ANC has—the politics of indigenous liberation within the MAS government have nonetheless been separated artificially from the project for revolutionary socialist transformation. The left-indigenous combined liberation struggle between 2000 and 2005, grounded in anticapitalism and indigenous liberation, has become under the Morales government a formulaic struggle of distinct stages. The MAS emphasizes indigenous liberation today, with socialist transformation placed on the back burner for fifty to one hundred years. Such a perspective fails to come to grips with the fact that the vast majority of the indigenous population also constitutes the bulk of the working classes and peasantry whose full emancipation cannot be realized under capitalism—even a capitalism cloaked in an "Andean-Amazonian" guise.[1] In this chapter and the next we demonstrate these trends for the first year of the administration, while Chapters Five and Six illustrate its deepening and consolidation over the following three years (2007–2010).

Even more serious than abandoning a politics of transition toward socialism today, the MAS administration and the class interests it serves tends to represent an important continuity with the preexisting neoliberal model—alive in Bolivia since the shock therapy of the mid-1980s. There were partial policy breaks with neoliberalism in the first year of the new government, in the areas of hydrocarbons (natural gas and oil), in foreign relations with Venezuela and Cuba, and in relations with the IMF. But even here, a decisive move to rupture ties with neoliberalism was ambiguous at best.

Regarding the CA, at the height of the recent left-indigenous struggles the popular classes envisioned an assembly that would structurally uproot the economic, political, and social status quo, building a new collective sovereignty from below of and for the indigenous proletarian and peasant majority. The vision included the organic participation of the central social movement, trade union, neighborhood, indigenous, and peasant organizations in the formation, deliberation, and execution of the assembly. The CA actually introduced by the Morales government, in contrast, precluded these revolutionary and participatory demands. Instead, it enshrined some of the worst characteristics of regular congressional politics. The MAS made a series of guarantees to the bourgeoisie of the eastern lowlands concerning the assembly's structure, conduct, and content. Appeasing the far right in this way contributed to the creation of new political space for the rearticulation of stronger right-wing forces in the shape of an autonomist movement in the media luna. While the Bolivian right had been incredibly weakened after five years of left-indigenous advance between 2000 and 2005, it subsequently began to rebuild its capacities. With its base in the departments of Pando, Beni, Santa Cruz, and Tarija, the autonomists obstructed the proceedings of the CA and increased the possibility of civil war at various junctures in 2006. The right was emboldened by the space provided to it, becoming more self-assured since expanding its geographic sphere of influence into the departments of Sucre, and, to a lesser extent, Cochabamba over 2006 and 2007.

Indigenous Liberation and the Political Economy of the MAS Government

[We are fighting for] a system in which the poor govern our country…We don't want to see our children dying in the countryside because of the absence of medical attention; not attending schools because they have no money; fainting in classes because they haven't had sufficient food…We want another system in which the majority is attended to with the riches that are ours. We want that, because if, to the contrary, that does not exist there will never be peace. The very Bible says that peace is the fruit of justice, and if there is no social justice, there is not going to be peace. This is the objective. I believe that Christ also struggled for that; and I don't know if Christ was a communist, but he also talked of these things. That is what we want, because capitalism is very wicked, perverse, bloodthirsty, inhuman, and terrorist. [2]

For the moment, I think we are, to use the old language, before merely democratic changes. That is to say, the decolonization of the state, the construction of equality, the appearance of collective rights: those, for Bolivia, comprise a gigantic revolution. For five hundred years the indigenous here had been considered animals without rights. [The fact that this is no longer the case] is already a gigantic step forward. Seen in the perspective of the world, it's not a big thing, but for Bolivia it's huge. And the possibility of deep transformations, more structural in nature, that will result in a historic culmination of workers' forces with indigenous-peasant forces; with this…maybe we'll be here discussing things beyond democracy, or capitalism with better distribution, [but the latter] represent the limited horizon in today's reality. [3]

The national liberation struggles in Southern Africa, from 1960 to 1990, were fought against European colonial occupation and white minority rule, and for Black majority rule. Liberation from these evils was a democratic victory that is rightly and widely celebrated, but political scientist John S. Saul correctly calls for a new struggle in Southern Africa, or "the next liberation struggle": a revolutionary transition to socialism, because black majority rule has not meant an end to capitalist exploitation in Southern Africa. [4] Similarly, in Bolivia, historic gains by indigenous peoples in the general elections of 2002, Morales's victory in December 2005, and the forcing of indigenous issues onto the national political agenda through popular struggle from below, have been important steps toward bringing an end to white-mestizo minority control of the state and an apartheid-like culture around race relations. These are democratic victories. At the same time, however, the MAS has taken steps against the next liberation struggle for socialist transformation, just as the ANC did in South Africa after the defeat of apartheid. The two lengthy passages quoted above, the first from mining trade unionist Miguel Zubieta, and the second from from future Vice President Álvaro García Linera, are representative of wider debates circulating throughout Bolivian society in 2005 regarding the character and form liberation was to take. Zubieta called for anticapitalist, revolutionary transformation. García Linera, on the other hand, called for democratic reforms that would leave capitalist social relations fully intact. Across Latin America, one of the central paradoxes of the 1990s has been the emergence of neoliberal multiculturalism.[5] In reaction to massive indigenous mobilizations, states developed strategies to contain the radical potential of these movements through official "recognition" of cultural diversity, indigenous languages, and constitutional change. At the same time, while the cultures of indigenous peoples have been "recognized" by neoliberal states, the material conditions of these same people have been deteriorating.

The MAS has broken with neoliberal multiculturalism in some ways because it has slowly implemented specific and moderate reforms to the neoliberal economic model it inherited, what I call reconstituted neoliberalism in the second half of this book. At the same time, however, the MAS is attempting to artificially separate the cultural and anticolonial revolution to end oppression of indigenous people from the socialist revolution to end class exploitation experienced by those very same indigenous workers and peasants who constitute the majority of the Bolivian population. Issues that were organically linked in the *combined liberation struggle* of the 2000 to 2005 revolutionary epoch have begun to unravel in the ideology adopted by the MAS in government.[6] This undoing is lost on many sympathetic analysts on the left.[7]

One fundamental function of the state under capitalism is to "reproduce the conditions for accumulation through the application of economic policies that guarantee the optimization of profits obtained by corporations."[8] In the first three months of the MAS administration the state played this role quite consistently in the realm of economic policy, broadly maintaining the neoliberal financial policy apparatus it inherited. This is evidenced, for example, by the fact that the new government officially reconfirmed the independence of the Banco Central de Bolivia (Bolivian Central Bank, BCB). The government agreed with the BCB to maintain a regime of fiscal austerity, pledging to run a deficit of less than 3.2 percent in 2006, while capping inflation at 4 percent or lower.[9] The financial press reported "a surprise visit" in early May by President Morales to the headquarters of the Association of Private Banks of Bolivia, where he was quoted as asking this body for regular meetings through which they could "make their proposals known and to make adjustments, with the sole purpose of looking after economic stability."[10] By forfeiting control of financial policy to the BCB and committing to a macroeconomic program of austerity, the government was preventing the state from "assuming discretional measures to stimulate economic activity and to affect (or privilege) specific classes or class fractions. In this way, the supposed neutrality of economic policy guarantees the predominance of the largest capitalists, obliging the state, on the contrary, to cover strictly those obligations which favor private investment and the reproduction of the labor force without significantly affecting corporate profits."[11]

In an April 2006 BCB report, the bank positively assessed the first three months of the MAS government, especially with regard to its control of inflation. The BCB report also made clear its recommendations for strict limits to salary increases in the public sector as well as for continued austerity in public spending.[12] Following closely on the heels of the report, public statements by government officials as well as leaks to the press indicated that the promised increase in the minimum salary from 440 to 880 bolivianos per month would not be forthcoming.[13] The actual increase was a relatively paltry raise of 13.63 percent, announced on Labor Day, May 1, 2006.[14] Reviewing the first year of the Morales administration, the Economist Intelligence Unit reported that "the non-financial public sector ended 2006 with an estimated fiscal surplus equivalent to 6% of GDP, an unnecessarily high level of savings for a country with immense investment needs and one that has benefited from debt forgiveness initiatives leading to a reduction in the public sector debt stock from 80% of GDP in 2004 to 54.6% of GDP in 2006." The briefing goes on to show that "despite booming revenues, which are also underpinned by strong external demand for Bolivian commodities, public investment expansion by the central and regional governments has been, at best, modest…Despite an overall 31% year-on-year increase in infrastructure investments in 2006, social investment shrank by 6% according to estimates from the Unidad de Análisis de Políticas Económicas y Sociales (Udape), a think tank linked to the Ministry of Planning."[15] In the first year, then, in terms of macroeconomic and labor policy, there were discernible continuities between the MAS regime and its predecessors.[16] It is a truism that the neoliberal structures of the past cannot be overcome overnight. But over the course of the first year we do not even see modest initial steps in confronting this past. The failure to fulfill the electoral promise to increase dramatically the minimum wage went practically unnoticed in Bolivian society, as the small raise actually introduced was surreptitiously enacted on the same day as the wildly popular "nationalization" of the hydrocarbons industry—more on that in a moment.

The most comprehensive economic strategy of the MAS government to date, the Plan de Desarrollo Nacional 2006–2010 (National Development Plan, PDN), was released on June 16, 2006.[17] Its content stresses the democratic and cultural revolution of indigenous liberation. However, the political economy of the document signals only modest breaks with the general neoliberal development model of previous years. The plan is fundamentally predicated on the continuation of an export-led economy based on non-value added, primary natural resource commodities, most importantly hydrocarbons and mining minerals, the exploitation of which will continue to be controlled fundamentally by transnational capital. Existing export agri-business will also play a driving role in the national development model. In order to ensure the competitiveness of the economy, the plan's basic foundations will be oriented toward reducing aggregate domestic demand, maintaining low inflation, respecting the independence of the central bank, and therefore securing a tight lid on salaries and a legal framework that will prove attractive to transnational capital seeking to invest in export sectors.

It is true, as we will see in greater depth below, that the new contracts signed with transnational petroleum companies concerning the exploitation of Bolivian hydrocarbons, as well as elevated prices for exports to neighboring Argentina and Brazil, provided substantial new revenue for the Bolivian state in the midst of Latin America's commodity boom. With the new state revenue, the PND indicates that the government will increase public investment to 11.9 percent of GDP by 2010. However, the bulk of this investment will be directed toward basic infrastructure and the financing of prefectures and municipalities, as well as to various support mechanisms for enhancing the small-scale production of the petty-bourgeoisie, linking them to niche markets, and creating virtuous ties between small-scale producers and transnational capital in nontraditional export markets. Only 12.8 percent of the new public investment is designated for the industrialization of hydrocarbons in areas where state participation has increased—refineries and commercialization. Between 2007 and 2015, according to the PND, the government plans to invest only US$25 million in hydrocarbons. At the same time, the MAS foresees an increase in foreign direct investment in (and therefore control over) the fundamental means of production as a percentage of GDP. Without greater public investment in hydrocarbons and other key sectors, industrialization over the long term, under the domain of the state and social control, will prove unviable.[18] The PND, in other words, does not steer a clear development path away from transnational domination of Bolivian hydrocarbons and mining based on the extraction and export of primary natural resource commodities.

Bolivian sociologist Lorgio Orellana Aillón reminds us:

> Neoliberalism is a regime of accumulation that promotes and expands the businesses, power, and hegemony of a commercial-financial oligarchy, strongly articulated to transnational corporations and private international banking, whose network of interests overlaps with the production and exportation of primary materials in Bolivia. Given the elevated organic composition of capital required for the exploitation of minerals and hydrocarbons and for the mechanized exploitation of agro-industry, the *attraction of fresh capital* and external credit has a strategic character for the interests of this oligarchy.[19]

In his reading of the PND, Orellana Aillón argues that because it does not envision an end to transnational private control of the objective factors of production in the fundamentally important primary export sector, the PND is not a "post-neoliberal" document, and because it is the central policy framework on economics released by the government, the latter, too, cannot be described as revolutionary, nationalist, or post-neoliberal.[20] Political economist Susan Spronk agrees with Orellana Aillón that neoliberalism "is more than a set of economic policies. [It is] a form of class rule that emerged as a response to the crisis in western capitalism in the 1970s." However, she argues that while the MAS is neither nationalist nor revolutionary it does not follow that the government is neoliberal by default.[21] My own sense is that moderate reforms to neoliberal policies were initiated by the MAS government in the hydrocarbons sector in its first session in office, and in terms of government relations with the IMF (deciding not to renew the Stand-By Arrangement when it expired in March 2006). This partially distinguished the MAS government from the unambiguously neoliberal administrations of Lula in Brazil and Bachelet in Chile, for example, or the hard right administrations of Uribe in Colombia and Calderón in Mexico.[22] However, there was an undeniable pattern of considerable neoliberal continuity in major policy areas as well as in the class interests being served by the political economy of the MAS government during its first term in office. As this becomes entrenched over the four years of the first term in office, one could comfortably call the new development model a type of reconstituted neoliberalism as I argue at length in Part II of this book.

What is most important for the scope of this chapter, however, is that just as constitutions can look good on paper while their relationships to social reality are tenuous or inconsistent, national development plans and the real implementation of those plans are often at odds. While analyzing the content of the PND is critical, we cannot rely on this alone. We need always to return to the contingency of the dynamic context of social forces on the ground, and examine how these forces relate to those occupying the state apparatus. When we do so, we can see more clearly how the implementation of the PND is actually highly contested from both the right and the popular movements. The inevitability of a neoliberal outcome over the longer term under the MAS government is therefore not preordained. The extent to which the PND may be modified in practice, and the MAS pushed into conducting deeper reforms, is left open as one of various possible outcomes.

Hydrocarbons

One of the arenas of deepest contradiction and social struggle is the hydrocarbons industry. Bolivia has long been rich in natural resources. Unfortunately, they have served mainly to line the pockets of foreign pillagers and their respective empires, whether in colonial or republican times. Today, natural gas plays the role that silver and tin played in earlier historical eras.[23] Since 1997, new discoveries in the country secured Bolivia's position as second only to Venezuela in South America with respect to natural gas reserves. Bolivia's proven and probable natural gas resources in 2005 measured some 48.7 trillion cubic feet, with lesser oil reserves of 856.6 million barrels.[24] Over the last decade, demand for natural gas has increased steadily in neighboring Argentina, Brazil, Chile, and Uruguay, and Bolivia is the only country that currently enjoys the capacity and geographical proximity to meet that demand in a cost-efficient manner.[25]

Under the first administration of Gonzalo Sánchez de Lozada (1993–1997), the hydrocarbons sector was privatized through the Law of Capitalization and the Hydrocarbons Law of 1996 as part of a more general drive to privatize state-owned enterprises (SOEs). The World Bank and the IMF were sources of external pressure during this period. The Bank, in particular, was the most important provider of conditional loans behind the Hydrocarbons Law of 1996, facilitating and evaluating each stage of the reform.[26] As with other SOEs, the privatization of Yacimientos Petrolíferos Fiscales Bolivianos (YPFB) was euphemistically termed "capitalization." Under this process, YPFB was divided into three separate companies—Empresa Petrolera Chaco, Empresa Petrolera Andina, and Transredes—and 50 percent of each was sold to multinational petroleum corporations for a total sum of US$834,944,022.[27] Today, the major players in the hydrocarbons industry are Brazilian state-owned Petrobras, Repsol (Spain), Total (France), and BP and BG Group (Britain).

Levels of foreign direct investment, exploration, production, and export of hydrocarbons accelerated quite dramatically following privatization.[28] Between 1997 and 2001, for example, private investment in the industry increased from US$296 million to US$401.3 million.[29] Investments of private hydrocarbons companies also accounted for over half of FDI in Bolivia after 1996.[30] What is singularly remarkable, however, is the declining proportional take of the Bolivian state over time as production in new reserves (at 18 percent royalty rates) increased relative to existing reserves (at 50 percent royalty rates), and the international prices of oil and gas shot skywards:

We see that gas production has gone up by 376 per cent [between 1999 and 2004], oil production by 44 per cent and gas prices have risen by 80 per cent and oil prices by 78 per cent. In all, the sector's turnover has risen by 303 per cent. However, while these trends are overwhelmingly positive...the share that the state is receiving each year has been consistently declining. Although the value of revenue generated in royalties and taxes for the state is going up—it increased by 198 per cent between 1999 and 2004—the state's share in the companies' turnover is actually going down. The Bolivian government has captured a significantly lower proportion of benefits in 2004 than it did in 1999.[31]

At the same time, the intensified activity in capital-intensive hydrocarbons exploitation created very few jobs, and those that were created were mostly highly skilled technical positions such as lawyers, managers, and engineers.[32] This low rate of employment creation today is compounded by the fact that when YPFB was "capitalized" thousands of unionized workers were laid off.[33] Furthermore, it is imperative that we consider the environmental destruction wrought by the construction of pipelines, increased exploitation and production, and oil and gas leakages and fires during the intensification of these processes with the boom in FDI post-privatization. All these factors have serious implications for human health, water sources, fisheries and livestock, indigenous and other rural community livelihoods, and Bolivia's wealth of biodiversity.[34]

What is most damning to the neoliberal model in the hydrocarbons sector, however, are the figures showing how much YPFB contributed to the Treasury between 1990 and 1996, prior to privatization, compared to what the private companies contributed between 1999 and 2004, after privatization and before the moderate reforms to the neoliberal model in 2005 and 2006. Between 1990 and 1996, YPFB contributed US$1,790.6 million to the Treasury, compared to US$1,238.6 million contributed by the companies between 1999 and 2004, a difference of US$552 million:

So by simply comparing royalties and taxes (excluding sales taxes), we see that YPFB was a higher contributor to the Treasury than the companies are post-privatization. But it is also critical to remember that YPFB's contribution came without the costs of the reform, subsidies, profit remittance, or any risks of tax-avoidance or contract-abuse. As YPFB's operations were significantly smaller-scale, Bolivia was also receiving higher benefits without communities having to bear the same level of environmental costs…This reduction in benefits to Bolivia is occurring in the context of a huge increase in investment, production, and exports, as well as increasing prices.[35]

After Sánchez de Lozada was forced to resign in October 2003, his replacement, Carlos Mesa, tried to reach a compromise between the irreconcilable demands of the left-indigenous movements on the one hand, and the IMF, World Bank, and foreign petroleum companies on the other. Mesa passed a new hydrocarbons law in May 2005 that introduced a tax system similar to that of the early 1990s, prior to privatization. He introduced an additional 32 percent flat tax on the value of oil and gas production that, in addition to the 18 percent royalties, meant an ostensible return to a 50/50 take between the state and the private companies.[36] The social movements quickly rejected the partial measure, while, at the same time, it was denounced as confiscatory by the foreign petroleum companies. In late May and early June 2005, hundreds of thousands of protesters occupied La Paz once again, with the nationalization of gas as one of their leading demands. This process set the stage for Mesa's resignation and Evo Morales's electoral victory in December 2005. When the new MAS government took office in January 2006, it held a clear mandate to nationalize the industry.

Three months into the new MAS government Morales announced the nationalization of hydrocarbons through presidential decree 28701. However, it quickly became apparent that "nationalization" amounted to little more than rhetorical flourish and populist theater. The government emphasized that the decree established a new regime of royalties and taxes whereby 82 percent of profits would now go to the state, and only 18 percent to private companies. In reality, however, this new 82/18 relationship was only a transitory measure of 180 days duration invoked to pressure the companies into new contracts. There was never any guarantee that these new contracts would yield an arrangement as favorable as the transitory measure built into the decree. Despite the aggressive language of total state control, it was not clear in the decree what was being expropriated, if anything. Perhaps most important, however, were the juridical ambiguities around the weight of a decree versus a law. In the Bolivian legal system, where a law contradicts a presidential decree the former is supposed to supersede the latter. In other words, however radical sounding the presidential decree, wherever it contradicts the existing Hydrocarbons Law 3058 (introduced by Mesa in May 2005), Law 3058 is supposed to prevail. The areas of divergence and contradiction between the law and decree predictably transcended debates among constitutional experts and became the stuff of heated political contests and contention that spilled over into the streets as part of the general social polarization in 2006.

Despite the ambiguities of the initial decree, in October 2006 the Morales government announced the signing of forty-four new contracts with twelve petroleum companies, including the two biggest players, Petrobras and Respol, for a period of thirty years.[37] The contracts were widely perceived as an enormous political victory for the Morales government, and Morales declared his mission accomplished, the government had nationalized hydrocarbons. With the new contracts it is estimated that the state's hydrocarbons revenue "will surpass the $282 million a year received from 1998–2002, to a total sum of $1.3 billion a year in 2006. According to Evo Morales, this figure will reach $4 billion a year by 2010, which represents approximately 100% of Bolivia's annual GDP and will allow the MAS-led government to undertake ambitious social projects."[38] Revenue infusions have also been secured through new export agreements with Argentina and Brazil. Convenio Marco, a new project of Argentine-Bolivian energy integration, was initiated in June 2006. Under the auspices of Convenio Marco, 7.7 million cubic meters of gas was to be transported to Argentina daily until December 31, 2006, at a fixed price of US$5 per million British Thermal Units (BTU). Beginning in 2007, a longer term flexible price arrangement has been based on the prices of various related petroleum commodities on the international market. By some estimates, this represents a 48 percent increase in the sale price of gas to Argentina, which could mean annual increases of US$110 million in state revenue.[39] In mid-February 2007, an agreement between Bolivia and Brazil was also confirmed. The Bolivian government claimed that it would now receive an increase of US$144 million in state revenue from this deal.[40]

Under the new contracts and export agreements there has been an undeniable increase in state revenues, which brings to an end the unadulterated giveaways of the Sánchez de Lozada years. It is also clear, however, that the new contracts do not amount to a nationalization of the industry. They reinforce the primary-export model of development and militate against the development of a serious industrialization policy and reconstitution of YPFB. The first fundamental flaw in the new agreements with the foreign petroleum companies is that the Morales government recognized the existing shared-risk contracts which had been signed by Sánchez de Lozada without congressional approval, and which were therefore illegal.[41] Royalties and taxes to be paid to the state under the new contracts are variable in part based on the weight of past investments. If these are inflated, therefore, revenue that ought to be going to the state will be diverted to private hands.

The Morales administration also misled the public by portraying the new agreements with the transnationals as service contracts, rather than operations contracts or shared production contracts. According to the Brazilian company Petrobras, under the new contracts of October 2006, each petroleum company executes the entirety of its operations at its own expense and receives direct payment defined in relation to recuperation of costs, prices, volumes, and investments, all elements of shared production contracts according to Law 3058.[42] In the case of Petrobras, this meant that the company would continue production in a number of the largest gas fields in Bolivia. The new contracts ensured that Petrobras maintained ownership of all its current shares and that all the reserves in the relevant gas deposits could be included in the declared value of the company on the stock market.[43] According to the most comprehensive report available to date, this held true for gas reserves in all the concessions of all the petroleum companies active under the new contracts.[44] Another important early concern was that it would be highly improbable that YPFB would be meaningfully reconstructed under the new institutional and legal arrangements. With respect to the basic financing of the state company, there were serious ambiguities and uncertainties from the outset. In the two largest gas fields, San Alberto and San Antonio, for example, the royalties and taxes were divided along these lines: 18 percent in royalties paid to the departments in which the fields are located, 32 percent in direct taxes (IDH) to the Bolivian Treasury and another 32 percent directly to YPFB. However, while contracts guarantee the 50 percent composed of royalties and IDH, the remaining 32 percent destined for YPFB was contingent upon the pace at which transnationals recuperated costs and past investments as well as the volume of their production.[45] This raised serious questions regarding the security of funds for the reconstruction of YPFB.

Additionally, YPFB was supposedly to become the principal agent of commercialization and prime regulator of petroleum operations in Bolivia in the new setting; in fact, its assigned regulatory role was a minor one. For example, transnational petroleum companies continued to fix their own basic expenditures and employee salaries, which, along with other components, constituted costs that had to be recuperated. YPFB had no authority under the new contracts to determine these expenditures and employee salaries. The state company could only verify the validity of the declared recuperable costs presented to them by the private company.[46] We know already of the YPFB's weak regulatory capacity during the period following privatization in the late 1990s and early 2000s. As a consequence, there was good reason to be skeptical about its new capacity to prevent fraud and abuse on the part of the foreign petroleum companies operating in the country after Morales came to office. As Uruguayan journalist and sociologist Raúl Zibechi points out,

> The problem with not nationalizing hydrocarbons is that the reformulation of the state-owned YPFB…is not real. The new contracts require that YPFB not make investments or assume risks or responsibilities, but rather, act as an overseer for hydrocarbon companies…The agreement signed with Argentina, which raises the price of gas supplied to this country, as well as the supply to Brazil, which makes up 30% of the energy used by the powerful São Paulo industrial belt, will provide a considerable boost to state revenue, but consolidate gas exports without industrialization. In practice, it will render large profits in the short term but create problems in the long run.[47]

Let us now turn from the politics of hydrocarbons to the politics of the Constituent Assembly and the right-wing autonomist forces, the other major areas of contention in 2006.

Constituent Assembly and Right-Wing Autonomist Reaction

> Where is this Constituent Assembly going to come from? There is no longer going to be a Congress. There is no longer going to be a government...We will organize ourselves in a Constituent Assembly where there will be workers, peasants, carpenters, shoe-shiners, women, and men...We will need to define what kind of country we want, what kind of economy we want...We are going to do these things...after a *pachakuti* as the Aymaras and Quechuas say, after a grand revolution, as socialists and Marxists say. In our federation we've said that if one has an old shoe, what should one do, save it or throw it out? Obviously, throw it out brothers. This system is an old shoe, rotten and full of corruption. We have to destroy it once and for all, so that a new system can be born in its place...If in the end we are going to struggle for this revolution, to follow through with this, we are only going to be able to do it through social movements. It will be the insurgency of the Bolivian people.[48]

In 1990, through the Indigenous March for Territory and Dignity led by indigenous movements from the department of Beni in the northern Amazon, the conception of a Constituent Assembly to refound Bolivian society, state, and polity, was brought to the center of Bolivian political life.[49] Of pivotal importance was the challenge this posed to internally colonial race relations within Bolivia. While 1990 signaled the formal articulation of the demand, we can trace the latest wave of struggle to decolonize the state to the end of the Pacto Militar-Campesino (Military-Peasant Pact, PMC) in the early 1970s and the emergence of an independent, indigenous-peasant *katarista* movement. The various threads in the ideology of *katarismo* emphasized the revindication of indigenous pride and the organization of movements dedicated to indigenous liberation. The ideology and its attendant political currents were mostly confined to the rural Aymara altiplano and the cities of La Paz and El Alto. While the kataristas, for all intents and purposes, fragmented and disappeared organizationally in the 1990s, facets of the movements' ideological heritage nonetheless fed into the left-indigenous struggles of the early 2000s.[50]

In the Cochabamba Water War of 2000, the push for a Constituent Assembly took on an enhanced intensity and breadth as a plethora of social movement and trade union organizations adopted it as an over-arching goal. The drive in 2000 was led by the Coordinadora, the principal popular umbrella organization of the Water War. Oscar Olivera, the most visible leader of the Coordinadora, expressed the will of many in the following passage:

> The Constituent Assembly...should be understood as a great sovereign meeting of citizen representatives elected by their neighbourhood or-ganizations, their urban and rural associations, their unions, their communes. These citizen representatives would bring with them ideas and projects concerning how to organize the political life of the country. They would seek to define the best way of organizing and managing the common good, the institutions of society, and the means that could unite the different individual interests in order to form a great collective and national interest. They would decide upon the modes of political representation, social control, and self-government that we should give ourselves for the ensuing decades. And all these agreed decisions would immediately be implemented...Let us be clear: Neither the executive branch nor the legislative branch, not even the political parties, can convoke the Constituent Assembly. These institutions and their members all stand discredited for having plunged the country into disaster.[51]

Such a vision of transformative, fundamental change guided subsequent calls for a Constituent Assembly in the rural rebellions of the altiplano in 2001, and the October 2003 and May–June 2005 Gas Wars.

On March 4, 2006, the MAS government officially responded to these demands with the Law of Convocation of the Constituent Assembly and the Referendum Law for Departmental Autonomies. Elections for the Constituent Assembly and the referendum were thus scheduled for July 2, 2006. The law on the Constituent Assembly fell far short of the revolutionary sentiments underlying Olivera's words. It was com-promised from the outset by three basic facts: the MAS did not enjoy a majority in the Senate and thus entered into negotiations with the far right; the MAS leadership preferred a "social pact" with right-wing social forces inside and outside of Congress; and, finally, insofar as there was to be popular participation in the Constituent Assembly the MAS favored participation through the party rather than through the organic social movements, trade unions, neighborhood assemblies, and indigenous organizations that were behind the project in the first place.[52] Consequently, there were numerous obstacles to the participation of autonomous popular indigenous and left organizations built into the law, as assembly deputy candidates were required to run as members of established political parties or "citizen groups," the latter of which were overwhelmingly right wing.

The electoral law on the Constituent Assembly determined that there would be 255 assembly deputies. Two hundred and ten would be directly elected, with the three top candidates of the seventy electoral districts becoming deputies. The remaining forty-five deputies would be determined proportionally on the basis of relative majority, with five deputies representing each of the nine departments. However, there was a dramatically disproportional clause built into the assembly law that ensured that the process would not lead to structural reforms, never mind revolutionary change:

> In each electoral district the party or organization that comprised the relative majority could only send two representatives, according to a curious "minority protection" rule…In accordance with this resolution, even if a party secures over 75% of the votes in its district, as long as one of the minority parties receives more than 5%, this latter party will get the "third" minority representative. This clause assured not so much the "plurality" proclaimed at the time, as a means to assure representation for a small minority of ad hoc right-wing organizations with some local clout. Without this clause, these groups would not attain representation in the Assembly.[53]

After the July elections, the assembly was designed to convene on August 6, 2006, in the colonial city of Sucre for six months to one year. At the end of this process, the proposed constitution would require the backing of two-thirds of the 255 deputies, and the support of 51 percent of the Bolivian electorate in a popular referendum. The minority protection rule meant that even if the MAS won a majority in every electoral district, they could win a maximum of only 158 assembly deputy positions, less than the 170 required to control the process with a two-thirds majority and hasten the implementation of a transformative constitutional agenda.[54]

The results on July 2, 2006, despite the limited parameters established by the electoral law, reflected the strength of the Bolivian indigenous left. As Dunia Mokrani and Raquel Gutiérrez point out, the most straightforward aspect of the elections was "the electoral disaster suffered by Bolivia's right wing, although it was not completely wiped out as a political force...The years of massive indigenous and popular organization in Bolivia between 2000 and 2005 managed to topple the monopoly over party and institutional representation held by economic and political elites."[55] In their reasonable estimation, "the right's political representation in the Assembly comes to 99 seats out of the 255 total, or 39% of the Assembly. This percentage is not enough to pass an article proposed for the new constitution, which required two-thirds majority, but it is sufficient to veto the changes proposed by other factions, which requires only 33% of the vote."[56]

Reaffirming their December 2005 electoral status as the dominant national party, the MAS won 50.7 percent of the popular vote in the July elections. In addition to the decline of the right, trends in the regionalization of political struggle were reestablished in formidable ways in these elections. For example, the MAS won substantial majorities in the departments of Chuquisaca, La Paz, Cochabamba, Oruro, and Potosí, while they lost in Tarija, Santa Cruz, Beni, and Pando. The same day as the Constituent Assembly elections, Bolivians were asked to respond "yes" or "no" to a referendum question on departmental autonomies, fundamentally a right-wing initiative as we will see below. At the national level, 57.6 percent opposed the right-wing formulation of departmental autonomy. However, and this is critical, "yes" won by a significant margin in the departments of Tarija, Santa Cruz, Beni, and Pando. These electoral results, coupled with the reformism of the MAS and the belligerence of the right, also found expression outside of institutional politics in the increasingly successful, extra-parliamentary activism of the right around autonomist demands and obstructionist tactics within the Constituent Assembly over the next number of months.[57] In order to understand this development we need to trace the historical origins and class composition of the autonomist movement in the media luna departments of Beni, Pando, Santa Cruz, and Tarija.[58] With that basis, we can then begin to map the polarization of social forces on the right and left as the first year of the MAS government progressed.

During the period of neoliberal hegemony in Bolivia (1985–2000), capitalists in the departments of the media luna, and particularly those in the most economically dynamic and populated department of Santa Cruz, had direct access to the central Bolivian state apparatus through the three main right-wing political parties: the MNR, ADN, and MIR. The wave of left-indigenous resurgence in 2000 began to significantly affect the security of this access. To recap: the Water War and altiplano insurrections, in 2000 and 2001, respectively, threatened the governability of neoliberal capitalism by shutting down parts of the country and raising demands for indigenous liberation and anticapitalist measures; Morales came a close second to Sánchez de Lozada in the presidential elections of 2002; the MNR, ADN, and MIR suffered dramatic reversals in electoral performance beginning in 2002; Morales and the MAS took office in January 2006 after winning an unprecedented majority in the December 2005 elections; and the July 2006 Constituent Assembly elections reconfirmed the implosion of the political right within the electoral game. All these threats to capital have led to the resurgence of demands for departmental autonomy by the bourgeoisie in the media luna departments, with the thrust of the campaign being directed from the headquarters of the Comité Pro Santa Cruz (Pro Santa Cruz Committee, CPSC).

During the nineteenth century and first half of the twentieth, Santa Cruz was a backwater department in the Bolivian republic, reflecting the uneven development of capitalism in the country: "Santa Cruz elites were owners of agricultural plantations that used forms of debt peonage to produce goods for regional markets, and in a much more limited fashion, for the national market to the West."[59] However, by the 1950s, state largesse began to be directed toward the eastern department in an effort to foment agro-industrialization in the one part of the country untouched by the 1953 agrarian reforms that had been initiated in the wake of the 1952 National Revolution. As a result of these state initiatives, "traditional haciendas" in Santa Cruz were "replaced with modern and increasingly extensive agribusinesses that produce: sugar, wheat, cotton, soy, and beef for both national and export markets."[60] National resource extraction also took off, particularly in timber and oil by the mid-twentieth century.

The failure to implement land reform in Santa Cruz left an indelible print on the department's agrarian class structure, just as the reversal of agrarian reform over time has had important impacts elsewhere in the country. At the national level, large and medium landholders possess 90 percent of usable land, whereas community and small-scale producers account for the remaining 10 percent. Within this mosaic, land is most concentrated in the department of Santa Cruz, with Beni and Pando having only slightly less concentration.[61] The *cruceño* agrarian elite fought the nationalist populism of the MNR revolutionary government in the 1950s, and supported the reactionary coups by General René Barrientos in 1964 and Hugo Banzer in 1971.[62] Under the latter regime, which persisted until 1978, the cruceño bourgeoisie was at the receiving end of massive state subsidies (which incidentally contributed to the unsustainable accumulation of debt taken on by the Bolivian government during the Banzer era, setting the stage for the debt crisis of the early 1980s). James Dunkerley observes, "Banzer's economic strategy had two main goals: the attraction of direct foreign investment by removing all but the most minimal constraints on capital, and the fostering of rapid, export-led growth centred on Santa Cruz."[63] Cotton, coffee, sugar, and timber were promoted for export, in addition to the longstanding subsidies for oil exploration and export. While their class power continued to derive primarily from concentrated landholdings, the cruceño agrarian bourgeoisie was able to diversify its interests during the agro-export boom of the 1970s by investing in finance, industry, and the service sector.[64] An unspoken feature of this diversification, of course, was the intense participation of cruceño capitalists in the highest echelons of the cocaine industry by the late 1970s and early 1980s.[65] Between 1985 and 2000, the economy in Santa Cruz was the most dynamic in the country and the department's capitalists were correspondingly the most influential proponents of the neoliberal model.

At the outset of the twenty-first century, Santa Cruz was responsible for 40 percent of Bolivia's export revenue and 42 percent of its tax revenue.[66] As a proportion of its contribution to the country's GNP, Santa Cruz continues to lead in agriculture, finance, commerce, industrial manufacturing, electricity, gas, and water. The department attracts more FDI than any other region of the country, and leads in terms of total exports, nontraditional exports, imports, and use of cellular phones and the Internet.[67] Rubén Costas, a principal spokesperson for the cruceño bourgeoisie explains that cruceños "are more than 25 percent of the Bolivian population…generate almost half of the national taxes, and carry on [their] backs the major part of the economy."[68] Bolivian sociologist César Rojas Ríos correctly points out that the dominant cruceño ethos predictably valorizes business, the benefits of export, competition, wealth and fame, "free market" globalization, ostentatious living, and a social pyramid with the agro-industrial and petroleum elite at the pinnacle.[69]

Julio Enrique Kempff Suárez, general manager of the Federación de Empresarios Privados de Bolivia—Santa Cruz (Federation of Private Entrepreneurs of Bolivia—Santa Cruz, FEPB-SC) talked with me about what kind of Bolivia his federation was fighting for in 2005:

> We want a Bolivia with peace, in which we can work without blockades, without conflict…We are in favor of globalization. We are in favor of a market economy. We believe that is the road that nations need to follow in order to develop. We are in complete opposition to the radically distinct vision that dominates the western part of the country…Not only the MAS but also MIP, led by Felipe Quispe, proposed exactly the opposite: to return to a statist regime; to isolate us from the Western world; to say no to globalization; no to the FTAA; no to free trade zones; no to integration; to return to the era of the Incas, or something similar.[70]

Moreover, it is imperative to highlight the racism underpinning the dominant ideology in the department of Santa Cruz, and, more broadly, in the other departments of the media luna. A complex mythology of the particularity of the Bolivian lowlands emphasizes the region's comparatively whiter colonial heritage, a mythology through which the lowland ruling class stresses their ties to the Spanish conquistadores.[71] However, the bourgeois racist mythology of the current period also incorporates indigeneity, in the subordinate manner of the noble savage, emphasizing the strength of the racial mixing between white Spanish descendants and lowland indigenous peoples, who are typically subsumed in this discourse into the largest lowland indigenous nation, the Guaraní. This lowland, exceptional *mestizaje* (ideology of racial mixture) is encompassed in the notion of a *nación camba* (camba nation), extending across the regions of the media luna:

> Who are these "camba" sons of this eastern soil? Once a generic (and derogatory) term for "lowland Indian," across the second half of the 20th century regional mavens of high and popular culture gradually have re-fashioned "camba" into both a self-appellation and a shorthand for a special mestizaje. This unique mixing is supposed to have produced, and to explain, lowland exceptionalism within the Andean Indian nation of Bolivia. Militant cambas describe "camba-ness" as if it were a goal-directed zeitgeist unfolding in Bolivian history, borne of the original synthesis of two noble razas [races].[72]

The notion of a camba nation is set against the *collas* of the five majority-Andean-indigenous departments outside of the media luna. "Colla" can be traced back to *Kollasuyo*, one of the five departments of the Inca empire. In contemporary Santa Cruz, however, the term *colla* has been highly racialized, referring, pejoratively, to the large number of Andean indigenous migrants from the altiplano who have come to the department in search of employment. The proverbial threat of a herd of collas at the gate is employed—more and less subtly—by a variety of currents within the autonomist movement, stoking widespread xenophobia in the departments of the media luna. The leadership of the autonomist right uses a polished language to express these sentiments, careful to avoid the crude racial epithets one hears commonly in the streets of Santa Cruz. The department of Santa Cruz, "is a region that in spite of feeling like it contributes a lot to the country is not taken into consideration in the decisions being made over the country's future," according to Oscar M. Ortiz Antelo, general manager of the Cámara de Industria y Comercio (Chamber of Industry and Commerce, CAINCO). According to Ortiz, the expanding capitalist growth

in Santa Cruz is spurring unreal expectations on the part of impoverished residents of the highland departments. The consequent wave of
migration into Santa Cruz is creating "a certain tension in the region"
because there are not enough jobs for these migrants who then become
a drain on social services, according to Ortiz. Given the scenario as he
sees it, Ortiz says that cruceños feel discriminated against by the cen-
tralist national state.[73] On this view, the white-mestizo ruling class of
the eastern lowlands becomes the principal victim of racial oppression
in the country.

As Kent Eaton argues, in the face of the advances made by left-indigenous movements, the various fractions of the cruceño capitalist
class have been able to close ranks under the banner of autonomy,
where autonomy is generally understood to mean: "(1) regional control
over natural resources (e.g., land, timber, gas, and oil), (2) the right to
retain control over two-thirds of all tax revenues generated in the department, and (3) authority to set all policies other than defense, currency, tariffs, and foreign relations."[74] For example, the Cámara
Agropecuaria del Oriente (Eastern Agricultural Chamber, CAO), the
Federación de Ganaderos (Cattle Ranchers' Federation), the Cámara de
Hidrocarburos (Hydrocarbons Chamber), and CAINCO, have proved
capable of working together effectively in recent years through their
shared peak organization, the FEPB-SC. In 2004, the FEPB-SC broke
ranks with the Bolivia-wide business association, the Confederación de
Empresarios Privados de Bolivia (Confederation of Private Entrepreneurs of Bolivia, CEPB) to devote itself to the autonomist movement.
This has lent a certain popular credibility to its claims that the FEPB-
SC represents the territorial interests of Santa Cruz, and in related ways
to the whole media luna, rather than the core interests of a small group
of capitalists. The autonomist movement as a whole has, in this way, effectively incorporated, and/or co-opted, various sections of non-elite
civil society organizations, trade unions, and indigenous movements.[75]

Together, the fractions of the capitalist class represented in the
FEPB-SC finance and control the primary political tool in the autonomist struggle, the Pro Santa Cruz Committee (CPSC). The December
2005 prefecture elections witnessed, as we know, the victory of right-

wing candidates in each of the media luna departments. Likewise, in the departmental autonomies referendum in July 2006, the yes vote won in all media luna departments. In Santa Cruz, the yes campaign garnered an impressive 71 percent of the popular vote. Therefore, several components of the institutional apparatus of the state at the departmental level were captured by the autonomist movement in the early years of the Morales government. Moreover, in addition to the moderate faces of the CPSC and the prefectures, the rougher side of the coalition for autonomy is visible in the Nación Camba (Camba Nation)—an organization with more overtly racist positions than the CPSC, although the memberships of both overlap—and the proto-fascist youth league, the Unión Juvenil Cruceñista (Cruceño Youth Union, UJC), which is widely known for its violent assaults on indigenous peasants and indigenous urban poor, particularly during moments when these latter groups have attempted to mobilize for their rights in around the city of Santa Cruz. The formation of private paramilitary forces by large landowners seeking to protect their property rights against incursions by landless peasants has also been widely documented.[76] Finally, it has been noted in separate reports by journalists that Colombian mercenaries were active in Santa Cruz during the early stages of the Morales administration, working for sections of the ruling class who had been preparing for the possibility of civil war.[77] This is the multifaceted coalition of actors representing the autonomist project in the Bolivian lowlands.

It is important not to exaggerate the strength of the autonomist forces in this period, however. In historical perspective, the shift in the strategies of the Santa Cruz–based bourgeoisie from contending for the national state to battling for the autonomy of four departments should be interpreted unambiguously as a bourgeois retreat in the face of left-indigenous advance. It is emblematic of how the ideology of the free market, foreign investment, and racism has suffered enormous blows outside of Santa Cruz, Beni, Pando, and Tarija.[78] Even within the media luna, the presence of popular forces of left-indigenism such as the Confederación Sindical de Colonizadores de Bolivia (Union Confederation of Colonizers of Bolivia, CSCB), the Coordinadora de Pueblos Étnicos de Santa Cruz (Coordinator of Ethnic Peoples of Santa Cruz, CPESC), the *Movimiento Sin Tierra* (Landless Movement, MST), and dissident factions within the Central Obrera Regional—Santa Cruz (Regional Workers' Central of Santa Cruz) had not been effaced. Recall as well our discussion of the electoral results of December 2005 in which it was noted that the MAS did better than anticipated within Santa Cruz.[79]

At the same time, it is important not to underestimate the *regional successes* enjoyed by the autonomist movement in the early years under Morales, in terms of gaining popular appeal within the media luna for a struggle that, in essence, protects the interests of a privileged minority.[80] Some evidence on this score is catalogued in the following passage:

> Of great importance are the two days in June 2004 and January 2005 when hundreds of thousands of *cruceños* answered the call issued by the CPSC to demonstrate on behalf of autonomy for Santa Cruz. More than 350,000 people participated in the second of these events, the so-called Second Great Open Town Hall, which made it Bolivia's largest-ever public demonstration. Subsequent to this second and larger rally in January 2005, the "Agenda of January" came into use as shorthand in Bolivia to describe Santa Cruz's autonomy movement, in contrast to the "Agenda of October (2003)," which refers to the leftist movement that ousted Sánchez de Losada. In the period between these two demonstrations, the CPSC collected approximately 500,000 signatures in support of a referendum on autonomy and led a civic strike in November 2004 in the attempt to force the national government to hold this referendum.[81]

We need not accept the questionable figure of 350,000 participants, nor the erroneous claim that this was the biggest demonstration in Bolivian history, to agree with the basic fact that the movement for autonomy had won many adherents in the four media luna departments. "The national program in October [2003] was to nationalize gas and hold a Constituent Assembly," Félix Patzi points out. "Another program was born in January [2005], a program of the rich. They demanded autonomy conceived of as the preservation of the current land and capital structure."[82] The autonomists effectively wielded popular social forces behind a bourgeois agenda during the first year of the Morales administration, primarily focusing on the process of the Constituent Assembly, a subject to which we now turn.

Almost immediately following the start of the Constituent Assembly proceedings in early August 2006, it became clear that the autonomist movement intended to exercise its veto power within the confines of the assembly when possible, and in the streets when necessary. Political tensions first mounted precipitously when the MAS announced in August that the "two-thirds" rule for the Constituent Assembly would only apply to the final text of the draft constitution at the end of the process, whereas the decisions leading up to the final text would be determined by a simple majority. Moreover, defining the specific procedural rules that would govern the assembly would also be determined by simple majority.[83] The MAS, of course, held a simple majority in the CA, and therefore these announcements galvanized the autonomist right of the media luna, which denounced what they claimed was authoritarian maneuvering on the part of the government.[84] In mid-August, the right formed a decisive regional bloc within the media luna departments to challenge the "hegemonic plans of the MAS." On August 21, the CPSC declared itself in a "state of emergency." At issue was not simply the applicability of the two-thirds rule, but whether or not the CA had the authority to "refound" Bolivia—as the MAS and social movements contended—or simply to moderately reform the existing constitution—the position of the CPSC and its allies. On August 24, the autonomist forces—including the political party, PODEMOS—charged the MAS with attempting an *autogolpe* (self-coup) along the lines of Alberto Fujimori in neighboring Peru in the early 1990s.[85] PODEMOS subsequently boycotted the CA sending it into an indefinite recess, while on September 8, the autonomist movement in all four departments of the media luna hosted massive demonstrations and a civic strike. In the back and forth of Bolivian street politics, indigenous peasants aligned with the MAS then mobilized in Sucre where the Constituent Assembly was being held to protest the actions of the autonomist movement in the east.

The intensity of political conflict in this period was palpable. Vice President García Linera called publicly on the popular left-indigenous social movements to defend the government with arms if necessary against autonomist destabilization tactics, although he quickly retreated from these statements. Minister of Government Alicia Muñoz accused the prefect of the department of Pando of encouraging the formation of paramilitary groups to destabilize the national government. Meanwhile, a report solicited by the Argentine embassy in La Paz from the Grupo de Apoyo a las Colectividades Extranjeras argued that there was a 56 percent probability of imminent civil war in the country.[86] By way of compromise, the MAS offered to accept a "mixed voting system" rather than a simple majority, such that certain articles of the proposed constitution that were particularly contentious would require two-thirds support to pass, in addition to the two-thirds that would be required to approve the final text at the end of the process. PODEMOS rejected the offer as did the party's allies in the autonomist movements in the departments of the media luna. The extra-parliamentary activism of the autonomists therefore continued, although visible indications of imminent civil war subsided temporarily. These processes as a whole took a toll on the Morales government and the CA itself in terms of public perception. From a high of 80 percent in the immediate wake of the May Day "nationalization," support for the president plummeted to 52 percent by the end of September 2006, according to polls. Similarly, support for the CA fell from 69 percent in August to 45 percent in September 2006.[87]

A report issued by the conservative, pro-imperialist International Crisis Group documents further deterioration and intensification of conflict between November and December 2006.[88] In mid-November 2006, the government made new attempts to compromise with the far right of the media luna. However, the right again met government initiative with obstruction. In particular, the Unidad Nacional (National Unity, UN) party began a hunger strike that eventually grew to include two thousand participants across the country. In December 2006, right-wing violence around the CA intensified, including attacks on the offices of important nongovernmental organizations (NGOs) working for indigenous rights and supporting the interests of the landless peasants in Santa Cruz. On December 8, the civic committees of Beni, Pando, Tarija, and Santa Cruz issued an ultimatum to the government, threatening to declare de facto autonomy if the government refused to bend to their demands. In response, supporters of the government in the social movements announced that in the event of de facto autonomy they would traverse the country and physically occupy the city of Santa Cruz in defense of the government. On December 11, Morales called on the armed forces to defend national unity, provoking statements from the autonomist movement that bloody repression of their just cause was about to be orchestrated by the MAS government. The government subsequently reneged on their hard-line position and offered new negotiations with the media luna civic committees on the themes of the CA and regional autonomy. In an apparent initiative to increase their bargaining power, the four media luna departments decided to stage yet another public performance of their strength through the public formation on December 18, 2006, of the Junta Autonómica Democrática (Democratic Autonomy Committee, JAD).

Over the next several months, tensions within and outside the CA persisted just below the surface, but tenuous agreements were struck to allow the assembly to proceed. On February 14, 2007, compromise on the procedural rules was achieved between the multiple parties and citizen groups involved. The players in the assembly process therefore had six months to draft an entire constitution, if they were to proceed according to schedule. At that stage, the unresolved underlying conflicts and the frail nature of the compromise appeared to foreshadow an inevitable collapse of the process at some point in the coming months. An early report on the new basis for the assembly spoke to its ambiguousness and fragility:

> The voting process approved with the revision of Article 70 is lengthy, complicated, and still contains some gray areas…If each article of the new constitution is approved by the commissions and the entire body of the Assembly by two-thirds, the final text of the constitution will be submitted to the Bolivian public for approval by popular referendum. However, this is unlikely given the contentious nature of many of the articles to be debated, the potential for continued obstructions, the short time limit and the general disorganization of the Assembly…If there are articles that do not receive two-thirds approval, the debate on the article will move to a committee. This committee will attempt to reach consensus, but if that is not possible, there is an option to allow the Bolivian public to chose between two versions of controversial arti-

cles in a popular referendum. It is still unclear whether this vote would take place as part of the final approval of the text by Bolivian voters or would occur in a separate referendum.[89]

Based on the fundamental impasse of the first six months, it seemed impossible to imagine that consensus would be achieved on any article of import over the following six months. Fashioning two versions of each controversial article for Bolivians to vote on in a referendum (or referenda) seemed complex at best and highly implausible in the political conjuncture of that period. In any case, if, in the end, the process did not implode, the new draft of the constitution was seriously unlikely to embody the revolutionary and transformative visions expressed by left-indigenous movements between 2000 and 2005. The autonomist movement would undoubtedly attempt to veto social change of any depth, in all likelihood pushing the terrain of battle once again outside of state-mediated institutions.[90]

Conclusion

The first three chapters of this book have charted some of the broad trends in Bolivian political economy and society during the first year of the Evo Morales government. It has been argued that the Morales administration needs to be understood against the backdrop of the history of the 2000 to 2005 revolutionary epoch of left-indigenous resurgence that preceded it. The electoral victory of the MAS in the elections of December 18, 2005, represented a break on the potential for revolutionary transformation in an indigenous-liberationist and socialist direction because the MAS is a moderately reformist party and because the self-organization and self-activity of the popular classes and oppressed indigenous nations have declined in the wake of the elections. The trajectory of the MAS as a party is best analyzed in terms of its shifting class composition, ideology, and political strategy over time. In the late 1990s and early 2000s the party was unambiguously anti-neoliberal and anti-imperialist, had a core social base of indigenous cocaleros in Chapare, Cochabamba, and concentrated primarily on extraparliamentary activism. Since 2002, however, the leadership of the party has increasingly come under the tutelage of a mestizo urban middle-class intelligentsia, its ideology has shifted to moderate reformism, and its strategy has been one of emphasizing electoral politics and, especially, winning over the urban middle class. The most influential currents in the party do not believe that a transition to socialism is possible in the current context and therefore seek instead to develop Andean-Amazonian capitalism.

In terms of indigenous liberation, the electoral victory of the MAS was a democratic gain in the sense of putting indigenous issues at the center of the political agenda, where they can no longer be ignored. However, that democratic gain is a compromised one. Indigenous liberation for the MAS has been separated from the struggle for socialist transformation, and without a simultaneous struggle for both emancipatory aims the depth of each will be steadily hollowed out. Most disconcerting is how the MAS government's policy, and the class interests it serves, has in many fundamental ways continued the neoliberal trajectory. Possible exceptions during its first year in office were limited to hydrocarbons, foreign relations with Venezuela and Cuba, and the rejection of a new Standy-By Arrangement with the IMF. The examination of hydrocarbons has demonstrated that the reforms instituted under Morales in this arena cannot be meaningfully understood as nationalization, but rather as moderate reforms to the royalties and tax regime that mean more revenue for the Bolivian state but leave ultimate control of the industry in the hands of petroleum transnationals. Our analysis of the Constituent Assembly has also illustrated the limitations of this process and the ways in which it precluded the sort of revolutionary, transformative, and participatory assembly envisioned by the left-indigenous forces of 2000–2005. It is also clear that the willingness of the MAS to negotiate with the autonomist right, and to reign in its own social bases from radical mobilization, allowed the latter's political capacity to grow substantially over 2006 and to become increasingly obstructionist inside and outside the institutions of the state and the Constituent Assembly. The window of opportunity afforded to the MAS and the popular movements by right-wing collapse in 2005 was not seized upon, and the right has consequently become stronger and increasingly capable of countering new reforms. One more hopeful scenario might arise out of the right's belligerence. It might provide the impetus necessary for left-indigenous movements to begin to mobilize strategically and independently from the MAS government, escaping the limited parameters of the Morales reform agenda. In such a fashion they could defend the Morales government from imperialism and the autonomist right, as well as specific social reforms that improve the conditions of the indigenous proletarian and peasantry majority. They could do all this while organizing and mobilizing to force the government into more direct confrontations with the logic of capital. The left wing of the MAS, for its part, may eventually come to terms with how social pacts with the autonomist right are doomed to failure, and that the government's survival and reformist aims depend on a head-on confrontation with capital and the support of an organized and mobilized mass base. But this is only one possible scenario, and not the most likely one, at least as it is possible to tell at this stage in the process.

While the domestic scenario at the end of the first year of the Morales administration militated against the structural transformation of social relations, the international and regional contexts were more favorable than they had been in recent times. While U.S. intervention by way of nonmilitary "democracy promotion" remained a threat, as did the multileveled facets of economic imperialism in this period of global capitalism, it was nonetheless apparent that the United States was suffering a crisis of imperial overreach in the Middle East, neoliberalism had been rejected ideologically by much of the Latin American population, the IMF's influence in the region was in decline, relations with Venezuela and Cuba were providing Bolivia with new room for maneuver, and the combative impulse of popular movements was on the ascent in many countries. Enhancing the possibilities for transformative social change inside Bolivia to take advantage of the international and regional contexts of which it is a part would have required, and continues to require, the rebirth of self-organization, self-activity, and strategic mass mobilization of the rural and urban left-indigenous movements that arose during the revolutionary epoch at the outset of this century. The rebuilding of the social power of these popular movements independent from the MAS is the only way forward in the short term. Only when the MAS cannot take for granted the support of the popular classes will it be forced to renege on debilitating social pacts and compromises with the right. Following the 1952 National Revolution, popular social forces struggling for socialist transformation lost this independent power and the MNR—a populist party leading the revolution at the time—steadily capitulated to the right, reversing over time the reforms that were won in the revolution, reforms, it should be stressed, that were far more radical than the reforms of the current period. This set the stage for the right-wing coup of 1964 and a string of authoritarian regimes and counterrevolutionary impositions. The infamous Military-Peasant Pact was forged and until the mid-1970s the indigenous peasantry was pitted against the revolutionary miners and socialist transformation was thwarted. This is the ugly precedent. The hopeful one is the dramatic resurgence of militant mass insurrection and left-indigenous cooperation in combined struggle the likes of which we witnessed from 2000 until 2005.

Four

Dynamite in the Mines and Bloody Urban Clashes

Much of the academic and popular literature on Evo Morales and the Movement Toward Socialism, and the bourgeois-autonomist opposition of the media luna, has been centered on the conflict between the Bolivian left and right. In these discussions, the MAS is often inaccurately portrayed as the singular left protagonist in an epochal struggle for hegemony in the country. The scene on the ground is much more complicated than such a portrait allows. There were a number of instances over the course of the first year of the Morales administration in which popular social forces to the left of the party expressed their frustration with the reformism of the government and its unnecessary willingness to negotiate with the far right autonomist movement. This has sometimes led to confrontations between erstwhile allies of Morales and the MAS, such as the case in late September 2006 when, during a conflict in Parque Carrasco, two cocaleros were murdered by the state and called "narco-traffickers" by key ministers in the government. This was especially galling given the fact that Morales and the MAS party grew out of the milieu of anti-imperialist cocalero struggle in the region of Chapare, Cochabamba, in the 1980s and 1990s. Many on the Bolivian left saw this as capitulation to U.S. imperial intervention in the country by way of the American-led "war on drugs."[1] This was only one instance of many in which the impulses of the popular classes and oppressed indigenous nations have transcended the compromised politics of the government in power.

Political Economist David McNally reminds us that:

> Most fundamental to Marx's idea of revolution was the insistence that meaningful change can come only through a mass movement from below. Only by winning radical democracy for themselves, by conquering their own freedom, could the oppressed remake themselves as people capable of free self-government...Revolution thus has two interrelated components: changing of social rules and regulation (ownership, property, forms of government) and self-transformation...In short, the process of revolution—mass mobilization, participation in new forms of democracy, overturning old forms of domination, taking control of workplaces and communities—transforms the participants themselves.[2]

In an equally important passage, McNally teases out a key insight of Rosa Luxemburg's:

> Whoever wins an election in capitalist society attains *political office, not power.* After all, power in modern society is embedded in property—ownership of the means of production, distribution, and exchange—and the authority it confers. This power, represented by money, involves control over others, specifically over the labor and life-activity of those who comprise the working class...The great flaw of reformism is its belief that society can be radically transformed by changing governments while leaving the basic institutions and property relations of capitalism intact. The reality, however, is that rather than capturing power when they are elected, reformist parties are instead *captured by* power.[3]

For our purposes the premises of these two passages directs our attention in two directions: upwards, to the current MAS government in Bolivia and the structural limitations of its moderately reformist platform; and downwards, to the ongoing mass struggles from below that are attempting to push the current political and social processes in that country toward a transformative path while their participants transform themselves in the process.

This chapter seeks to fill a lacuna in analysis and reportage of the first year (January 2006 to January 2007) of the MAS administration in Bolivia through a detailed examination of two examples of popular revolt to the left of the MAS: the violent confrontations in a Huanuni mine in October 2006 and the "Cochabamba Conflict" of January 2007.

The example of the mines represents one source of serious potential for the rearticulation of an independent radical politics to the left of the MAS, whereas the Cochabamba Conflict is much more ambiguous in its medium- to long-term implications. The inspiring struggle for the resignation of a corrupt and right-wing departmental prefect was clearly a positive example of a groundswell of democratic politics from below that refused, if only for a short period of time, to succumb to the dictates of the MAS government. However, the declaration of a "parallel government" at the close of the conflict is best understood as ultraleft adventurism given that the social bases for such a project were no longer in place when the declaration was made.

After analyzing the Huanuni and Cochabamba scenarios, the chapter steps forward in time to presidential and vice-presidential recall referendums in August 2008 and right-wing destabilization campaigns that immediately followed, and ran through September. In these moments we see how the extreme right has responded to the government's unwillingness to confront it seriously, even as the same government treats the far left with derision. The role of the MAS in allowing room for the partial rearticulation of the autonomist right must be acknowledged and confronted. This strategic error on the part of the government led to the most serious instability in the country since Morales's tenure in office began.

Effective struggle to open pathways to socialism, indeed even for serious structural reform, will require the renewal of self-activity, selforganization, and strategic mobilization of popular movements autonomous from the MAS government. The precedent of the 2000 to 2005 indigenous-liberationist and anticapitalist struggles of an eclectic array of indigenous-left movements is a good basis on which to build. As this chapter seeks to demonstrate, the MAS government deserves the support of left-indigenous social movements throughout the country in its confrontations with the organized far right, concentrated in the eastern lowlands, and imperialism, concentrated in the U.S. state. Any reforms initiated by the MAS that improve the lives of the popular classes and indigenous nations also deserve the critical support of social movements as they seek to drive these reforms deeper and direct them into more direct confrontations with the logic of capital. With a clear analysis of the reformist character of the MAS government, popular movements seeking the fundamental overthrow of the combined social relations of capitalism and indigenous oppression in Bolivia will be in a better position to wage struggles that escape the limited parameters of the MAS's political agenda.

Class Struggle in the Mines

The policy and class dynamics in mining for the first several months of the new government indicated dramatic limits to the depth of reforms the MAS was willing to contemplate. In its electoral platform for the December 2005 elections, the party proposed the rehabilitation of the Corporación Minera de Bolivia (Bolivian Mining Corporation, COMIBOL) and the nationalization of the mines.[4] However, upon entering office, the MAS began immediately to promote new "shared risk" contracts between transnational mining corporations and the privileged sectors of the cooperative mining sector. This was set against a backdrop of rising commodity prices driven to a large extent by China's rapid economic growth. Nickel and tin prices increased more than 18 percent in 2006, for example, while Chinese officials estimated 8 percent GDP growth in 2007 after 10.7 percent in 2006, the highest rate registered since 1995.[5]

The case of the largest iron deposit in the world, Mutún, located in the department of Santa Cruz, is an important example of the early position taken by the MAS.[6] For decades Mutún lay dormant. Recently, however, spurred by the explosion of demand for iron in China, transnational corporations made clear their interest in exploiting the giant iron deposit. The MAS eventually granted Jindal Steel & Power, an Indian multinational, the prized exploiting license and mining was scheduled to begin on September 24, 2007. The government argued that the deal would result in US$200 million annually in tax revenue. However, some economists have pointed out that of the fifty million tons of iron that Jindal would likely extract each year, 95 percent would leave the country in raw form, with only 5 percent being industrialized in Bolivia. Mutún is thought to contain forty billion tons of ore, valued at approximately US$30 billion at today's prices.[7] A number of critical economists have pointed out that Mutún represents a failed opportunity of historic proportions. The MAS government was in a position to have used this window of opportunity to help reconstruct COMIBOL so that the state company could once again play a protagonistic role in the country's mines. Not only would this have assisted in wresting control from transnational corporate influence in Bolivia, it would have provided more revenue for meeting the needs of the impoverished population.

Since the mass privatizations and layoffs in the mid-1980s, the Bolivian mining industry has been essentially divided into two sets of workers. The first, organized through the Federación Sindical de Trabajadores Mineros de Bolivia (Mine Workers Union Federation, FSTMB), are employed by the state mining company COMIBOL. The FSTMB was the heart of arguably the most militant and revolutionary trade union movement in Latin America for much of the twentieth century.[8] The second set consists of self-employed cooperative miners, *cooperativistas*, organized through the Federación Nacional de Cooperativas de Bolivia (National Federation of Cooperative Miners of Bolivia, FENCOMIN). Many of the cooperative miners barely subsist and engage in intense self-exploitation in order to survive, while a privileged sector does much better. Much of cooperative mining functions on the same principles as private enterprises, whereby some coop members are in a position to exploit others. Wealthier cooperative miners contract work out to their "business associates" (poorer cooperative members) who are made to labor in the most horrendous working conditions. The workers in these relationships are not paid a salary, but instead receive a small portion of whatever they are able to extract from the mines. Increasingly, these workers are women and children. The workers in these settings, unlike COMIBOL workers, have no security, no fixed salaries, no benefits, and are not provided protection from existing labor laws.[9] In the recent past, the national leadership of FENCOMIN formed alliances with neoliberal political actors, including mining magnate and reviled ex-President Gonzalo Sánchez de Lozada.[10]

It is the privileged layer of cooperative miners that was initially represented in the MAS government through the Ministry of Mining and Metallurgy. Walter Villarroel, a former leader of the FENCOMIN and a registered member of the cooperative "La Salvadora" of Huanuni, was made minister of mining and metallurgy in the first MAS cabinet of January 2006. With the elevation in commodity prices, class struggle has intensified in the mines of the western altiplano. The privileged cooperative miners have accelerated their attempts to press the government into facilitating shared risk contracts between cooperative miners and transnational mining companies. They also have stepped up efforts to take over mines currently operated by COMIBOL, such as Huanuni, Caracollo, Barrosquira, Telamayu, and Colquiri. These takeovers and the politics of the cooperative miners have been resisted by the FSTMB. which has demanded that COMIBOL be restored to its former, formidable status as an important state enterprise.[11] Battle lines were drawn early for a bloody confrontation which would play itself out in October 2006, the outcome of which led to apparent shifts in the government's position on mining. The depth of these shifts is still unclear.

At a general assembly of the miners' federation, FSTMB, on July 4, 2006, miners agreed to mount pressure on the MAS government to nationalize the mines without compensation to transnational companies, to rebuild the state mining company, COMIBOL, and, finally, to establish collective workers' control of COMIBOL and the mines.[12] At the end of September, the miners initiated the concrete battle for these resolutions in a bold fashion. More than two hundred miners and one thousand indigenous peasant allies blocked the highways connecting Oruro to Cochabamba and Potosí, cutting off traffic flow to much of western Bolivia. Immediate demands included the creation of 1,500 new jobs and investment commitments for the reconstruction of COMIBOL into a functional enterprise. These transitional reforms were meant to prefigure full nationalization and workers' control in the future. President Morales himself had at various junctures called for the nationalization of the mining industry, although in practice the government had put its emphasis on safeguarding a secure investment climate for foreign capital. The government responded to the miners and peasants in September by publicly denouncing them as "provocateurs" and "Trotskyists."

Minister Villarroel told the press that the protesters were impeding the government's search for foreign investment to reactivate the mining sector. A frustrated Villarroel reminded the miners, "The government guaranteed legal security for foreign companies to invest in mining."[13]

In early October, the conflict intensified dramatically. The epicenter of events was a tin mine in the Posokoni Mountain in the community of Huanuni, but the wider repercussions of the situation quickly resonated throughout the country. The mine contains the largest deposit of tin in South America, and the tin's purity and accessibility make it a hot commodity. This was particularly so given current trends in the world market at the time. On February 22, 2007, for the first time in over twenty years, one ton of tin surpassed US$14,000 on the London Metal Exchange.[14] Huanuni is a town of 19,428 mostly indigenous inhabitants, located roughly 45 kilometers outside of the city of Oruro, in the Pantaleón Dalence province, in the department of Oruro. The Huanuni tin mine is primarily worked by employees of COMIBOL who are organized in the Sindicato Mixto de Trabajadores de Mineros de Huanuni (SMTMH), which, in turn, is affiliated with the FSTMB at the national level. Cooperative miners also work sections of the Huanuni mine, but in far fewer numbers.

On the afternoon of October 5, 2006, organized cooperative miners led an assault on the Huanuni mine in an effort to take it over. COMIBOL miners fought back and a running battle with exploding dynamite and street fighting spread from the mines into the town center over two days. Houses were burned to the ground, tires packed with explosives rolled down the mountainside into the town erupting in huge explosions, and the number of dead and injured escalated. The FSTMB and the Central Obrera Boliviana (Bolivian Workers' Central, COB) called on the government to send in troops to protect the state miners and the community from the violence initiated by the cooperative miners, but to no avail. Seven hundred police were sent in on October 5, but were apparently unable to stop the fighting, which persisted through October 6. The military was put on a "state of alert" but the executive order to intervene was not forthcoming. Morales, in the meantime, conspicuously refrained from making a public statement. Human rights ombudsman, Waldo Albarracín, and the minister of the presidency, Juan Ramón Quintana, were eventually able to broker a truce that ended the violence, but not before at least seventeen people were killed and numerous others injured.[15]

TABLE 4.1: CLASHES IN THE MINES, HUANUNI—OCTOBER 5–6, 2006

Participants	Demands	Govt Response
FSTMB FENCOMIN Townspeople Indigenous Peasant Movements	FSTMB: Nationalization; Rebuild COMIBOL; Workers' Control. FENCOMIN: Expansion of cooperative mines in the altiplano; alliances with transnational mining corporations; reduction of COMIBOL activities in mining industry	Initial support for FENCOMIN; Opposed FSTMB demands; Refusal to militarily protect FSTMB miners and families; in the aftermath, facilitated resignation of Minister of Mining and Metallurgy; promise to nationalize mining sector at undisclosed date in the future

On the surface, the state-employed miners of COMIBOL achieved some gains from their mobilizations and road blockades in September and their defense of the Huanuni mine in October. Villarroel was forced to resign from the Ministry of Mines and Metallurgy. He was replaced by José Guillermo Dalence, an ex-leader of the FSTMB. Additionally, Hugo Miranda Rendón was granted the position of interim President of COMIBOL. Until this appointment, Miranda Rendón had been the workers' representative on the directorship of COMIBOL. Moreover, Morales publicly admitted that "until now in the issue of mining we have not complied with the Bolivian people."[16] Morales then reasserted the intention of the MAS to nationalize the mining industry.[17]

However, the underlying conflicts hardly disappeared. In early February 2007, twenty thousand members of the cooperative miners' federation, FENCOMIN, launched a large protest in La Paz against the nationalization of the mines. The MAS government subsequently shifted its plan of "nationalization" to a watered-down proposal to increase taxes on private mining companies.[18] Nonetheless, on February 9,

Morales repeated the theatrical tactics he employed during the 2006 May Day presidential decree on natural gas,[19] this time announcing the nationalization of the Empresa Metalúrgica Vinto tin smelter, the fourth-largest in the world, as military troops stood by his side.[20] However, as is explained in Chapter Six, the Vinto tin smelter remains isolated from general mining policy. Transnational mining corporations continue unequivocally as the major players in this economic sector. The Bolivian government claims, for example, that in this specific instance the sale in 2005 of the Vinto smelter to Glencore, a Swiss multinational, was based on fraud. Dalence, the new minister of mining and metallurgy, claims that "the plant was taken from the Bolivian people fraudulently and we are reclaiming it." At the same time, Dalence's message to transnational mining capital more generally was as follows: "All foreign companies that operate within the legal framework have our guarantee that they won't be touched." As the *Economist* editorializes, "In October he said it was the turn of mining [to be nationalized]. Yet with Mr. Morales, whose rallying cry is 'Bolivian resources for the Bolivian people,' sometimes the symbolism and the rhetoric is more ambitious than the reality."[21]

In summary, the conduct of the MAS administration in general mining policy and specifically in the case of the Huanuni crisis confirms the theses advanced at the outset of this chapter. The independent revolutionary socialist demands and strategies of the FSTMB miners were denounced as provocative and "Trotskyist" by MAS officials. The MAS sought to avoid open class conflict in the mines and characterized the relationship between workers and transnational mining corporations in non-zero-sum terms. The interests of the two distinct groups were not seen as conflicting. FENCOMIN was favored as a counterweight against the radical demands of the FSTMB because the latter's politics would necessarily clash with the interests of transnationals. Morales, at various junctures, employed a radical rhetoric of "nationalization" but its meaning in the mining industry was highly ambiguous, accompanied as it was by assurances to transnational companies that they would not be touched if they continued to play by the rules, as "partners" not "bosses."

¡*Cochabamba de pie, nunca de rodillas!* Cochabamba on Its Feet, Never on Its Knees!

A second challenge to the MAS administration from the left occurred during what I refer to here as the Cochabamba conflict, beginning in late December 2006 and coming to a gradual close by the end of January 2007 (see Table 4.2). The conflict illustrates the extent to which the MAS was willing to facilitate mobilization of generally loyal social sectors during its first year in office, within strict parameters to achieve or sustain a favorable balance of forces at particular conjunctures vis-à-vis the autonomist right. On the other hand, it also exemplifies the ways in which popular movements were sometimes capable of transcending these set parameters and forging an autonomous path to the left of the government, even if only temporarily. Further, the Cochabamba conflict highlights the manner in which the MAS was willing to opportunistically withdraw its most loyal bases—the cocaleros, for example—from mobilizing tactics that threatened to transcend moderate, legalistic reformism. It also seems clear from the events in Cochabamba that, at least in early 2007, the social bases closest to the MAS were still, by and large, willing to comply with the line of the party issued from La Paz at the end of the day. The Cochabamba conflict suggests that while there was a limited presence of political currents to the left of the MAS in some of the major social movements, their influence was ephemeral up to that point in time. Finally, in the case of the Cochabamba Conflict, the far left's call for the formation of a parallel revolutionary departmental government was ultimately reckless adventurism because the social forces necessary to realize such a government were no longer mobilized.

TABLE 4.2: CHRONOLOGY OF THE COCHABAMBA CONFLICT

> *December 15, 2006*—Cochabamba Prefect, Manfred Reyes Villa, proposes a new referendum on departmental autonomy for Cochabamba despite the fact that 63 percent of the department's electorate voted "No" in the last nationwide departmental autonomies referendum held only months earlier, on July 2, 2006.

December 20—A popular assembly of cocaleros, factory workers, teachers, university students, and others, is held in the Plaza 14 de Septiembre, the central plaza in downtown Cochabamba. The assembly rejects the prefect's call for a new referendum. A tear gas grenade is tossed into the crowd, and the social movements accuse functionaries of the Prefect of culpability in the incident. Indigenous peasants, cocaleros, and urban popular sectors in Cochabamba initiate a vigil outside of the offices of Reyes Villa demanding his resignation.

December 21—The Central Obrera Departamental (Departmental Workers Central, COD) hosts another popular assembly of social movements and trade unionists in which it is decided that protests against Reyes Villa be postponed until after Christmas and the New Year to ensure greater participation.

January 4, 2007—Rural and urban popular movements mobilize in Cochabamba city and re-open vigil outside of the offices of the prefect, and occupy Plaza 14 de Septiembre.

January 8—Social movements reinforce their occupation of the Plaza 14 de Septiembre and set fire to the entrance of the prefect's office building. Reyes Villa escapes in a bulletproof car and flees to La Paz. Protesters demanding Reyes Villa's resignation are tear-gassed by police.

January 9—Negotiations to pacify the region are convened, first by Vice Minister Fabián Yacsik, and then by minister of the presidency, Juan Ramón Quintana. Negotiations are a failure.

January 10—A "civic march" is organized by supporters of Reyes Villa, demanding that "campesinos" (peasants), respect the city. The civic march declares the attempted burning of the offices of the prefect a "humiliation." The Civic Committee of Cochabamba, which is aligned with Reyes Villa, announces an indefinite civic strike. The presence of a proto-fascist youth group is reported for the first time in Cochabama. The group calls itself Juventud por la Democracia (Youth for Democracy, JD), and is modeled on the Unión Juvenil Cruceñista (Cruceño Youth Union, UJC) of Santa Cruz.

January 11—The most violent confrontations of the Cochabamba conflict take place. Right-wing "civic groups" and the JD clash with rural and urban popular movements in the Plaza de Las Banderas,

Plaza 14 de Septiembre, and Plaza Colón. Two people are killed—one on each side—and more than two hundred are injured, the majority of whom are of the popular movements according to press reports released by journalists upon visiting the hospitals. Many of the injured are gravely injured by bullets, beatings, and other outcomes of the fierce street fighting.

January 12—Social movements insist on the resignation of the prefect in a massive concentration of tens of thousands in the Plaza 14 de Septiembre. Reyes Villa retreats from his call for a new referendum for departmental autonomy in Cochabamba. Leaders of the cocaleros and other indigenous peasant sectors announce the lifting of road blockades of the interdepartmental highways in response to Reyes Villa's partial concession and pleas from the MAS government to end the blockades and guarantee free transit of people, goods, and vehicles. Nonetheless, some of the rank and file of the peasant unions refuse to lift the blockades and mainstream media reports indicate the persistence of intermittent and/or permanent blockades in various parts of the department contributing to ongoing traffic congestion or paralysis.

January 13—Ramón Quintana meets with social movements closely aligned with the MAS, seeking to define a basis upon which dialogue with Reyes Villa might be initiated. Reyes Villa accepts dialogue with the government in theory, but demands that negotiations take place in Santa Cruz, where he now is located after having traveled from La Paz. The rank and file of the cocaleros and other indigenous peasant movements return to the streets demanding the resignation of Reyes Villa. The MAS refuses to negotiate with Reyes Villa in Santa Cruz and accuses the prefect of Cochabamba of reneging on his duties as prefect by abandoning the department in a moment of crisis.

January 16—Reyes Villa refuses to resign in a televised message from Santa Cruz addressing the entire country. Reyes Villa assigns Johnny Ferrel, secretary general of the prefecture, the duties of the prefect for the duration of Reyes Villa's exile in Santa Cruz. Tens of thousands of cocaleros, indigenous peasants, peasant irrigators, the Central Obrera Departamental (Departmental Workers' Central, COD), university students, informal proletarians, formal workers, neighborhood organizations of the poorer zones of Cochabamba, teachers, and many others, hold a popular assembly in the Plaza 14 de Septiembre. A "legal exit" to the crisis through a proposed law that might make possible the forced resignation of Reyes Villa through a referendum is suggested to the assembly by leaders, affiliated with the MAS, of the peasant irrigators, the COD, and the cocaleros, among others. This is not coincidentally the position of the MAS government from La Paz. A large part of the rank and file reject this position of the leadership, denounce the social movement and trade union leadership loudly, and demand the resignation of Reyes Villa immediately. While there are divisions in the rank and file, currents of the radical left are able to hold significant sway in this moment. A Revolutionary Prefecture Government is declared, consisting of fifteen members of an executive committee who represent various social movement and trade union sectors. Tiburcio Herradas Lamas is elected president of the executive. A successful occupation and takeover of the offices of the COD is staged by the new parallel government. The MAS immediately denounces the popular departmental government as illegal and undemocratic and asserts that Reyes Villa remains the principal, legitimate political authority of Cochabamba who cannot be removed through street demonstrations or popular assemblies.

January 17–20—The Revolutionary Prefecture Government is unable to translate its declarations into actions and the exercise of power. The MAS successfully draws away from the parallel government the rank and file of the cocaleros, indigenous peasants, and parts of the COD. Meanwhile, attempts at mass mobilizations and a civic strike by radical social movements in El Alto and the altiplano do not receive mass support in the last instance. The latter movements were demanding the resignation of the right-wing Prefect of La Paz, José Paredes, in an act of solidarity with the Cochabamba popular movements against the destabilizing tactics of right-wing autonomist forces throughout the country.

January 22—Highly attended festivities take over the streets of La Paz as the MAS government sponsors celebrations of its first year in office. The Cochabamba conflict all but disappears from the national political scene.

This table was compiled through a qualitative analysis of the following media sources between December 15, 2006 and January 22, 2007: Los Tiempos, La Prensa, La Razón, Bolpress, El Deber, and Econoticias.

Cochabamba entered the international media spotlight briefly during the Cochabamba Water War of 2000, when a popular rural and urban movement rose up against a World Bank–driven privatization of the city's water.[22] This rebellion became a powerful referent in the global justice movement internationally. On the domestic scene it sparked the insurrectionary left-indigenous cycle of revolt that lasted for the next five years. The narrative of the Cochabamba conflict under investigation here begins on December 15, 2006, when right-wing Cochabamba prefect, Manfred Reyes Villa, proposed a new referendum on autonomy for the department. This proposal was issued during an open-air town hall meeting,[23] even though roughly six months earlier, on July 2, 2006, 63 percent of the department's electorate rejected autonomy in a nationwide referendum. Hence, while Reyes Villa was elected with 47.6 percent of the vote in the prefecture elections of December 2005 (the MAS came second with 43.1), by no stretch of the imagination did he enjoy a mandate for establishing departmental autonomy. His actions on December 15, therefore, were perceived by the Bolivian left generally, and in particular by the popular movements in Cochabamba, as a bold unilateral shift of Cochabamba's official departmental politics toward an alliance with the autonomist right of the media luna.

It would require willful blindness to miss the connections between Reyes Villa and the autonomist movement of the media luna. Most obviously, it was Reyes Villa's announcement on December 15 that he was planning on holding a new referendum on autonomy that provoked the Cochabamba conflict in the first place. When he fled Cochabamba in a bulletproof car at the outset of the worst clashes he headed toward La Paz where he met with the prefects of the media luna. From there he subsequently took refuge in Santa Cruz for the duration of the Cochabamba crisis. From Santa Cruz, the leading umbrella organization of the autonomist movement, the Comité Pro Santa Cruz, organized repeated demonstrations in the eastern part of the country in defense of Reyes Villa and against the alleged authoritarianism of the MAS government and the popular uprisings opposed to Reyes Villa in the streets of Cochabamba city. Finally, personnel from the offices of the Cochabamba prefecture have been accused by many popular movement actors of having been part of the formation of the Juventud por la Democracia (Youth for Democracy, JD), a violent, proto-fascist youth group in Cochabamba modeled on the Unión Juvenil Cruceñista (Cruceño Youth Union, UJC) of Santa Cruz.[24]

It was in the interests of the MAS government, therefore, to prevent an extension of the media luna's influence into Cochabamba through the person of Reyes Villa, without at the same time undermining their negotiations with the bourgeois autonomist forces over the Constituent Assembly's content and procedural rules. This was a delicate balance to manufacture, indeed. The MAS government, through its bases in the *regantes* (peasant irrigators) and cocaleros of Cochabamba, as well as through the masista leadership of Cochabamba's Central Obrera Departamental (Departmental Workers Central, COD), appears to have attempted to mobilize demonstrations and road blockades with the aim of simply constraining the capacity of the prefect of Cochabamba and the Cochabamba Civic Committee to align themselves more fully with the autonomist movement of the media luna.[25] It was on this basis that cocaleros, indigenous peasant sectors, the COD, and popular urban movements began their vigil in front of the offices of the prefect on January 4, 2007. However, the demands emanating from the grassroots of the rural and urban social movements that gathered in Cochabamba radicalized substantially as protesters were first repressed by police on January 8 and then were led into vicious battles by violent counter-demonstrators in the street fights of January 11, leaving two dead and more than two hundred injured, many seriously. This context of concentrated struggle, confrontation, repression, and violence—in addition to influence exercised in the demonstrations and assemblies by organized, Trotskyist university students—led the mobilized popular forces on the ground to escape temporarily the limits of the MAS party line and forcefully call for the immediate resignation of Reyes Villa.[26]

The first escalation of social movement tactics and demands can be traced to January 8. Social movements reinforced the numbers of protesters who were already occupying the central plaza of the city, the Plaza 14 de Septiembre, and continued the vigil in front of the offices of the prefect. As the day progressed, however, crowds attempted to gain access to the building of the prefecture. While prevented from taking over the prefecture by volleys of tear gas canisters fired by the police, protesters were able to set fire to the door of the building and two cars in the streets. One witness reported, "Dumpsters were knocked over, piles of garbage were on fire, two cars were burning, and the door to the government office was completely burned and in flames. Not a single police officer was on the plaza any longer because they all had taken cover inside the government headquarters. Every few minutes a window would open and tear gas canisters would be fired into the plaza. If we were lucky, a valiant person would rush to the canister, pick it up, and throw it back at the police...At the end of the day the conflict had resulted in 33 injured, destroyed vehicles, and an entire part of the center plaza burned down."[27]

It was during these events that Reyes Villa escaped in a bulletproof vehicle headed toward La Paz.[28] The following day, the central government sent Vice Minister Fabián Yacsik, and Minister of the Presidency Juan Ramón Quintana, to Cochabamba to initiate negotiations with the social movements and representatives of the prefect and his allies in the Cochabamba Civic Committee. None of the stakeholders were willing to entertain negotiations, however, their positions having been substantially hardened after the incidents on January 8. Two days later, on January 10, a "civic march" was staged by right-wing middle- and upper-class supporters of Reyes Villa. During the march, racist and patronizing epithets were shouted about the largely indigenous rural and urban popular movements present in the city. The Civic Committee declared an indefinite civic strike.[29] By this time, the official position of the MAS government with regard to the social movements was for them to respect the legitimacy of Reyes Villa. Government officials said he could not be overthrown through popular assemblies and street demonstrations because he was democratically elected, despite the obvious unpopularity of his position on departmental autonomy.

Elsewhere in the country the events in Cochabamba were beginning to have an impact. In La Paz, the prefects of the media luna departments met with Reyes Villa, while in Santa Cruz a gathering of the right-wing civic committees of these departments was scheduled for the following day during which tactics were to be defined as to how best to defend three goals: support for Reyes Villa, the "defense of democracy," and the push for the two-thirds procedural rule in the Constituent Assembly, which would favor the media luna's political allies.[30] The rising tensions between January 8 and 10 in Cochabamba and elsewhere set the stage for the most concentrated day of violence in the Cochabamba conflict, January 11.

Violent street battles erupted in the late afternoon. On the one side, primarily middle- and upper-class supporters of the Cochabamba Civic Committee and Reyes Villa—organized in "civic groups," the JD, and neighborhood associations from the wealthy *zona norte* (northern zone) of the city—were pitted against the other side—cocaleros, trade unionists, indigenous peasants, factory workers, municipal workers, popular neighborhood associations, teachers, construction workers, and the urban poor. Supporters of Reyes Villa were armed with wooden clubs (some with knives attached to their ends), baseball bats, metal pipes, golf clubs, tennis rackets, and some firearms. The popular movements were armed with many similar makeshift weapons, with the addition of dynamite sticks and the absence of firearms.[31] Detonations of dynamite and gunshots echoed throughout the city streets. Most of the fighting was restricted to battles with wooden clubs and hand-to-hand combat; however, the mobilized right wing also fired into the crowds. Barricades were erected in the zona norte to prevent incursions by the popular movements, while the latter erected their own barricades in the city center, paralyzing most of the city. Police were instructed by the central government not to repress anyone, and therefore restricted their interventions to minimal tear-gassing of spaces separating the two sides in the conflict in attempts to keep them apart from one another. Military troops did not arrive in the city until the early hours of January 12.[32]

Forty-two-year-old cocalero Nicómedes Gutiérrez was fatally shot in the chest, while twenty-year-old Cristian Urrestia was attacked and killed by social movement sectors when he was separated from the rest of his allies in the pro–Reyes Villa bloc. In addition to the two fatalities, more than two hundred injuries were reported, many of them serious, including gunshot wounds to the chest and life-threatening head injuries.[33] Solidarity demonstrations by popular sectors in the rebellious

city of El Alto were organized by FEJUVE–El Alto (the United Neighborhood Associations of El Alto) and Central Obrera Regional—El
Alto (Regional Workers' Central of El Alto, COR–El Alto) in which
hundreds of demonstrators tried to block access to the main airport in
the western part of the country, located in that city. In Santa Cruz,
meanwhile, the right-wing civic committee declared a 24-hour strike in
defense of the rule of law and Reyes Villa, and resolved to convoke a
cruceño assembly on January 12.[34]

   During this time, Morales was in Nicaragua attending the inaugu-
ration of newly elected president Daniel Ortega, and did not return to
Bolivia until the early morning of January 12.[35] García Linera was
therefore acting-president of the country in Morales's absence and he
expressed the government's official distance from the radicalizing social
movements on the ground in Cochabamba: "The government reaffirms
the search for solutions to the tensions and political conflicts through
dialogue and respect for the constitution."[36] Both García Linera and
Ramón Quintana stressed the fact that they respected the constitution
and recognized the legitimacy of Reyes Villa as prefect of Cochabamba.
At the same time, García Linera blamed Reyes Villa's intransigence for
the violence. Reyes Villa, for his part, fixed the onus on the MAS government, which he accused of manufacturing the entire crisis through
the mobilization of its social bases in Cochabamba. Reyes Villa reiter-
ated that he would not resign.[37] On the ground in Cochabamba, numerous sources reported the discord between the radicalizing position
of the social movements and the calming words of reconciliation, compromise, and negotiation on offer from the MAS government. For example, Julio Salazar, leader of the Federación de Trabajadores del
Trópico de Cochabamba, a central peasant union federation of the cocalero movement, told the press that because of the violence on January 11 the peasants no longer considered Reyes Villa the prefect of
Cochabamba, demanded a new prefect to take his place, and announced that they would not cease pressure tactics, including mass
mobilization and road blockades, until Reyes Villa resigned.[38]

   The following day, on January 12, violence was circumvented by the
presence of more than 1,500 military troops in the city, which had ar-

rived overnight. A tense calm saturated the city, with only sporadic confrontations between anti-riot police and university students.[39] Popular
social movements continued to occupy the city center and persisted in
demanding the resignation of Reyes Villa. Meanwhile, Morales had returned from Nicaragua and addressed the country with two televised
speeches. In the morning he asked the social movements in Cochabamba
to avoid vengeance and cease all violence. In the second presentation in
the evening he suggested that the MAS government was drafting a proposed law for consideration in Congress that would allow for the revoking of political authorities from their positions—including prefects—by
popular referendum, rather than through mobilization in the streets.
The executive also offered to mediate dialogue between social movements in Cochabamba and Reyes Villa, but Reyes Villa insisted that any
negotiations had to take place in Santa Cruz, where he had now based
himself after traveling from La Paz. At the same time, Reyes Villa retreated from his earlier position regarding the new referendum on departmental autonomy that he had called for on December 15.[40]

Again, the sentiments of the rank and file of the social movements still occupying the city did not closely parallel the position of
the MAS government. Reyes Villa's ostensible concession was too little, too late, in their eyes. A popular assembly organized by the COD
in the Plaza 14 de Septiembre, for example, closed the day by passing
three resolutions: that Reyes Villa must resign immediately; that
measures of mobilization and pressure tactics be intensified to accelerate his forced resignation; and that in order to best compel the resignation, social movements ought to take over and occupy the prop-
erties owned by the prefect in Cochabamba.[41] At the same time, the
government registered some success in having various cocalero and
other peasant sectors in the department lift road blockades in rural
areas, even if some blockades continued to impede the flow of interdepartmental traffic.[42]

Between January 13 and 15, a general stalemate persisted, with Reyes
Villa continuing to refuse to return to Cochabamba, the social movements maintaining their contention that he must resign, and the MAS attempting to mediate between the two sides through negotiation and dia-

logue.[43] On January 16, an unsuccessful attempt was made by Trotskyist currents, mostly rooted in the public university of Cochabamba, to build on the discontent of the rank and file and push the contradictions of the Cochabamba conflict toward a revolutionary, parallel departmental government. At a popular assembly convened by the COD that day, between ten thousand and thirty thousand[44] people—cocaleros, regantes, rural and urban teachers, poor neighborhood activists, high school and university students, transport workers, unorganized sectors of the urban poor, and others—gathered in the Plaza 14 de Septiembre. The majority of the speakers vehemently spoke against the legal exit to the crisis proposed by the MAS government. Rather, they called for such measures as the strengthening of the struggle against Reyes Villa, his immediate replacement by a new prefect, and revolutionary struggle against the Bolivian oligarchy. The crowd chanted "*Possession! Possession!*" which was a call for the take over of the prefecture by the popular assembly.

There were but a few speakers at the assembly who adopted the MAS line being issued from La Paz. Omar Velasco, secretary general of the COD, representing this line, said he realized emotions were heated but that the social movements nonetheless had to stay within the boundaries of legality. Omar Fernández, leader of the regantes and a MAS senator, also called for a legal exit, while Víctor Mitma of the COD echoed Morales in calling for calm and an end to violence. Fernández argued, "The assembly is sovereign and its resolutions must be obeyed, but within legal parameters."[45] Likewise, Severo Huanca, secretary of the Seis Federaciones del Trópico Cochabambino, the central organization of the cocaleros, supported a legal exit and respect for constitutional rules.[46] These speakers were pilloried with insults from university students, transport workers, and other sectors of the crowd. The moderate leadership of the cocaleros and the COD were attempting to pass resolutions in the assembly completely at odds with the sentiments of the crowd.[47] The moderates ended their speeches with a call for a legal path to Reyes Villa's resignation as well as a trial of responsibilities for the Cochabamba prefect regarding his role in precipitating the violent deaths of January 11. One reporter with the conservative Santa Cruz newspaper *El Deber* noted, "The discontent [with the position of the moderate leadership] was almost unanimous [*casi general*]."[48]

3Pressure from below at the popular assembly grew to a level where the departmental councilors of Cochabamba who were present in the plaza felt compelled to convene an emergency meeting in the offices of the COD. The social movements in the plaza demanded that the departmental councilors censure Reyes Villa and name a new prefect. Over dissenting voices of moderate social movement and trade union leaders affiliated with the MAS, the councilors present did in fact resolve to censure Reyes Villa and to ask the social movements in the plaza to elect a new prefect. However, by this stage divisions in the rank and file had become more visible, as the leadership of the social movements and unions closely aligned with the MAS pressured the bases to disband from the assembly. Meanwhile, Marco Ríos, leader of the most vocal sector of the radical left, the Federación Universitaria Local (Local University Federation, FUL), spoke in favor of the creation of armed antifascist groups to defend transformative change against the reactionary political tactics of the media luna autonomist forces. At this point, according to various accounts, the cocaleros, the COD, the regantes, and the Federación Bartolina Sisa retreated with their memberships, leaving in the plaza only a fraction of the ten thousand to thirty thousand initially gathered, with the FUL playing a predominant leadership role in the remaining group.[49] The reduced group declared the formation of a parallel Revolutionary Departmental Government and elected fifteen representatives—primarily university students, transport workers, and representatives of neighborhood associations—to the parallel government's *comité popular*, or popular committee. Tiburcio Herradas Lamas became the president of the new "revolutionary" formation.[50] After unsuccessfully attempting to enter the offices of the prefecture, which was protected by police forces, the new "parallel government" convened a press conference at the COD offices and invited the media to another press conference scheduled for the following morning. Meanwhile, Reyes Villa had taken advantage of the confusion and returned to Cochabamba under the protection of the police.[51]

The inability of the parallel government to carry through with their declarations became obvious almost immediately. The MAS government produced a barrage of public statements, press conferences, and televised addresses denouncing the formation of a parallel government as illegal. Morales pledged his support for the legality of Reyes Villa's control over Cochabamba. Alex Contreras, the official spokesperson for the Presidential Palace, said that, for the executive, Reyes Villa continued to be the first political authority of Cochabamba and that the government would not recognize any popular departmental government comprised of radical groups of the extreme left: "We do not recognize the popular departmental government. We respect legality and the Political Constitution of the state."[52] Alfredo Rada, vice minister of coordination with social movements, echoed Contreras: "We consider these radicalized groups of the ultra-Left."[53] García Linera said that while protests are legitimate, the measures adopted by social movements in relation to the revolutionary parallel government are illegal, and that it is imperative to respect democratic norms and rules.[54]

On the afternoon of January 17, Morales met with leaders of the indigenous peasant unions of Cochabamba, the cocaleros' federations, and the COD and was able to persuade them to opt for the still ambiguous legal strategy of seeking Reyes Villa's resignation by way of an uncertain proposed law for revoking the mandates of political authorities. In the absence of support from these key sectors, and in conjunction with the inertia, immaturity, and limited political organizational capacity of the radical left, the Revolutionary Departmental Government had completely dissolved by January 18, 2007, only two days after its bold declarations. It proved entirely incapable of exercising power, even while Reyes Villa remained spectacularly unpopular in the department. Herrada Lamas declared that the parallel government had been betrayed. He questioned the rural and urban union leadership's loyalty to the MAS, and asked why the radical resolutions of multiple popular assemblies had been abandoned.[55] By January 22, the Cochabamba conflict had faded from the national political scene as massive festivities celebrating the first year of the MAS administration kicked off in La Paz. So long as the underlying contradictions that spurred the conflict remain, however, it is only a matter of time before they rise to the surface once again.

In summary, the Cochabamba conflict illustrates how the MAS sought to mobilize its social bases so as to circumvent advances by the far right in Cochabamba while retaining explicit control over the protests. Most importantly, the MAS sought to mobilize its social bases so as to circumvent advances by the far right in Cochabamba while retaining explicit control over the protests. The demands of the mobilization were to be strictly defined by the MAS itself rather than the grassroots assemblies on the scene. When they transcended the acceptable limits the social movement participants were quickly denounced by the government. The rest of the chapter shifts our attention to a different form of extra-parliamentary conflict evident during the early years of the MAS government—that is, a series of right-wing destabilization campaigns.

Recall Referendums, Right-Wing Destabilization, and the El Porvenir Massacre

"Summing up the aims of the new regime, Villarroel uttered his most memorable refrain: 'We are not enemies of the rich, but we are better friends of the poor.' This impossible pledge to favor the poor without estranging the rich—couched in a language of intimate ties—encapsulates the military populist's ambitious but doomed reformism." Thus writes historian Laura Gotkowitz of Colonel Gualberto Villarroel's government in the early 1940s.[56] Villarroel was captured and hanged by protesters in the Plaza Murillo in La Paz, just outside the Presidential Palace, on July 14, 1946. The tin-mining and large-landowning oligarchy that had been threatened by the reforms of military populism in the post–Chaco War period of the late 1930s and early 1940s began its restoration after Villarroel's lynching.[57] It would be a tragedy of immense proportions for left-indigenous forces and the Morales government to follow the paths of Villarroel in the late 1940s and the MNR of the 1950s. Viewed together these experiences represent the signature failure of left-wing populism when it does not confront the economic and political power bases of the urban capitalist and agrarian landowning elite, even in situations when popular mobilization and radicalization have been positioned to make these sorts of inroads on elite control of society.

More than four hundred observers from the Organization of American States (OAS), the Latin American Council of Electoral Experts, and parliamentarians from Europe and Mercosur countries (Argentina, Brazil, Uruguay, and Paraguay) were present for the recall referendums of eight departmental prefects and President Morales and Vice President Álvaro García Linera on August 10, 2008.[58] All stood to lose their jobs or reinforce their support base. Referendum day went relatively smoothly, with turnout an exceptional 83 percent. Voters were asked to decide whether prefects and the president and vice president should continue in their positions. In the case of Morales and García Linera, voters were also asked whether they favored the continuation of the government's process of change. The results are depicted in Tables 4.3 and 4.4.

TABLE 4.3—PRESIDENT AND VICE PRESIDENT

Department	%Vote in Favor August 2008	% Vote National Elections December 2005
Chuquisaca	54	54
La Paz	83	67
Cochabamba	71	65
Oruro	83	63
Potosí	78	58
Tarija	50	32
Santa Cruz	38	33
Beni	42	17
Pando	53	21
Nationwide	68	54

Source: Derived from BIF 2008, 2.

Perhaps the most striking component of the results is that Morales and García Linera increased their nationwide support by 14 percent compared to the December 2005 elections. Their support increased in every department save Chuquisaca. On the question of prefects, too, right-wingers Manfred Reyes Villa of Cochabamba and José Luis Paredes of La Paz lost their posts—although the deeply undemocratic Reyes Villa initially said he would not step down. In accordance with the ref-

erendum law, Morales appointed interim prefects in these departments
until new elections were scheduled.

TABLE 4.4—DEPARTMENTAL PREFECTS (GOVERNORS)

| Department | % Vote December 2005 | August 2008 | |
		%Vote In Favor	%Vote Against
La Paz	38	36	64
Cochabamba	48	35	65
Oruro	41	51	49
Potosí	41	79	21
Tarija	46	58	42
Santa Cruz	48	67	33
Beni	45	64	36
Pando	48	56	44

*Source: Derived from BIF 2008, 2. The department of Chuquisaca had just had a new
prefect voted in, and thus did not hold a referendum.*

Many on the left have taken the results as a triumphant victory for
the MAS's "democratic and cultural" revolution.[59] These unadulterated
celebrations seem to neglect some crucial components of what the referendum has meant.[60] The autonomist right never expected to oust
Morales and García Linera at the national level. Of course, Reyes Villa
(Cochabamba) and Paredes (La Paz) did not want there to be a recall
referendum in the first place. They objected when PODEMOS, the
main right-wing party that holds a majority in the Senate, supported
the referendum law because they expected to be kicked out by the voters who hated them. But in terms of the short-term strategy of the autonomist right, Reyes Villa and Paredes were relatively expendable.
What counted was gaining the bourgeois respectability of legal recognition for departmental autonomy in the core media luna departments.
The illegal and widely condemned autonomy referendums in those departments earlier in 2008 were insufficient for moving forward with
the concrete enactment of "autonomy," asserting departmental control
over natural gas and agro-industrial wealth.

After these latest legal referendums, right-wing autonomists maintained their control of five of nine departments—Pando, Beni, Santa Cruz, Tarija, and Chuquisaca. What is more, they increased their popular support in these departments, and laid the basis for a destabilization campaign against the Morales government, the assertion of new controls over their department's natural resources, and the beginnings of a campaign (ultimately unsuccessful) to prevent the MAS's reelection in 2009—if toppling it through extra-parliamentary means proved impossible beforehand.[61] The referendum results promised to reinforce "the de facto division of the country" and concede "to the subversive separatists a halo of legality they did not possess earlier."[62]

The Morales government seemed to be clinging to a naive faith in the eastern lowland oligarchy's openness to negotiation. Morales sought to combine some of the demands of the autonomists with his government's objective of introducing the draft of a new constitution—approved by the Constituent Assembly in Oruro early in 2008—to a popular referendum. The Morales administration appeared to be convinced that "Andean-Amazonian" capitalism was compatible with a softer version of bourgeois departmental autonomy in the media luna. But the right-wing autonomists wanted nothing more than to see this project of the MAS fail, for the government to stumble from one debacle to the next, and almost immediately showed clear signs of renewed destabilizing energies following the referendum.

The Belligerence of the Autonomists

In the immediate aftermath of the referendums Morales and García Linera invited the opposition prefects to La Paz to negotiate. But the right signaled that it was completely uninterested in achieving any national agreement or social pact with the MAS government. Rubén Costas, the prefect of Santa Cruz, had this to say in the wake of his resounding victory: "This insensible, totalitarian, masista, incapable government has neglected the development of the people and only seeks to concentrate power and transform us into beggars before it." When denouncing the alleged role of Venezuela's Hugo Chávez in propping up the Morales regime, he indulged in the same racist epithets characteristic of the Venezuelan opposition: "No to the big foreign monkeys!"[63]

After showing up at negotiations with the government on August 14 for a few hours, the five right-wing prefects of Chuquisaca, Pando, Beni, Tarija, and Santa Cruz ceremoniously broke off talks in a ritual that had clearly been rehearsed. Gathering together in Santa Cruz immediately after the La Paz meeting with Morales, the prefects called for a civic strike and mobilizations for August 19, Chuquisaca's prefect called for a new illegal referendum on departmental autonomy and insisted again that Sucre should be the new capital of the country, and all five departments declared that "national authorities" are unwelcome in their territory until various demands were met.[64] In the early evening of August 13, 2008, nine Molotov cocktails were hurled at the Santa Cruz offices of the indigenous rights organization, Centro de Estudios Jurídicos e Investigación Social (CEJIS). The police took over one hour to respond.[65] Costas interpreted the results of the referendum as a new mandate to drive forward the bourgeois autonomist agenda in Santa Cruz and the rest of the media luna. He announced a host of illegal initiatives: the formation of a departmental Legislative Assembly; creation of a new departmental tax agency designed to control and collect taxes on natural resources in the department; and the election of subgovernors within the department of Santa Cruz.[66]

None of this should have been surprising given the seditious recent history of social forces behind autonomy. In the period immediately prior to the August referendums, a group of two hundred autonomist reactionaries took over the Tarija airport, successfully impeding a planned meeting between the presidents of Venezuela, Argentina, and Bolivia. A tiny group of thirty-five autonomists were able to take over another airport. And a vehicle, in which the minister of the presidency, Juan Ramón Quintana, was traveling, in the eastern lowland city of Trinidad, was shot at by autonomist forces.[67] The Morales government backed away from enforcing the law in each of these cases. Heinz Dieterich a German-Mexican sociologist is correct to point out, "the counterrevolution has conquered 'liberated zones' in which the central government cannot enter."[68]

The Material Bases of Autonomy

Recent reports on the relationship between natural gas and agro-industry and the autonomy conflicts in Bolivia confirm what I have argued in this book. Concentration of land in Bolivia is the worst in the world after Chile. Much of the concentrated landholdings are located in Santa Cruz. Branko Marinkovic, leader of the Pro–Santa Cruz Civic Committee, to take but one example, reportedly owns some 12,000 hectares (30,000 acres) of land.[69] Tarija, with only 4.9 percent of Bolivia's population, accounts for 60 percent of the country's natural gas production and 85 percent of gas reserves. Santa Cruz follows with 22.3 percent of production. In excess of 82 percent of natural gas production, then, is located in these two media luna states. Under the current complex arrangement of distributing hydrocarbon revenue—split between the national government, the national gas and oil company YPFB, prefectures, municipalities, and universities—the four media luna departments receive 30 percent. Meanwhile, the other five departments (with 79 percent greater population than the media luna) receive only 19.7. This should be considered alongside the fact that in 2007 the media luna departments had a per capita income of roughly 1.4 times that of the other five.[70] As Tom Lewis suggested at the time, "The present political conjuncture in Bolivia is indeed contradictory. In principle, regional self-determination and the peoples' right to immediately recall their elected officials are pillars of democracy. But in today's Bolivia, 'regional autonomy' means handing over the country's wealth—lock, stock, and barrel—to the most reactionary sectors of the Bolivian ruling class and to continued exploitation by the transnational corporations."[71]

The Government's Reformism: Soft on Oligarchs, Hard on Workers

The MAS bears considerable responsibility for allowing the autonomist right to partially reconsolidate itself over this period. In crafting the Constituent Assembly in 2006, the government distorted the revolutionary notion of the assembly envisioned by left-indigenous move ments between 2000 and 2005. The government sought continuously either to demobilize autonomous rural and urban protest—such as invasions and occupations of large landholdings by landless peasants in the east in 2006, and urban revolt against Reyes Villa in Cochabamba in late 2006 and early 2007—or to strategically mobilize its bases against the media luna (especially the cocaleros of the Chapare region), but within very strict perimeters, predetermined by government elites.

As we have seen above, when, in October 2006, the government faced mobilizations of state-employed miners in Huanuni, who were demanding nationalization and workers' control, the miners were denounced by government officials as "Trotskyists" and "provocateurs." Later that month when private cooperative mining interests, allied with transnational mining companies, attacked the state-employed miners, the government initially supported the cooperative miners rhetorically, and failed to send in the army to circumvent the bloodbath that followed. More recently, the same miners, with the support of the COB, struck against the MAS's neoliberal proposal for a new pension law. The state's coercive forces violently broke up a road blockade in the department of Oruro, leaving two miners dead and approximately fifty others wounded—some gravely.[72] Contrast the treatment of the miners with that of the two hundred proto-fascists who took over the Tarija airport. The government had committed itself to fiscal austerity, low-inflationary growth, and central bank independence. Its mining and labor market policies contained deep continuities with the antecedent neoliberal model. Its "agrarian reform" had failed to make consequential inroads on the landholdings of the agro-industrial elite of the eastern lowlands.[73]

While the reforms in the hydrocarbons sector cannot be called nationalization, they have, in combination with elevated international prices, generated vast amounts of new revenue for the state. As a consequence of reforms of the hydrocarbons industry under the Mesa government in 2004, and subsequent reforms in 2006 by the Morales government, the Bolivian state has reaped impressive benefits from the high prices of natural gas. But as one report by a center-right Bolivian economist suggests these revenues have not in fact been redirected to desperately needed social projects: "public investment has increased significantly over the past two years, rising from $629 million in 2005 to $1,103 million in 2007. Most of the new funds have been spent on roads and other infrastructure totaling close to 60 percent of total investments in 2007. Social investment has decreased over this period to less than 30 percent of total investments in 2007."[74] While revenues for the state have increased, real wages have declined when inflation is taken into account.[75]

Revolutionary Advances or Populist Complacency?

The fact that Morales and García Linera enjoyed 68 percent popular support in the wake of the recall referendum was indeed an opportunity to move forward with a more direct confrontation with the logic of capital. But the government needed to veer drastically away from conciliation with the eastern lowland oligarchy, and recognize that there were zero-sum class questions that could not be avoided. No justice for landless indigenous peasants would be forthcoming without expropriations of large landholdings. There could not be justice for workers while real wages were falling and miners were being killed in the streets. There could not be a "democratic and cultural revolution" in Bolivia so long as Guaraní indigenous people remained literally enslaved to masters in parts of the country. There could not be authentic democracy without workers' control and democratic social coordination of the economy. All this necessitated confronting capitalists and imperialism. While such a route had been made more difficult by the renewed legitimacy of the autonomist movement following the referendums, the rearticulation of the right was not yet complete. "Autonomy" has only ever been an objective for the right when it has been too weak to conquer state power at the national level. Neoliberalism by 2008 was perceived as an entirely exhausted and illegitimate project by much of the Bolivian population. The autonomist right, though, had no alternative to offer, other than autonomy and the destabilization of Morales's "dictatorship." There was still an opportunity to circumvent right-wing counterrevolutionary efforts. Such a victory over the right, such an advance toward socialism from below and indigenous liberation, could not be a consequence of the benevolent goodwill of leaders such as Evo Morales or Álvaro García Linera, however. Then, as now, it depended on the rejuvenation of popular indigenous and left forces in rural and urban areas across Bolivia. By providing the right with breathing room, the Morales administration left the window open to counterrevolutionary assault. And it arrived in late August and early September 2008.

Oligarchs on the March: A Coup in the Making?

On September 10, 2008, Minister of Government Alfredo Rada accused the right-wing autonomist leader Branko Marinkovic and Santa Cruz prefect Rubén Costas of orchestrating a wave of violence as part of a "civic governors' coup d'état." Rada accused Marinkovic of having just returned from the United States where he allegedly received instructions for fomenting the coup attempt. "Bolivia on the brink," is a phrase too often uttered by passing journalists unaccustomed to the country's regular politics of the streets. But events of the first two weeks of September 2008 could not be passed off as the ordinary business of protest. Rather, a right-wing coup attempt was in the offing in the five departments governed by the right-wing opposition. The critical media luna departments were joined in part by far-right elements in the government of the department of Chuquisaca. These right-wing autonomists seemed not to have achieved sufficient support within the military to carry out a successful coup, but the passivity of the Morales government in the face of ferocious racism, violence, and the takeover of state institutions and airports on an unprecedented scale, did not bode well for the future of Bolivia.

One indication of the seriousness of the situation was that Morales announced that U.S. ambassador Philip Goldberg was no longer welcome in Bolivia and would be asked officially to leave the country in the coming hours. Morales accused Goldberg of meeting with the oppositional prefects of the five departments in rebellion, to help coordinate what had become a full-scale destabilization campaign. The campaign was led by the Consejo Nacional Democrático (National

Democratic Council, CONALDE), which brought together the prefectures and civic committees of Santa Cruz, Beni, Pando, Tarija, and Sucre, under the banner of "departmental autonomy." These prefectures and civic committees in turn represented the agro-industrial, petroleum, and financial elite of these departments. While they were led by the bourgeoisie, the autonomists had won over substantial sectors of the popular classes by manipulating real democratic desires for decentralized "autonomous" self-governance, as opposed to alienating central state control. If the civic committees and prefects were the pretty face of autonomism, a growing network of proto-fascist youth groups linked to them were its clenched fist in the streets.

The immediate objective of the autonomist right was to destabilize the Morales government and to weaken left-indigenous forces throughout the country. One longer term goal was to reaffirm and consolidate private elite control over the natural gas and agricultural wealth of the country that was increasingly under threat due to widespread popular sentiment in favor of expropriation, nationalization, redistribution, and the establishment of social control over Bolivia's riches. A related long-term objective of the autonomist right was to reconquer state power at the national level.

The Post-Referendum Conjuncture

Again, we ought to remember that Evo Morales and Álvaro García Linera won the support of nearly seven of every ten Bolivians in the August recall referendum. At the same time, however, right-wing prefects consolidated power in five of the country's nine departments. While the Morales and García Linera line since the referendum had been moderation and calls for negotiation and dialogue with the far right, CONALDE launched massive and coordinated direct actions: road blockades; racist attacks against unarmed pro-government rallies; terrorization of poor, mainly indigenous neighborhoods in the eastern lowlands by gangs of proto-fascist thugs; armed assaults on military and police personnel guarding public institutions; occupations and shutdowns of airports; looting and burning of state offices; and the vandalizing of state-owned media outlets.

In so doing, the autonomists established real power in most of the departments of Santa Cruz, Tarija, Beni, and Pando, and urban areas of Chuquisca, particularly the departmental capital of Sucre. It became literally unsafe for the president and state representatives to visit these areas. Momentum was on the side of the right, and they were in no mood for negotiation.

Morales and his government refused to declare a state of emergency and thus the right-wing advanced and brutal acts of racist violence in over half of the country's territory continued apace with impunity. "We are not going to declare a state of emergency," stated vice minister of Social Movements Sacha Llorenti. "We are not going to succumb to the provocation," Llorenti continued. Likewise, Foreign Affairs Minister David Choquehuanca said, "This is a government of dialogue…. The groups committing the violence, violating laws and human rights are small. We call on these violent groups to return to negotiations."[76]

But a state of emergency, in combination with the concerted mobilization and organization of popular left-indigenous forces throughout the country, might have allowed the government to reestablish constitutional order and detain and bring to justice right-wing subversives bent on destroying a government that enjoyed the support of 68 percent of the population. It would have helped to guarantee military and police protection of state property and basic rights for the civilian population in the face of racist terror. It would have helped to provide a means of defense against right-wing autonomists wielding guns and Molotov cocktails.

It might have turned the tide against the colonial-era violence and public denigration of the indigenous poor in urban plazas of the major eastern lowland cities: whippings, beatings with clubs and two-by-fours, and punching, kicking, and swarming, captured on private and state media alike. All this was accompanied by disgusting racist epithets, and legitimated by the departmental prefectures and civic committees who said Morales's "dictatorship" brought it all on.

Jorge Soruco, a human rights activist in the department of Beni, conveyed the exasperation of popular sectors loyal to the government living in the five departments in rebellion: "This is racist dementia, madness that we can't allow. We are living in an era of insanity, where the people of the opposition…are confronting the people with situations of extreme violence."

A Late-August Festival of Hate against the Indigenous of Santa Cruz

After registering astonishing levels of support in the referendum, the MAS government declared that it was going to bring forward for popular referendum the draft of a new constitution approved by the Constituent Assembly in Oruro several months earlier. In celebration, indigenous peasant and working-class supporters of the government set off on August 29 for a peaceful march to the Plaza 24 de Septiembre, in the center of the city of Santa Cruz. A gathering of autonomists, organized in part by the Unión Juvenil Cruceñista (Cruceño Youth Union, UJC), were there to greet them.

According to the mainstream daily *La Prensa*, one UJC speaker at the autonomist rally declared: "We are not going to permit [the entrance of the masistas] into the Plaza. When we go to their communities, they treat us like dogs. We want independence. We don't want this damned race in our territory." Other chants and phrases used that day, according to the vociferously anti-Morales *La Razón* newspaper, included: "shitty collas," (colla is a racial slur used in Santa Cruz to refer to indigenous people from the western highlands), and, "Indians return to your lands."

After the speeches, the racists went on a rampage against the unarmed trade unionists and peasants, as well as any visibly indigenous person in proximity of the plaza. Indigenous women wearing the traditional *pollera*, or gathered skirt, were particularly vulnerable to beatings and racist taunts. One autonomist youth leader, Amelia Dimitri, was captured in video footage and photographs whipping an indigenous woman wearing a pollera. This occurred immediately after Dimitri addressed the crowd of autonomist thugs in a rousing speech. Hers was only the latest face of hatred on the autonomist right.

On national television, Bolivians watched as racist teenagers wielded clubs, whips, and two-by-fours against unarmed indigenous workers and peasants. Images of men and women with broken noses and shirts literally drenched in blood quickly made their way to YouTube, private and national state media, and the front pages of the local newspapers. These were the "democracy supporters" supported by imperialism against the "dictatorship" of Evo Morales. But where were the police? Where was the military? The MAS government refused to act, calling instead for negotiations.

In the following weeks the pace of events intensified further, such that during September 9 and 10, Bolivia was perched on a precipice, below which laid the defeat of left-indigenous power—on the rise since the wave of insurrections between 2000 and 2005—and the conquest of power by imperialism and the rich and the white-mestizo elite who have long ruled the country, and who retain control of economic power despite Morales's electoral victory.

The Makings of a Coup Attempt

The latest phase of pressure tactics in the media luna departments began in earnest with the initiation of a road blockade on August 25 in the Chaco region of the department of Tarija, followed a week later by parallel road blockades in the departments of Beni and Santa Cruz. This latter period also saw the occupation by force of several public institutions in Santa Cruz, as well as an attempt by the proto-fascist UJC to take over the police barracks in the capital city of that department, also named Santa Cruz. As many analysts have pointed out, the actions by the autonomist right over this period merely represented the latest consolidation of their power in the eastern lowlands, given that for most of 2008 it had been impossible for the president and other government officials to safely visit major cities in the eastern lowlands, due to airport occupations and violent acts perpetrated against state ministers.

On September 10, at least twenty-two state entities were occupied and taken over by the youth wing of the Pro–Santa Cruz Committee and their sister organizations in the departments of Santa Cruz, Beni, Tarija, Pando, and Sucre. The right-wing occupiers declared that they would transfer power of these state institutions to autonomous departmental authorities. In Pando, for example, the prefect, Leopoldo Fernández, named a departmental director of the National Agrarian Institute (INRA). President of the Beni Civic Committee Luis Alberto Melgar, and vice president of the Pando Civic Committee Ricardo Shimokawa, announced that the occupations and mobilizations in their departments to date were just beginning. Among the state institutions taken over across the country were the state television channel, Televisión Boliviana, and radio station, Patria Nueva. The airports of the eastern lowland cities of Trinidad, Guayaramerín, and Riberalta were also seized by autonomist forces. Two natural gas stations were seized, and twenty-nine different road blockades were erected on the highways of these five departments.

Despite presidential authorization to protect state institutions, the National Police and Military Police lost control of these entities, as they were forcefully driven from their stations by violent mobilizations of the far right. University students, proto-fascist political youth gangs, functionaries of the departmental prefectures, and an array of other social sectors, including organized housewives (*amas de casa*), participated in the right-wing autonomist assaults on public institutions and confrontations with the coercive apparatuses of the state. These street actions were directly linked, however, with the finely dressed men occupying the highest institutions of departmental power—the prefectures and the civic committees. And these men represented the agro-industrial, petroleum, and finance capitalists. Indeed, many autonomist politicians had millions of their own money invested in these sectors.

The Scope of the Right-Wing Assault

Santa Cruz, where the confrontations between the National Police and the Military Police and the UJC were most intense, witnessed the takeover of the National Tax Services (SIN) offices, the National Agrarian Institute (INFRA), and the state telecommunications company (ENTEL).

The offices of Televisión Boliviana and Nueva Patria in Santa Cruz were initially broken into at night by young thugs who damaged equipment and lit parts of the offices on fire. Security of the premises was then reestablished by state forces for a period of time on the morning of September 10, until bands of the UJC effectively drove the police forces away with Molotov cocktails. The state then lost control entirely of their state media companies in the city.

Right-wing autonomist forces also launched violent attacks against various indigenous NGOs and human rights organizations, such as the Centro de Estudios Jurídicos y de Investigación Social (CEJIS). CEJIS on two earlier occasions in 2008 was attacked with Molotov cocktails. The El Trompillo and Viru Viru airports were taken over by the state military to ensure they were not taken over by autonomist forces. In Tarija, where road blockades set up in August persisted late into September, right-wing autonomist forces took over government tax offices (SIN), the offices of the National Agrarian Institute (INRA), and the border state's migration offices. Perhaps most importantly, they also managed to occupy the offices of the superintendent of hydrocarbons. Given that roughly 82 percent of natural gas production occurs in the department of Tarija, this was of major concern.

In the department of Beni, the Jorge Henrich airport was taken over, and its runways blockaded with transport trucks and piled debris. The offices of the Administration of Airports and Aerial Navigation (AASANA) were taken over. Likewise, the airport of Riberalta was shut down. Also in Riberalta, the doors of the offices of Televisión Boliviana were damaged, although the mob didn't manage to enter the premises. The Bolivian Postal Service (ECOBOL), ENTEL, and the Migration offices were also taken over in this city. In the community of Guayaramerín, autonomist activists violently seized the offices of the National Customs office and the airport terminal. Elsewhere, in the city of Villamontes, the Civic Committee took illegal control of a natural gas station, giving it the capacity to turn off supplies to the Yacuiba–Río Grande Gas Pipeline (GASYRG), the main natural gas source for Brazil.

In Sucre, the Unión Juvenil de la Chuquisaqueñidad (Youth Union of Chuquisaca, UJCh—Sucre is the capital of the department of Chuquisaca) and associated organizations, took over the tax offices and other state institutions. These protests were led in part by the notorious

Roberto Lenin Sandóval, who was then awaiting trial for his participation in the right-wing takeover of state institutions several months earlier, as well as for his role in racist attacks against indigenous peasants as part of the Chuquisaca Conscience movement.

However, unlike in the other four departments controlled by the right, Chuquisaca's autonomist actions against the central government were limited to the capital of Sucre, as the countryside continued to be controlled by indigenous peasants overwhelmingly aligned with the Morales government. "The reactionary rampage in the lowlands is the result of a desperate, cornered minority that has been given considerable breathing room by a weak, vacillating central government that nevertheless enjoys massive popular backing," explained historian Forrest Hylton, who was on the scene in Bolivia. "The opposition has demonstrated the central government's inability to impose the rule of law amid public/private terror against its supporters—a spectacular triumph for any right-wing movement."

As mentioned earlier, on September 10, President Evo Morales took belated action against what appeared to be a mounting coup attempt by expelling U.S. ambassador Phillip Goldberg for meeting with autonomist leaders in the lead-up to the coordinated chaos of the preceding weeks. As noted, according to Morales, the United States was behind this attempted coup. This was an atypically bold anti-imperialist measure by the Bolivian government and was almost immediately followed by Hugo Chávez's expulsion of the U.S. ambassador to Venezuela, Patrick Duddy. Unfortunately, Morales' anti-imperialism here was unaccompanied by measures against the domestic sources of antidemocratic, right-wing belligerence.

On September 11—a date infamous in Latin America as the anniversary of the 1973 fascist coup in Chile—the foreseeable fatalities of reactionary violence took place, though on a scale that exceeded most expectations. Indigenous peasants in the department of Pando set off from the community of El Porvenir on their way to a gathering in Cobija, the department's capital. Along the way, they were intercepted by paramilitaries, some using official departmental vehicles. Machine-gun terror left at least fifteen peasants dead, more than thirty injured, and more than one hundred missing. These figures were arrived at by a preliminary investigation of the Asamblea Permanente de Derechos Humanos de Bolivia (Bolivian Permanent Assembly of Human Rights, APDHB). Desperate peasants fleeing their would-be assassins leaped into the adjacent river—well known for its abundant populations of crocodiles and venomous snakes.

The Face of Fascism

The central government finally declared a state of emergency in Pando. Then-prefect Leopoldo Fernández was arrested and transferred to the capital city of La Paz, along with several other of his cronies, to await trial for involvement in the massacre. President Morales appointed an interim military prefect, Landelino Rafael Bandeira Arce. A brief political portrait of Leopoldo Fernández reveals the character of the contemporary Bolivian right. He is a descendant of big-player families in the rubber and nut industries of the northern Bolivian Amazon. Since the late nineteenth century, these industries have been notorious for subjecting their workforce—local indigenous workers and migrant workers from the Andean region—to conditions of extreme exploitation, and even servitude.

Fernández was one of the key producers in the nut industry in the eastern lowlands, and a major operator in the ranching sector as well. He got his political start during the most brutal dictatorships of Luis Garcia Meza (1980–81), and Celso Terrelio and Guido Vildoso (1981–82), Fernández was a director of the Instituto Nacional de Colonización (National Institute of Colonization, INC), in Pando. It has been well established that Garcia Meza in particular paid for the "services" of loyal regional civilian and military functionaries by handing out large tracts of land. Fernández, as a director of INC, was in charge of administering huge parcels of fertile territory. Through these and other channels Fernández was able to transform Pando into something like his personal fiefdom.

His political power was on display again during the second presidency of ex-dictator Hugo Banzer, and Vice President Jorge "Tuto" Quiroga (1997–2002), when he worked variously as congressperson, prefect, and minister of government. Until his recent imprisonment, the movers and shakers in the logging, agro-industrial, and nut sectors of Pando's economy—like the Sonnenschein, Hecker Hasse, Becerra Roca, Vaca Roca, Penaranda, Barbery Paz, Claure, and Villavicencio Amuruz families, who together own almost a million hectares of fertile territory—had operated with impunity under Fernández's protection.

The Regional Response

In the wake of what quickly became known as the Massacre of El Porvenir, Chilean president Michelle Bachelet called an emergency meeting of the South American Union (UNASUR) in Santiago on September 15. The outcome was the Declaration of La Moneda, a document signed by twelve governments, denouncing the secessionist violence that was attempting to undermine the Morales government. While this display of South American unity and independence from American imperialism was to be celebrated, analyst Guillermo Almeyra rightly pointed out that much of the solidarity only runs so deep. Cristina Fernández and Lula da Silva, the presidents of Argentina and Brazil respectively, were motivated principally by their countries' dependence on the continued flow of Bolivian natural gas to their markets.

Meanwhile, the solidarity of other signatories—like Colombia, Peru, Chile, and Uruguay—along with that of the Organization of American States (OAS), is predicated on Morales reaching a negotiated conciliation with the far right, rather than imposing the popular democratic will in support of fundamental, transformative change in the country. In other words, the regional solidarity effectively isolated the Bolivian extreme right, but the domestic process still had to transcend the boundaries of a negotiated exit—preferred by many regional governments—if the outcome for the popular majority was not to be severely compromised.

By the end of September twenty thousand mostly indigenous peasant supporters of the government mobilized and marched to the outskirts of the major eastern lowland city of Santa Cruz to denounce the massacre and to demand the radicalization of the process of change in the country. This march received public support from some sectors of the MAS leadership, but only very tepid and conditional support from the president himself. Road blockades had been lifted temporarily—although no demobilization had occurred—after Morales called for this so that negotiations with the extreme right, taking place in the city of Cochabamba under the auspices of the OAS, could continue without interruption. In these negotiations, the right consistently illustrated its unwillingness to concede any of its central demands. And despite the fact that Morales was behind the lifting of the road blockades, the still-mobilized peasants threatened to resume their siege of Santa Cruz a month later if the autonomist forces had not yet given in substantially at the negotiating table.

Meanwhile, the Bolivian Workers' Central (COB) was divided. The leadership entered into an uncritical pact with the MAS government, but leading sectors of the COB, such as the miners' federation (FSTMB), continued to call for working-class independence—meaning that the working class will act militantly against any right-wing threats to democracy, but will not allow the Morales government free reign to give in to the old neoliberal order. The Factory Workers of Cochabamba also called militant working-class mobilizations against the autonomists, suggesting that a just solution could not be found at the OAS-mediated negotiating table.

During its first two and a half years in office, Morales's administration conceded repeatedly to the demands of the extremist autonomist right of the media luna departments while offering only moderate reforms to its popular constituency. It declared socialism to be an impossible aim in the country for fifty to one hundred years, and instead sought to implement "Andean-Amazonian" capitalism, a model which tries to reconcile the conflicting interests of imperialism and capital on one side and those of the impoverished peasantry and working classes on the other. The right wing used the space provided to it by the MAS to rearticulate its political bases, from historic lows in 2003 and 2005 to a situation of dominance in half the country, including in the richest and most populated department of Santa Cruz, by mid-2008. This was the backdrop that needed to be taken into account when political forces considered the meaning of the August referendum.

Sectors of the left understood this dynamic and sought in mid-2008 to move toward greater working-class and peasant independence from the government, so that more sustained pressure for change could be applied from below by popular forces, even as they defended the government against the domestic right and imperialist machinations. On August 1, 2008, the executive committee of the COB released the following resolution:

> The Bolivian Workers' Central, loyal to its glorious history of revolutionary struggle, will never be a political instrument of the oligarchy and imperialism. Our iron commitment is with the defense of the democratic political process opened up in the heroic days of October 2004 [sic, 2003] and May–June 2005 with the blood of the Bolivian people and workers. We are convinced that the revolutionary, patriotic and popular forces have to unite in a single front to crush the oligarchy and imperialism, but not at the cost of giving up our social rights that have been curtailed by neoliberalism, much less of getting caught up in the political games [pongueaje político] of this or any other government.

The documents calls for the unity of the workers and the Bolivian people, solidarity against the oligarchy and imperialism, and for driving out right-wing elements within the MAS.

Oscar Olivera wrote this passage as part of an open letter during a collective hunger strike of factory workers in Cochabamba around the same time:

> The workers of yesterday and today should feel proud of our identity, of being the producers of the material goods that we and others need to live, proud that we are those who use the strength of our arms and our minds and our hearts to transform Mother Earth's, Pachamama's, gifts for our well-being. We have managed to resist. We have managed to subsist as an organized body. We have been able to salvage some of our rights, and we have passed into a long and dark tunnel in these years of invisibility and now we are inclined to make ourselves visible again by showing our indignation for our working conditions. We are also doing this because of the indifference of our current government, which for more than two years has ignored us. In spite of the fact that we workers struggled to put this government where it is today, our leaders have forgotten about us. We have been struggling in the streets since April for BREAD, WORK and HOUSING because they don't listen to us, they don't see us, they don't feel us, because they no longer live like us, the simple working people who live from their own work and not others' work. We ought to feel proud because with our struggle, we are pushing for the so-called "process of change" to be not just a slogan, but also a reality. The only way to change things, to change our working condi-

tions and our lives is through unity, organization, mobilization, the recuperation of our memory, of our values. We must remember our fa-
thers and grandfathers, our mothers and grandmothers, our older
brothers and sisters and we must ask them face to face if what we are
doing today is OK and what else we are missing in order for their inher-
itance to be preserved and augmented, so that the well-being of our
sons and grandsons, and all of dignified life, is forever preserved.

Unfortunately, it would be wildly misleading to suggest that the
COB's resolution and Olivera's statement reflected the leading ideas of
left-indigenous sectors on the ground in Bolivia in mid-2008. Rather
there had been a demobilization of independent political action from
below and an increasing reliance on elite negotiations between the
MAS leadership and the autonomist oligarchy—when the latter decided to participate. Nonetheless, these sentiments were incipient signs
of more independent working-class actions to come in 2009 and 2010.

Conclusion

Through an examination of the Huanuni and Cochabamba eruptions,
this chapter sought, first, to demonstrate that the possibility of a transition to socialism in the near to medium term was explicitly denied during the first year of the Morales administration through the implementation of Vice President García Linera's "Andean-Amazonian capitalism."
Under this development model, popular-class indigenous interests are
subordinated to the interests of capital in the MAS's asymmetrical,
multiclass coalition, because the government is committed to the foundational macroeconomic pillars of neoliberalism—fiscal austerity, low-
inflationary growth, flexible labor markets, and central bank independence. Its second objective was to show how this same overarching
model of development led it into ill-fated negotiations with, and toler-
ance of, the extreme right of the media luna departments, allowing
room for its partial rearticulation, destabilization campaigns, and the
El Porvenir massacre of September 2008.

This chapter has illustrated that during the first year of the MAS
administration the government mobilized its social bases at various

junctures but within strict parameters defined by the government itself. This was apparent both in the case of the Cochabamba conflict when the demands of social movements eventually transcended the goals of the MAS, and in the MAS's response to the FSTMB's protests leading up to and during the October 2006 crisis in the Huanuni mine. Evo Morales is not a charismatic leader in the sense of classical populism, but as the first indigenous president of the republic he is seen to be a direct representative of the historically excluded and oppressed indigenous majority. Ideologically, the MAS often employs radical rhetoric, particularly with regard to "nationalization" in various sectors of the economy. In reality, however, "nationalization" has a remarkably restricted scope and assurances are constantly made to important sectors of foreign and domestic capital alike that their fundamental interests will not be jeopardized. Furthermore, despite large increases in state revenue from soaring natural gas prices it was demonstrated that social spending has been notably austere. All this suggests that we need to pay diligent attention to the practice of the MAS rather than parroting its rhetoric. The negligence of some analysts in this regard has led them to exaggerate the radical nature of the current administration.

This chapter has attempted to draw out some of the complexities of the Bolivian process and the character of the MAS government. The mining confrontations of October 2006, the urban street battles in January 2007, and the racist violence in Santa Cruz and El Porvenir are but a few windows into a whole series of dynamic and unpredictable class struggles that played out in the wider political setting of the administration's first year. The traditions and initiative of the popular classes and oppressed indigenous nations, displayed so powerfully in the early years of this century, will need once again to express their social power independently of the MAS if their aims and objectives are not to be defeated or tamed beyond all recognition under the current government. With this kind of renewal of self-activity a deepening of social reforms can be forced along, and even the foundations for social transformation constructed. At the same time, the strategic, autonomous mobilization of the popular sectors is also the best barrier to the advance of the counter-revolutionary autonomist movement in the media luna departments.

Top: In a march from El Alto to La Paz on May 16, 2005, a young protester marches with a sign: "Bolivia will not be a colony of the Yankees or the transnationals."

Bottom: The leaders of the Bolivian Workers' Central (COB) march from El Alto to La Paz on May 16, 2005. The bottom of their banner reads: "The emancipation of the workers will be the work of the workers themselves."

Top: Militant-indigenous proletarian activists gather outside the offices of the Federation of Neighborhood Councils of El Alto (FEJUVE-El Alto) during the Second Gas War of May–June 2005.

Bottom: Graffiti in El Alto demands "Gas for All" during the Second Gas War of May–June 2005.

Top: Tens of thousands gathered on May 23, 2005, in the Plaza San Francisco of La Paz, with the *whiphala*, the multicolored indigenous flag, a symbol of popular resistance against neoliberalism and racial oppression.

Bottom: Military police near the Presidential Palace in La Paz during a lull in street battles in the Second Gas War of May–June 2005.

Top: Military police stand watch over El Alto in the lead-up to the Second Gas War in 2005. The capital city of La Paz is situated behind them in the valley below.

Bottom: This image from May 25, 2005, shows how the streets of La Paz were filled every day with masses of protesters by the end of the month, setting the stage for neoliberal president Carlos Mesa's forced resignation on June 6, 2005.

PART II

Consolidating Reform, 2007–2010

Five

The Ideological Structures of Reconstituted Neoliberalism

"A crisis consists precisely in the fact that the old is dying and the new cannot be born; in this interregnum, a great variety of morbid symptoms appear."

—Antonio Gramsci

"A state crisis does not necessarily lead to a new state. There can be internal adjustments, in [social] forces, alliances, and politics, and there can be a reconstitution of the old state...the national revolutionary state of 1952 had phases of internal mutation and of reconfiguration that permitted it to survive a little bit longer...."

—Álvaro García Linera

"To occupy the presidential office and to obtain a parliamentary majority does not serve the interests of the exploited in any way if the power of the bourgeoisie and the regime of big private property continue intact."

—Radical Bolivian journalist in El Alto

On December 6, 2009, Evo Morales won a decisive mandate for a second term in office with an astonishing 64 percent of the popular vote. The turnout was close to 90 percent.[1] This latest electoral victory marked the peak of a wave of successes in the polls, including 67 percent support for his administration in the recall referendum of 2008, and 61 percent approval of the new constitution in a popular referendum held on January 25, 2009.[2] The December 2009 elections represented the most profound level of institutional consolidation in the apparatuses of the state for any political force in recent Bolivian memory. Morales was the first president in Bolivia to be reelected in successive terms, and the first to win with a larger percentage of votes when elected for a second term.[3] For the first time since the 1952 National Revolution, a party won a massive majority, and control of both houses of the legislature, providing the MAS with the power, among other things, to reconfigure the reactionary judiciary. The MAS controls 25 of 36 Senate seats, and 82 of 130 seats in the House of Deputies.[4] Morales also made important gains in the departments of the media luna, the heartland of the country's autonomist right wing. In Tarija, Morales actually won a majority of votes, and in Beni, Pando, and Santa Cruz, he increased his support substantially. Most importantly, in this regard, he won 41 percent of the popular vote in the department of Santa Cruz, the principal axis of the eastern bourgeois bloc.[5] In the departmental elections for governors, mayors, and departmental assemblies held on April 4, 2010, moreover, the tide continued to turn in favor of the MAS. Of the nine governorships, the MAS won six (Chuquisaca, La Paz, Cochabamba, Oruro, Potosí, and Pando) and lost three to right-wing oppositions (Tarija, Santa Cruz, and Beni). This represented a significant shift from merely three MAS governorships (Chuquisaca, Potosí, and Oruro) in the 2005 departmental elections. What is more, the race was tight in Tarija and Beni, and reasonably close in Santa Cruz. The winning opposition won 49, 53, and 43 percent to the MAS's 44, 38, and 40 percent, in Tarija, Santa Cruz, and Beni respectively.[6]

The current conjuncture, at the close of the latest electoral cycle and in the midst of the opening months of the government's second term, provides an ideal time once again to take stock of image and reality in contemporary Bolivian political economy. Unfortunately, on both the right and the left internationally, hyperbole has often substituted for serious reflection and analysis of the Bolivian scenario. In the weeks before the elections, for example, Judy Rebick, a prominent figure on the Canadian left who recently traveled to Bolivia, suggested that the MAS government is "reinventing democractic socialism. They are in the process of creating a plurinational state with equal rights for all nations and people, redistributing land, providing free health and education for everyone, creating what they call a pluri-economy that includes public, private, co-operative, and communitarian. In four years of power they have eliminated illiteracy, reduced extreme poverty by 6%, instituted a senior's pension for the first time, nationalized hydrocarbons, and achieved a 6.5% economic growth [sic]. They are showing that a government that acts in the interests of the majority really can succeed and that an alternative is truly possible."[7] Naomi Klein, one of the most prestigious voices of the global justice movement, remarked that, "Bolivia is in the midst of a dramatic political transformation, one that has nationalised key industries and elevated the voices of indigenous peoples as never before."[8]

The Canadians were not alone. In various Latin American countries, leftists greeted the victory of Morales in Bolivia as an unequivocal advance toward socialism. Atilio Borón, a well-known Argentine intellectual, suggested that Bolivians had just elected "a president committed to the construction of a socialist future for his country."[9] For Mexican radical, Ana Esther Ceceña, the continuation of the Morales-García Linera administration for an additional four years signified an opportunity to "deepen a creative pathway which does not repeat the exhausted roads of developmentalism," but rather "invents fresh pathways" toward the "conceptualization and construction of no-capitalism." She asks, rhetorically: "Will Bolivia be the example which offers the key for beginning that new era of humanity, the era of living well [vivir bien] in no-capitalism?"[10]

These positions were reflections of Morales's recent rhetorical embrace of what he now often refers to as Bolivia's advance toward "communitarian socialism." Addressing the crowds amassed outside of the Presidential Palace in La Paz following his December 2009 election victory, for example, Morales noted that the win provides a space and opportunity to "accelerate the process of change and deepen socialism."[11] Later that month, at the climate talks in Copenhagen, Morales served as a beacon of hope for activists raging in the streets against the hypocrisy, arrogance, and suicidal tendencies of powerful state leaders who were consigning the future of the world's ecosystems to oblivion in secret corridors and meeting rooms.[12]

The Bolivian president named capitalism itself as the key enemy of nature. At the subsequent World People's Conference on Climate Change and the Rights of Mother Earth, held in April 2010 in Cochabamba, Morales had this to say: "We are here because in Copenhagen the so-called developed countries failed in their obligation to provide substantial commitments to reduce greenhouse gases. We have two paths: either Pachamama or death. We have two paths: either capitalism dies or Mother Earth dies. Either capitalism lives or Mother Earth lives. Of course, brothers and sisters, we are here for life, for humanity and for the rights of Mother Earth. Long live the rights of Mother Earth! Death to capitalism!"[13]

The same symbolism that has triggered the imaginations and aspirations of some leftist intellectuals, as well as many progressive activists throughout the world, simultaneously sparked the ire of decrepit cold warriors in Washington and conservatives in Latin America. Hawkish pundits, such as Mexico's ex-leftist, Jorge Castañeda, have lined up behind U.S. imperialism's branding of Morales as one of the scarier components of a disconcertingly immoderate current within the wider left turn that has gripped regional politics over the last decade.[14] The *Economist* refers to Morales as a "socialist of Amerindian descent," bent on "refounding" the country as an "Amerindian socialist republic." The magazine reports that the December 2009 elections were a "thumping endorsement for the social revolution," he is leading.[15] According to the *Washington Post*, the Bolivian president is a "leftist" driven by his quest to "tighten state control over the impoverished economy."[16]

Mapping Intellectual Currents in Bolivia under Morales

Bolivia has long been marginalized from mainstream international political discussion and affairs. Even the rest of South America has often forgotten the existence of its landlocked indigenous core. This general context helps to explain the easy descent into simplistic caricatures that we have seen rehearsed in many sources on the left and right cited above. The complexity of developments in Bolivian social, political, and economic life under Morales has predictably generated more serious analysis at home. Broadly speaking, Bolivian scholarship and intellectual life has divided into three camps, reflecting, to varying degrees, fractures and articulations of actual social and political forces on the ground.[17]

There are, in the first instance, warriors of the ancien régime. These are intellectuals who defend the social hierarchies and economic and political structures of capitalist development consolidated in the neoliberal era since 1985. This group can be fruitfully divided into two further subcategories. There are the conservatives, on the one hand, who tend to exaggerate the radicalism of the MAS government and see its replacement as necessary for the preservation, or, in some cases, restoration, of the old social structures of neoliberalism. On the other hand, there are the liberals, who share a nostalgia for the old power structures, but who see in the Morales administration the best possible defense of those structures under the given conditions of neoliberal crisis in contemporary Bolivia. The liberals tend to have a more realistic assessment of the limited scope of the socioeconomic reforms introduced by the Morales government thus far, but are nonetheless concerned that the parameters for any future social, economic, and political change be tightly circumscribed.

A second broad and eclectic intellectual camp includes figures that are relatively uncritical in their loyalty to the MAS. This group embraces advocates of moderate and culturally circumscribed multiculturalism (that is to say, supporters of indigenous cultural advance disassociated from socioeconomic transformation), social democrats and populists of various inclinations, and anticapitalists who either see the seeds of profound transformation in the changes already instituted by the Morales government or perceive in those changes only modest encroachments on neoliberalism, but understand these meager steps to be the "realistic" or "necessary" extent of reform at the moment given the structural constraints of global capitalism.

A third camp, to which this book hopes to make a modest contribution, takes an array of positions broadly in favor of revolutionary indigenous liberation and anticapitalist transformation of the Bolivian state, society, and economy. Defense of the MAS government against any and all right-wing threats from domestic and/or imperial forces is a priority for this group; however, they tend to argue that the actual breaks with neoliberalism have been exaggerated by the government's pageantry and have been generally outweighed, in fact, by various continuities in Bolivia's neoliberal political economy. Strategically, this critical left-indigenous camp emphasizes that authentic transformation cannot depend on the benevolence of the Morales–García Linera leadership, but rather will spring forth from the self-activity, self-organization, and tactical mobilization of the exploited and oppressed themselves, acting autonomously from the MAS government.[18]

It is hardly surprising that in the context of effervescing social movements, and now a government that describes itself in socialist terms, the central concern of mainstream sociologists and political scientists writing about Bolivia over the last number of years has been the specter of revolution and the concomitant necessity of containing the rebels from below and reestablishing order from above. For radical intellectuals, who saw the reigning neoliberal order in Bolivia over the course of the 1980s and 1990s as fundamentally premised on racialized class injustice, the period of rebellion threw up different concerns from those of the mainstream.[19] The question arising from the context of insurrection from a radical vantage point was rather how this ideological discontent, and its expression in the rising cycle of anti-neoliberal protest in the first five years of the twenty-first century, might be channeled into a fully-fledged societal and political transformation of the country's structures in the interests of the indigenous proletarian and peasant majority.

The Order Fetish: Conservative and Liberal

Conservatives, such as Franz Xavier Barrios Suvelza, believe that a praetorian society such as Bolivia's cannot survive the sort of "politicization"—i.e., increasing involvement in democratic politics of the popular classes—that is occurring under Morales; a reassertion of explicitly "a-political" and "a-democratic" realms of the state is consequently required. "The contention here," Barrios Suvelza contends, "is that the current process of change in Bolivia involves a tendency… to reshape the style of the state in the direction of an unbounded and uncon-strained democracy, one lacking restraint on the passions—what we might call in Stoic terms a pathetic state."[20]

"Pathetic" in this sense refers to "a style of state where democratic and politicized forces have come to permeate the state."[21] We are to re-coil in horror at "the way in which democracy has overflowed into the decision-making sphere," during the Morales government, "to the detriment of a-democratic and apolitical state functions."[22] This is the sort of political philosophy marshaled recently in Honduras by Roberto Micheletti and his cronies as they sought to justify to the world their military coup d'état in late June 2009 against the democrat-ically elected Manuel Zelaya.

That the work of José Luis Roca is treated as serious scholarship in one of the more important edited volumes to appear on contemporary Bolivian politics in recent years is a further sign of how an otherwise defanged far right has retained a certain tenuous hold in public intel-lectual life, particularly in the media luna departments. Unimpeded by the actual historical record, Roca's recent intervention in scholarly de-bates on "regionalism" maintains that regionalist conflict in Bolivian history effectively subsumed class and ethnic tensions under its um-brella, and continues to define the central axis of division in the coun-try to this day. Roca lines up ideologically behind the autonomist forces of the media luna—and particularly those of its leading edge, the fero-ciously right-wing and rabidly racist elite of the department of Santa Cruz—against the alleged centralism of La Paz.

The solution to pervasive regionalist conflict in Roca's view is to devolve autonomous powers to each of the nine departments—as the eastern bourgeois bloc of the media luna has demanded. This will sup-posedly result in the long-desired decentralization of political power and perhaps ensure the ongoing viability of Bolivia as a unified coun-try. Of course, this amounts to willful obfuscation of the massive con-centrations of natural gas deposits, large agro-industrial landholdings, and industrial and financial capital in the departments of Santa Cruz and Tarija at the expense of the rest of the country. A radical redistribu-tion of the country's wealth down the social hierarchy—along geographical, ethnic, and class lines—is one of the urgent necessities of the day. The demands for autonomy emanating from the eastern low-lands—whatever their rhetoric to the contrary—reflect a political cam-paign to halt through destabilization each and every modest movement by the Morales government toward that end.[23]

The underlying sympathy with right-wing authoritarianism in Roca's writings reveals itself plainly in his treatment of different epochs in Bolivian twentieth-century history. The period after the National Revolution in which universal suffrage, agrarian reform, and the na-tionalization of the mines was achieved is described as "one of harsh political repression."[24] After the 1964 right-wing military coup, how-ever, things seem to improve: "The period of military government from 1964 to 1982 brought with it greater regional participation in the way the country was run…Its most creative phase was under the military government of Hugo Banzer (1971–78), when regional development corporations were set up in the nine departments, funded by oil and other natural resources royalties or by treasury transfers. Santa Cruz managed to provide itself with the public works and essential services it had demanded for so long, ushering in a period of exceptional prosper-ity."[25] For those readers unfamiliar with the history of the Southern Cone, Banzer was a close ally of the notorious Augusto Pinochet in Chile and the barbarous junta that ruled neighboring Argentina in the late 1970s and early 1980s. He pursued like-minded policies at home—the foundations, in effect, of Roca's "exceptional prosperity."

Roca also cites approvingly the notoriously racist *Pueblo Enfermo* (Sick People), written by historian Alcides Arguedas in the early twenti-eth century.[26] Roca agrees with Arguedas that the imaginative and cre-ative qualities of some subsections of the Bolivian population can be celebrated, but that we simply must lament "the obstinacy of the Ay-maras of La Paz."[27] Roca's chosen people of the media luna are refresh-ingly modern, broadly supporting "neocapitalist development and market economics." The largely indigenous departments of the west, by contrast, are "strongly influenced by traditionalism," desiring a retro-gressive "return to pre-Hispanic societal modes across Bolivia."[28] This analysis is roughly as sophisticated as that of Gabriela Oviedo, an ex–Miss Bolivia who infamously intervened in public affairs several years ago. She remarked to the beauty pageant press that she hated how outsiders think of Bolivia as a country populated merely with short Indians. Ovieda wanted us to know that she is from the eastern side, where the elite are tall, white, and very often have a brilliant command of the English language.[29]

On the economic front, conservative Juan Antonio Morales, president of the Central Bank of Bolivia between 1995 and 2006, is perhaps the only intellectual in the country who still fundamentally believes in the entirety of the orthodox neoliberal model that was first introduced in Bolivia in 1985. J. A. Morales worked closely with Harvard economist Jeffrey Sachs in the mid-1980s and early 1990s, the latter renowned internationally for his role in designing the country's "shock therapy" of that epoch. To the extent that J. A. Morales admits some of the failures of the neoliberal reforms of the 1980s and 1990s, he deflects critique by pointing to the inauspicious character of the international political economy in that period. "Following the failure of the state-capitalist model in the mid-1980s," Morales argues, "Bolivia went from an open economy in which the private sector predominated and where the country inserted itself into international markets for trade and investment. The structural reforms of the 1990s had a major impact, but they took place at a time of unfavorable terms of trade and a progressive disenchantment among the public concerning the lack of results and the failure to honor the promises to make the model acceptable."[30] In other words, the only failure of neoliberalism in Bolivian history is that it was never fully implemented at a propitious moment in the international political economy. It follows that, to the extent that Evo Morales deviates from the model, Bolivia will regress.

Horst Grebe López, president of a conservative economic think tank in La Paz, has also taken up the neoliberal mantle in the era of MAS hegemony. "The panorama in the mid- to long-term is worrying," he told a *Financial Times* reporter on the eve of the December 2009 elections. "We have great needs for investment in strategic sectors, we have to increase private investment in sectors that create employment and we have to guarantee the legal security and property rights for foreign investors." The state's priority, as the neoliberal mantra has suggested for the last three decades, is to establish a competitive environment to which global capital might be attracted. Under the Morales regime, "the investments are minimal, the administration is very bad, production is falling."[31] Grebe sees a worrying shift in Bolivian government policy away from the rationality and moderation of its center-left neighbors: "The political shifts that we are awaiting in Brazil, Chile, and that we have seen in Uruguay show that the tendencies of our neighbours in South America are towards a more rational combination between the market and the state."[32]

The liberal guardians of order tend toward a more realistic account of the actual reforms implemented by Morales, as distinct from the president's radical sophistry. Unlike conservative critics, they are predisposed to accepting the Morales regime's existence insofar as there is no viable right-wing alternative and the regime continues to chart a path of moderation. Morales may even be a stabilizing force for good in their eyes. In the early twenty-first century, writes George Gray Molina, head of the United Nations Development Program in Bolivia, "much attention has shifted to the relative strength of social movements and the weakening of traditional political parties, democratic institutions, and the rule of law, among other dimensions of the state-society balance."[33] He cites a UNDP survey published in 2007 that found "Bolivians feel that laws are not enforced, because most feel that 'laws are unjust' and that 'unjust laws may be broken.'" He goes on to note that "Bolivian public opinion has identified the worst transgressors as 'the rich' and 'politicians.'" In addition to these worrying trends, Gray Molina is also concerned that "most Bolivians continue to advocate 'universal' enforcement of laws while at the same time reserving the right to transgress, protest, overturn law."[34]

For Gray Molina and other liberals, the political priority of the day ought to be constructing and preserving a modus vivendi, or institutional apparatus, of state-society relations capable of dampening the rising tide of radical discontent with the established order and consolidating the status quo—a status quo necessarily reconfigured along certain cosmetic lines, but with an unaltered underlying socioeconomic foundation. The best bet for liberals might just be to hazard some "institutional pluralism," allowing "state holes" to persist—"places where bureaucratic or legal state presence is tenuous…where authority, legitimacy, and sovereignty are continuously contested" by unions, indigenous communities, and social movements—so long as they are ultimately contained.[35] So long as the overarching system of liberal capitalist rule is not threatened at its core. By and large, Gray Molina concludes, state-society relations under Evo Morales express in many ways this objective. Indeed, a close examination of state-society relations under Morales reveal abiding continuities with the preceding neoliberal model and seem to be functioning to basic liberal ends.

In terms of cultural indigenous advance, ultimately within the parameters of neoliberal multiculturalism, the recent writings of Xavier Albó, a Jesuit priest and well-regarded cultural anthropologist, provide a useful historical panorama of the political struggles around ethnicity and—at least cursorily—their interaction with simultaneous processes of class conflict and state formation since the colonial period. Against standard views of uncontested colonial and neocolonial rule over a passive indigenous majority, Albó stresses the importance of waves of indigenous rebellion (and also indigenous elite collaboration with colonialists) stretching back centuries. Indigenous people did not "simply [adapt] a passive, prepolitical posture" in the face of domination, but rather were the agents behind "continuous struggles and rebellions" against the different authority structures of the colonial and republican periods.[36]

Albó is at his weakest when he introduces a clichéd trajectory of Bolivia in the post-1989 world. This is a scenario in which the "class-based approach" to popular struggle has been abandoned in favor of "a more ethnic paradigm."[37] In fact, as this book has stressed, struggles for socialism from below and indigenous liberation were deeply intertwined in the most powerful popular movements of the twenty-first century, exhibiting what I have called elsewhere "combined oppositional consciousness."[38] Albó is also far too lenient in his treatment of the small number of indigenous elite who abandoned their mass movement bases and cynically adapted to the neoliberal multiculturalism that became official state policy over the course of the 1990s—Victor Hugo Cárdenas, who became the first Aymara vice president of Bolivia during the height of neoliberal restructuring, is the most glaring example.

This mistaken historical rendering of the last twenty years of indigenous struggle leads Albó considerably wide of the mark when he suggests that in dealing with the neofascist right of the media luna departments, the MAS government has perhaps been insufficiently conciliatory. "Arguably," Albó suggests, the differing agendas of the eastern bourgeois and left-indigenous blocs have been "unnecessarily exacerbated by some of the [overly assertive] positions adopted by the MAS government."[39] Precisely the opposite is true. As has been documented, the MAS has allowed neofascist right-wing vigilantes to flourish and the departmental governments of the eastern lowlands supporting them have also operated with impunity. Unmoored from the structural realities of the actually existing political economy and racialized class structure of the country, Albó's political conclusions on the present provide little guidance. There are, nonetheless, residual strengths in Albó's framework, to be found in the interstices of his concluding hypotheses on the recurring dialectical tensions of Bolivian history: those between ethnic identity and national identity; ethnicity and class; rural and urban transformations and inequalities; and the scourge of regionalism.

The Loyalists

Despite a flurry of publications in the wake of Morales's election in 2005, a theoretically sophisticated, empirically rich, and comprehensive account of the social origins and political trajectory of the MAS has not yet been produced. Suggestive journalistic monographs by investigators sympathetic to the MAS have appeared,[40] as have descriptive texts of social movement-state relations under the Morales administration.[41] In spite of offering many important empirical insights, these works tend to lack historical and theoretical depth and often parrot uncritically official dispatches from the party. As a consequence, they offer, at best, only a partial picture of the present.

A paradigmatic case study is Jorge Komadina and Céline Geffroy's *El poder del movimiento politico.*[42] While frequently making assertions about the overarching course and significance of the MAS's development, the fundamental basis of the study is circumscribed geographically to the department of Cochabamba, and temporally to the period between 1999 and 2005. The theoretical framework developed at the outset of the book is a derivative combination of European new social movement theory, French poststructuralism, and American liberal institutionalism.[43] The political-economic backdrop of neoliberal crisis and its role in fostering the reemergence of left-indigenous social movements and the MAS itself is basically absent from the narrative.[44] The treatment of opposing analytical viewpoints frequently descends into caricature. And descriptive characterizations of well-known phenomena are presented as major theoretical breakthroughs. Nonetheless, the book is rooted in an impressive array of interviews, ranging from rank-and-file members of the party to officials nestled in its highest institutional echelons.

Komadina and Geffroy begin by distinguishing their analysis from "orthodox Marxist" critiques of the MAS as reformist rather than revolutionary,[45] liberal and conservative labeling of the MAS as populist,[46] and autonomist Marxist portrayals of the MAS as more social movement than political party. They attempt to situate the strategic and tactical orientation of the MAS vis-à-vis formal electoral politics and street protests over the last decade. A principal thesis advanced is that the 2002 general elections marked a substantive turning point for the party, shifting its preeminent objectives away from extra-parliamentary, insurrectionary-based change, toward electoral politics. The MAS certainly did not abandon extra-parliamentary activism altogether, lest the party lose its social base in the increasingly radical and well-organized rural and urban popular sectors. However, as Komadina and Geffroy correctly point out, to the extent that MAS militants took to the streets in the 2003 and 2005 Gas Wars, the party leadership offered support on a tactical basis, distancing themselves at all times from the more radical sectors of the movements in the streets, privileging negotiated constitutional exits to the state crises rather than revolutionary mass insurrection, and demanding moderated versions of the demands emanating from the social movements—especially those calling for a Constituent Assembly and the full nationalization of the hydrocarbons industry.

El poder del movimiento politico traces the origins of the party back to the coca growers' movement in the Chapare region of the department of Cochabamba, and the ongoing relationship between the coca growers' unions and the party structure. It fleshes out different facets of the structure of the MAS, but the overall arch of the established procedures and the formal and informal institutions of the party are never clearly depicted. Even more importantly, apart from the party's roots in the coca growers' movement, we learn nothing of its changing class composition over time. The party's relationship to urban unions, urban poor peoples' movements, and popular community struggles go virtually unexamined. The city is implicitly treated as a relatively homogeneous "middle class" domain, as distinct from a peasant-dominated countryside.[47] Because there is no empirical treatment of the changing class composition of the party over time, Komadina and Geffroy treat the shift in strategy beginning in 2002 as merely one more technical policy choice, rather than the political expression of growing urban and rural middle class influence over the bulk of the party's highest positions and leadership circles. The authors chart the progression toward a more ethnicized image within the MAS as the party sought to transcend its peasant roots in the department of Cochabamba and build a national coalition. The cultural and political significance of the party's use of the coca leaf and the multi-colored *whiphala*, or indigenous flag, are explored, as are the eclectic historical figures from leftist and indigenous movements of the past now celebrated by the party: Tupaj Katari, Che Guevara, Marcelo Quiroga Santa Cruz, and Luis Espinal, among others. In sum, Komadina and Geffroy's text is ideologically sympathetic to the moderately reformist trajectory of the MAS throughout the early 2000s, and hostile to what it characterizes as "orthodox Marxist" and right-wing critics of the party.

A recent collection, edited by Karin Monasterios, Pablo Stefanoni, and Hervé Do Alto, is ideologically similar, but much richer analytically.[48] Stefanoni, the editor of the Bolivian edition of *Le Monde Diplomatique*, is most effective in his treatment of domestic and foreign right-wing mythologies that have arisen to delegitimize the Morales administration. He demolishes the absurd—but nonetheless recurrent—assertion made by prominent fractions of the Bolivian right that Morales's government exercises reverse racism by excluding whites and mestizos from formal and informal spheres of political power. Stefanoni pulls apart their accusations and provides a systematic accounting of the ethnic and political diversity of the ministers who constituted Morales's first cabinet in 2006. He also demonstrates why we ought to dismiss as conspiratorial drivel the popular right-wing notion that Hugo Chávez was behind the rise in left-indigenous social movements in Bolivia since 2000 and is now effectively controlling the Morales government from behind the scenes.

Stefanoni shifts gears elsewhere in his contribution to the volume, in an effort to soothe the anxieties of the liberal right. Here he takes on the question of whether or not the MAS government is in fact "a government of the social movements" as their official discourse suggests. Stefanoni rightly points out that while symbolically indigenous movements receive more attention from the executive and legislative powers under the Morales government, it is also true that access to key ministries—especially those directly relating to the economy—have been completely closed to social movement influence. Strikes by teachers and doctors were declared illegal by the Morales government during its first year in office. Public sector workers received miniscule salary increases in 2006 and 2007, and the party has practiced strict fiscal discipline in its macroeconomic operations.

Nonetheless, Stefanoni sees the rise of Morales as embodying a "postneoliberal" turn in Bolivian politics and is, in the main, sympathetic to Vice President Álvaro García Linera's formulation of the MAS's economic project as "Andean-Amazonian Capitalism"—a multifaceted program that will supposedly see 36 percent of the economy eventually come under state control. Stefanoni implicitly follows García Linera's line that socialism is not feasible in the Bolivian context, at least at this present conjuncture, and that a "new moderated version of state capitalism" is the best that can be achieved.[49]

Stefanoni, in this and other writings, is adept at highlighting discursive contradictions at various levels within and between different officials of the MAS administration. "The discursive ambivalence of Evo Morales is evident," he contends, for example, "when, in international forums, he presents himself as the extreme defender of the Pachamama (Mother Earth). Meanwhile, toward the interior of Bolivia, he defends classic developmentalist and productivist positions, such as oil exploration in the Amazon, going so far as to make accusations against various NGOs for 'confusing' the indigenous" into opposing such initiatives.[50]

In November 2009, a few weeks prior to the December elections, I had the opportunity to interview the Bolivian ambassador to Canada, Edgar Tórres Mosquiera, a sociologist by academic training. I pushed him to respond to some of these discursive contradictions and to relate them to the material realities developing on the ground in Bolivia:

> JRW: On the one hand, Evo Morales speaks frequently in international forums from an anticapitalist perspective. He denounces capitalism as a system based on the exploitation of people, and particularly the poor. And he also denounces capitalism as a system that destroys the ecological systems of the world. On the other hand, though, we have Vice President Álvaro García Linera speaking within Bolivia about the impossibility of socialism in the current context in that country and promoting rather what he calls "Andean-Amazonian Capitalism." So, it seems to me that there is at least an apparent contradiction, discordance, between these messages. Can you explain this contradiction?

ETM: In the current conjuncture, we have to look at what is happening in Latin America. In Latin America the correlation of forces is in favor of the social movements. Bolivia has a very special particularity. What we have to do first in the current conjuncture is to strengthen the inclusion of more than 4.5 million who have been marginalized, excluded from the management of the state. In this sense, what Vice President Álvaro García Linera is doing is interpreting the reality of the Bolivian context. The Bolivian state has an historic debt to these sectors that have never benefited from health, education, or basic services. Therefore, in this first phase, first and foremost, we are emphasizing the inclusion of these social sectors that have never benefited from the way the state has been run. We have to overcome the social exclusion, marginality, illiteracy, malnutrition, [high levels of] mortality. These are fundamental stages if we are going to be able advance. If in this first phase we do not fulfill this historic role we will be running against the mandate of the indigenous peoples and the social movements. Therefore, it's very premature to launch a call for twenty-first-century socialism if we haven't fulfilled this first phase.

No dichotomy exists between the president and the vice president. What is more, there exists a harmony of focus, on the social. The intelligentsia within the Movement Toward Socialism believes that it is fundamental to complete these primordial, fundamental stages—as Foreign Minister David Choquehuanca says, to live well, not to live better. What does it mean to live well? We have to provide health and education to all those huge social sectors that have never had anything, to defeat illiteracy, malnutrition. These are things that you see every day in my country. This is something fundamental to understand.

Now, in those international forums, Evo Morales has spoken out against savage capitalism. What does savage capitalism mean? It means a capitalism in which profits are not distributed to the social sectors that need them. We understand that foreign investment is fundamental to move forward, but we don't want bosses with this investment, but rather partners.

In the long history of Bolivia all our natural resources have been pillaged, and none of the benefits stayed in our country. Our new proposal means that the big investors also have to share their wealth. This is the new model, the new focus that President Evo Morales is introducing.

There are no divisions within the leadership. It's only that we all recognize that each stage, each phase has to be fulfilled. And from there, we continue to move forward.[51]

Thus we are introduced, again, to the subtle ways through which the combined liberation struggle for indigenous liberation and socialist transformation of 2000 to 2005 has been altered into a struggle of distinct stages. The MAS emphasizes indigenous liberation today, with socialist transformation only a remote possibility, at some distant point in the future. The adjective *savage* is how Morales's anticapitalist rhetoric effectively morphs into a sharper mode of the standard anti-neoliberal rhetoric utilized by almost every politician in contemporary Latin America.[52] It implies that there might be a capitalism with a human face. It is perhaps unsurprising, therefore, that "Bolivia's stunning macroeconomic performance" has "garnered the leftist Morales administration praise from an unlikely source: officials at the International Monetary Fund." The Morales government employs populist rebuke of savage capitalists the way Barack Obama denounces Wall Street bankers—i.e., conflict in public conceals vast interpenetration of interests behind closed doors. The "nationalization" of hydrocarbons in May 2006, for example, "looked like a pretty radical act," but, "after the troops and the TV cameras left, it turned out that the government's policies weren't all that radical. Morales's reform amounted to a renegotiation of the country's multiple contracts with foreign oil companies, an increase in taxes on those firms, and a reestablishment of the public oil and gas company (YPFB), along with a declaration that the Bolivian government wanted 'partners not masters.'"[53]

In sector after sector, the rhetoric of reform runs deeper than practice. "Mr. Morales…decree[d] the renationalisation of the mining sector on February 9, 2007," the Economist Intelligence Unit points out, but "the decree applied only to a handful of former state assets and does not extend to private sector mines, development projects or exploration concessions. Most active mining projects in Bolivia fall into the latter categories."[54] For Luis Arce, minister of finance, "There are two kinds of private enterprise in Bolivia: a businessman that invests and generates work, has made good business during these past four years, and now is adhering to the process of change," he said. "And another dedicated to politics, simply being in the opposition and trying to live off the state as it has done in the past. That business sector is destined to die."[55] Savage capitalists are out, and humane capitalists are in. The fraudulent bourgeoisie is being replaced with its honest counterpart.

Existing alongside the essentially social-democratic intellectual loyalists, such as Stefanoni, are a contradictory set of anticapitalists. Of these, the political philosopher Luis Tapia is among the most eloquent. Tapia, alongside the current Vice President Álvaro García Linera and others, is a founding member of the radical intellectual forum La Comuna—"The Commune," after the Paris Commune of 1871.[56] His theoretical and political writings are essentially split in focus between interpretations of the opus of René Zavaleta Mercado (arguably the country's most important Marxist intellectual of the twentieth century) and incisive interventions seeking to understand and influence the trajectory of left-indigenous insurrectionary movements in recent years.

In a recent essay, he draws on the terms "constituent" and "constituted" power from the Italian autonomist Marxist Antonio Negri, but Tapia gives them an original spin in the context of Bolivian state formation and social struggle over the last two centuries. "Constituted power," Tapia explains, "tends to be identified with the constitution and with the various institutions that operate as a state at a particular place in time."[57] Constituent power, on the other hand, is formed "when projects or forces emerge that seek to change the relationship between the state and civil society, the arenas within them, the subjects involved, the relationships between them, and consequently the political form that society adopts. In this sense, a constituent power is something that emerges at points of crisis, or provokes a political crisis that, among other things, can lead to the reconstitution of a country."[58]

Tapia incorporates into this theoretical and analytical framework a sensitivity to historical and material processes and structures. "All constituted power has a history," he writes. Rather than emerging from the ether, "it is a political, social, and historical accumulation that brings with it learning and experience, as well as conflicts and contradictions, leading (on occasions) to development in particular aspects or (at others) toward exhaustion and decay."[59] Tapia thus reminds us that the first constitution of the Bolivian Republic that flowed out of its independence in 1825 ignored almost entirely the majority indigenous population of the new country. The political character of the situation had changed with independence from the Spanish conquistadores, but there had been no accompanying social revolution. "The constitutions of the nineteenth century acknowledged a political change—the replacement of Spanish colonial power by a new state that responded to the dominant economic and social power groups within it," Tapia points out. They "brought no social change as such."[60] The 1938 Constituent Assembly introduced for the first time an element of social change—a labor law, and other social reforms—as peasant and worker capacities for struggle developed. In 1952, the National Revolution carried things further, ushering in new changes out of the context of profound crisis in the social order. Perhaps more than any of these other historical periods however, the terrain of class struggle and politics of indigenous resistance within the Constituent Assembly process of 2006–2007 showed the most promise for change because the assembly was taking place in tandem with the dramatic social and political upsurges from below between 2000 and 2005.

Ultimately, though, Tapia is far more critical of the shape the assembly took than are many Bolivian intellectuals on the left who have found it very difficult to criticize the Morales administration. Despite Tapia's very arguable belief that the MAS is a workers' party that has captured state power, he fully recognizes the compromised outcome of the assembly process: "The assembly became closely linked to the presence of political parties, both those of the opposition (which were against it in principle) as well as that of the ruling party, which, as leader of the executive, tended to subordinate constituent power to constituted power. In so doing, it limited the scope for change that had previously emerged from the waves of protest and which might well come about if the new political order included the full diversity of social organization in the design of new political institutions of government."[61]

The final theoretical contribution to the loyalist camp to be addressed here, and the most important, comes from Álvaro García Linera. The ways in which García Linera framed the state crisis and the character of social movements in multiple books and articles in the opening years of this century were profoundly influential, in the sense that they penetrated not only scholarly layers of academe, but the movements themselves, on different levels. In an essay published in 2008, derived from a lecture delivered in mid-December, 2007 at a gathering of La Comuna, García Linera provides his most detailed theorization of socio-political and economic developments in Bolivia since he became vice president in 2006.[62] It deserves our attention both for its theoretical sophistication, and its ultimately unpersuasive characterization of the MAS project as a potentially revolutionary resolution to the neoliberal state crisis, as understood in García Linera's own terms.

For García Linera, the state is the objective expression of the correlation of social forces and ideas in society at a particular moment.[63]

State crisis arises from problems in the extant correlation of forces; that is to say, a crisis erupts when there is no longer any social force capable of enforcing the totality of ordering dominant ideas of political life and society that would otherwise permit a moral correspondence between the oppressors and the oppressed. The crisis unfolds through the entire constellation of state institutions and norms, or the objective expression of the correlation of social forces and ideas in society at any one moment.[64]

Garcia Linera traces three phases of a process of state crisis beginning in 2000, and opens up the possibility that a fourth and final stage, a stage of resolution, was surfacing in the dying days of 2007. The spirit of the first phase, a crisis of the neoliberal state, took tangible form in the uprisings of the Cochabamba Water War. The ideas of the dominant bourgeois bloc—aligned with foreign capital, agro-exporters, financial capital, the political elite, and an array of imperial forces—had lost its capacity to define in a stable manner the political horizons of the country. The popular classes, comprised in their majority of indigenous people, were now actively mobilized against the neoliberal model of foreign direct investment, free-market globalization, exports of raw materials, and rule by elite-pacts[65] between traditional political parties.

Thus, the first stage of state crisis, a crisis of neoliberalism in the Bolivian context, began in 2000. However, as Garcia Linera is quick to point out, a "state crisis does not necessarily lead to a new state. There can be internal adjustments, in [social] forces, alliances, and politics, and there can be a reconstitution of the old state."[66] What transpired in the Bolivian case at hand was an entry into a second phase, one of "catastrophic equilibrium." Garcia Linera borrows the concept of catastrophic equilibrium from Antonio Gramsci, and interprets its significance in light of the social struggles in Bolivia in the early 2000s. The catastrophic equilibrium, for Garcia Linera, signified a second stage in the structural crisis of the Bolivian state. A confrontation between two political projects reigned across the country, a dominant neoliberal bloc in relative decline, and an ascending popular bloc of indigenous and left constellations, both with a capacity to attract support from and mobilize significant social forces. The showdown was playing itself out both in the formal institutional arenas of parliamentary politics and in the street battles of the cities and mobilizations in the countryside. There was no socio-political bloc with the capacity to enforce its hegemony over society as a whole and thus the state entered a period of cata-strophic equilibrium. A paralysis of the state thickened and congealed.[67]

The third stage, García Linera suggests, can be thought of as "as-cendant hegemonic construction," constituted by waves of intense so-cial conflict, interspersed with periods of relative stability. Here, García Linera's narration of the pendulum of conflict, stability, conflict, self-consciously mirrors the texts of Marx on the European crises of 1848 and their titanic class struggles.[68] In the Bolivian case, the insurrec-tional power of the October 2003 Gas War, and the accompanying emergence of the "October Agenda" of the popular left-indigenous bloc, evoked the partial victory of this political project, its relative pre-ponderance throughout society, and its capacity to attract social mobi-lization. For García Linera, this partial victory, or ascendant hegemonic construction, was institutionalized in the December 2005 elections when Evo Morales assumed the presidency.[69] However, it must be stressed that this ascendant hegemony remained fragmentary and in-complete, subject to mobilizational resurgence on the part of the bour-geois bloc, and the manifold tactics of right-wing destabilization.

Societies can live neither in a constant state of mobilization and conflict, according to García Linera, nor in perpetual stasis and stabil-ity. At some point in time, a "point of bifurcation," a restructuration of the social order must congeal in a resolution of the state crisis. From the vantage point of 2007, García Linera suggested that such a point had seemingly arrived. Possibilities for exit were the consolidation of a revolutionary, popular, indigenous, and national state, on the one hand, or the restoration of a reconstituted neoliberalism, on the other. Should the latter, counterrevolutionary scenario win the day, it would either be the outcome of a hegemonic rearticulation of the autonomist forces of the eastern lowlands in a manner that transcended their re-gional isolation, or the self-inflicted implosion of the revolutionary bloc whose ascendant hegemony had still only partially matured.[70] The old state would return, under new conditions.

By 2007, then, an epoch of ascendant hegemonic construction may have bled into a "point of bifurcation." This was, according to García Linera's uncharacteristically tentative analytical moves on this issue, a fourth, and final stage of the process of neoliberal state crisis initiated in 2000. Points of bifurcation, he suggests, may be resolved through insurrection, coercive military power, or democratic negotiation.[71] Shifting now, more straightforwardly, into his role as vice president of the republic, García Linera argues at this moment that the referendum on the new constitution would effectively channel the resolution of the state crisis into democratic institutions, and that the new constitution, if passed, would have as its nucleus popular indigenous sectors, but would also ensure the rights and interests of the middle class, and responsible capitalists, who pay their taxes and follow the rules of the law.[72] One could be forgiven if the revolutionary content of such a multiclass, constitutional consensus was lost on them.

Indeed, I want to argue that García Linera's theoretical formulations risk becoming the unwitting reflection of restored capitalist class rule in a reconfigured neoliberal state. Since García Linera's essay was published, the new constitution passed a popular referendum in January 2009, and the December elections later that year witnessed the institutional consolidation of MAS power within the apparatuses of the state. Following his theoretical framework, the neoliberal crisis, the catastrophic equilibrium, the ascendant construction of hegemony, and the point of bifurcation have now all seemingly been resolved. Neoliberalism should have been defeated, and a popular, indigenous, national, and revolutionary hegemony achieved. The next chapter, through an extensive examination of the economic structure of reconstituted neoliberalism, reveals some of the fundamental flaws in such a reading. Key factors in the vulnerability of García Linera's framework include its misconception of the MAS as a revolutionary party in direct continuity with the aims of the left-indigenous insurrectionary forces of the Water and Gas Wars, and the separation of the combined liberation struggle for indigenous liberation and anticapitalist emancipation into distinct transitional stages.

Conclusion

This chapter has sought to elucidate a cluster of critical issues at the nexus of conjunctural electoral results and their interpretations, and more deeply rooted intellectual and ideological patterns in Bolivian political thought during the era of Evo Morales. A number of theses were developed along the way. First, it was argued that Evo Morales's electoral victory in December 2009 reflected a profound institutional consolidation of formal political power within the apparatuses of the state. Second, these elections were greeted with a certain uncritical euphoria in Latin American and international leftist circles. The substance of these reactions tended to rely on the image of communitarian socialism crafted by the Morales government more than on any serious analysis of the concrete record of the MAS government in the sphere of political economy over the four years of its first administration. Third, more substantive and sophisticated theoretical and ideological clashes are unfolding in Bolivia itself, often reflecting long-standing political divides refracted onto the crisis of neoliberalism and the competing projects seeking to resolve that crisis in their favor. Liberal and conservative thinkers seek a restitution of a (reconfigured) neoliberal order, although with different strategies and tactics between them. An array of MAS loyalists project their own ideological proclivities onto the party's loosely knit political web of ideas, too often seeing in the radical words and pragmatic actions what they wished was there, and ignoring the rest. A third camp of critical left-indigenous currents sees a serious disjuncture between the image and reality of the MAS government, and, while defending the government against the domestic right and imperial interference, place more emphasis on the power of the exploited and oppressed to create and force transformative change through their own initiatives and struggles from below. The next chapter sets out to contribute modestly to this camp through a systematic analysis of the economic structure of reconstituted neoliberalism in Bolivia today.

Six

The Economic Structures
of Reconstituted Neoliberalism

"Even the IMF is happy with Bolivia's economy; imagine the irony of that."
—Gonzalo Chávez, Bolivia-based, Harvard-educated economist

Having described the ideological currents that are most alive in Bolivian politics and formal intellectual life under Evo Morales in the previous chapter, the focus now turns to political economy. The purpose here is to demonstrate why the development model implemented by the Morales administration over the entire four years of its first administration (2006-2010) is best characterized as reconstituted neoliberalism. In order to understand the constituent parts of reconstituted neoliberalism, we first navigate our way through an extended, historical treatment of the declining legitimacy of neoliberalism globally, and the principal schools of thought and developmental practice in Latin America over the twentieth century, paying particular attention to structuralism, neoliberalism, and neostructuralism. Out of this we arrive at reconstituted neoliberalism in the present, and the way in which it has taken on a particular form in the Bolivian case. Second, we move from this deep contextualization of the emergent development model of the MAS, into a concrete study of the composition of Bolivia's economic structure, overall growth, fiscal policy, and social spending between 2007 and 2010 to show empirically how this represents reconstituted neoliberalism. We also, in this section, chart out some of the social consequences of this model in terms of inequality, poverty, and urban working-class life. Third, we explore the regime of *proactive labor flexibility* pursued by the Morales government in the urban world of work. Fourth, and finally, we explore some illustrative instances of conflict from below that are emerging out of the popular classes in response to the gap between image and reality in the Morales development program.

Neostructuralism as Reconstituted Neoliberalism

The legitimacy of neoliberal capitalism as a model for development in the Global South had already experienced deep decline over a number of years prior to the breakout of the world economic crisis in 2008. In the midst of the crisis, that decline has only accelerated. Various academic, institutional, and policy-based responses have emerged that criticize the fundamentalist neoliberal framework in the fields of economics, development studies, and political economy.[1] The failure of neoliberalism to produce the development results its advocates promised throughout the Global South over the last several decades has led to a new consensus in mainstream academic and policy-making circles around a reconstituted neoliberal theory that sets aside some of the unbridled market mechanisms of the traditional framework. This latest theoretical derivation from purist neoliberalism is sometimes called "neoinstutionalism," or, less frequently, "neo-Listian" development economics, after the nineteenth-century German economist, Friedrich List.[2] The proponents of the new framework, Greig Charnock points out, "reject the market fundamentalism of the 1980s and early 1990s, represented by structural adjustment and shock therapy, and with these many of the assumptions about what the untrammelled free market can achieve." According to the new consensus, "the key to understanding both the developmental limits to and potentialities of the market lies, therefore, in the institutions that facilitate and/or hinder rational market action."[3] There is recognition that in order for the core foundations of the original market reform agenda to actually be carried out to maturity, a second generation of institutional shifts in state policies will be required. These shifts will necessarily jettison some of the basic facets of neoclassical rationality by allowing a greater role for state engineering. States must fashion institutions that promote policy stability, adaptability, and coherence and coordination of markets. The institutions must be of high quality and embody "public regardedness" rather than personalistic clientelism. As in the case of the original set of neoliberal reforms, however, under the guise of "content-free" institutional arrangements, the hidden functionality of these institutions is their basic utility for capital, and their ideological orientation toward global competitive capitalism.[4] This is true even of the leftist flank of the new institutionalism, which goes so far as to prescribe direct or indirect state control of selected means of production and allocation of resources for late-developers.

The particular Latin American expression of this international trend has found its principal outlet in the "neostructuralism" of the United Nations' Economic Commission for Latin America and the Caribbean (ECLAC) and closely related intellectual milieus since the mid-1990s. While neoinstitutionalism, and its Latin American incarnation as neostructuralism, signify an advance away from neoliberal dogmatism, it is nonetheless clear that the new development paradigm obfuscates key components of class relations under capitalism, pursues "success" within rather than against capitalism, and is wholly inadequate when seen from the encompassing Marxist objective of working-class emancipation from exploitation by capital.[5] This is the wider international and regional ideological context in which Bolivia's development model under Evo Morales has been fashioned.

Fernando Ignacio Leiva's excellent text, *Latin American Neostructuralism: The Contradictions of Post-Neoliberal Development*, makes an important contribution to clearing up relevant aspects of these muddy theoretical and analytical waters. The book weaves together a close analysis of over two decades of ECLAC, and ECLAC-related publications and documents, and an examination of the historical and material changes to the structure of Latin American capitalism over the corresponding period. Leiva sets out to evaluate the strengths and weaknesses of Latin American neostructuralism, the depth and breadth of its influence in reshaping Latin America's political economy, its overarching implications for Latin American politics and society, and the extent to which it represents an alternative to neoliberalism.

Structuralism, Neoliberalism, and Neostructuralism

An important part of Leiva's project is to distinguish between what he takes to be structuralist, neoliberal, and neostructuralist schools of thought within Latin American development economics. The most influential figure in classical Latin American structuralism was undoubtedly the Argentine economist Raúl Prebisch, who in his 1949 monograph, *The Economic Development of Latin America and its Principal Problems,* first conceived of the unequal relationship between an industrialized center and an agrarian, dependent periphery in the world economy. Within this international division of labor, countries that were dependent, agricultural exporters would tend to experience declining terms of trade, structural unemployment as a consequence of the limits to growth in traditional export sectors and subsequent nonabsorption of dispossessed peasant labor, and trade imbalances as a result of excessive importation of industrial goods and export of only raw agricultural and mineral goods. Prebisch headed Argentina's first central bank between 1935 and 1943 and was widely recognized for his expertise in Keynesian economics by the 1940s, but his influence in Latin American development economics really came to the fore during his time as executive secretary of ECLAC between 1949 and 1963, and then first secretary general of the United Nations Conference on Trade and Development (UNCTAD) between 1964 and 1969.[6]

ECLAC as an institution became the established heavyweight in Latin American economic research in the 1950s and 1960s and generated decisive policy advice for key figures in the region's national banks and finance ministries over these decades. ECLAC institutions in Chile and affiliated institutions elsewhere in Latin America developed educational programs on structuralist thought through which they "trained and indoctrinated middle-ranking Latin American personnel in central banks, development and finance ministries, and university faculties." By the 1960s, a large number of famous structuralist economists, sociologists, and political scientists taught alongside the likes of Prebisch in these programs. The teachers included Aníbal Pinto, Jorge Ahumada, Antonio Barros de Castro, Maria da Conceição, Carlos Lessa, Leopoldo Solís, Osvaldo Sunkel, Fernando Henrique Cardoso, Torcuato de Tella, Rodolfo Stavenhagen, Aldo Solari, and Francisco Weffort, among others.[7] While the structuralists hardly created the Import-Substitution Industrialization (ISI) growth model of the era, they did play an essential part in legitimizing existing ISI development programs, and providing research, analysis, and a theoretical framework for pushing the model further and consolidating it throughout Latin America. U.S. imperialism, for its part, tried to prevent the creation of ECLAC and attempted to discredit the institution once it was established fearing structuralist doctrine might radicalize and promote an acceleration of state-owned enterprises, provide subsidies for domestic as against foreign capital, and advocate an ever-larger sphere of state planning within the economy. While American foreign affairs officials opposed ECLAC, they enthusiastically promoted ISI and the opportunities it provided U.S. multinationals to leap tariff walls and build protected plants oriented toward growing domestic markets.[8] Structuralism, correctly constrained, in other words, congealed nicely with American capital's objectives in the region.

The hegemony structuralism enjoyed within Latin American economic thought and policy, and the legitimacy ECLAC achieved as an agenda-setting institution, suffered massive blows with the uneven geographic expansion of neoliberalism on a world scale beginning in the mid-1970s. At the international level, neoliberalism advanced as a political project of the ruling classes in the advanced capitalist countries—especially in the United States—to create or restore capitalist class power in all corners of the globe in response to the crisis of embedded liberalism in the late 1960s, the decline in profitability and the growth of stagflation by the 1970s, and the rise of leftist political threats to capital in the shape of radical popular struggles, labor movements, and peasant insurgencies across large parts of the world during that period.[9] The debt crisis of the 1980s opened up new imperial opportunities to take advantage of the leverage over Third World countries, including most of Latin America. The U.S. state, and, to a lesser but important degree, other core imperialist powers, utilized their control of the strategic international financial institutions—commercial banks, the multilateral lending institutions such as the International Monetary Fund (IMF) and the World Bank, and various regional banks—to push through structural adjustment programs (SAPs) in a vast number of countries.[10] SAPs, which were often imposed by IMF and World Bank conditionality, typically included demands for Third World countries to commit to fiscal austerity with minimal to zero deficits, cutbacks in spending for social services and subsidies for food and other basic necessities, reform of the tax system, liberalization of financial markets, unification of exchange rates, liberalization of trade, elimination of barriers to foreign direct investment (FDI), deregulation of industry, and strengthening of guarantees of private property rights.[11]

Against this international backdrop, virtually all Latin American countries between the mid-1970s and the mid-1990s engaged more or less rapidly in the fundamental restructuring of their economies along the lines of the Washington Consensus, moving decisively from ISI to Export-Oriented Development (EOD) development programs. In the 1980s, this transition in economics was accompanied by a shift away from authoritarian regimes toward highly constricted electoral democracies. But it is important to stress that neoliberalism was born out of Latin American state terror—backed by American imperial might— over the preceding decades. The systematic bloodbaths were necessary for the effective destruction of the political left, labor unions, and other popular class organizations. The mass movements, and revolutionary and populist projects, that had proliferated throughout large sections of the region since the end of the Second World War needed to be quite definitively expunged from the scene if neoliberalism was to take hold.[12]

Already by the late 1980s, however, the orthodox theory and practice of neoliberalism was called increasingly into question in Latin America. Social polarization and economic and social crises stood visibly in the way of realizing the harmonious society projected by neoclassical economic theory. This trend persisted until the explosion of protests and realignment of class forces by the end of the 1990s. It was out of the emergent contradictions of the late 1980s that neostructuralism was born in its incipient form, through ECLAC's publication of *Changing Production Patterns with Social Equity*, under the leadership of Fernando Fajnzylber.[13] "Given that the basis of a new and harmonious society did not emerge spontaneously from neoliberal structural adjustment," the neoliberal project responded to destabilizing internal contradictions and social conflicts by expanding the scope of its institutional restructuring without abandoning its "essential emphasis on the rationality of the market as the foremost organizing principle of social life."[14]

In the course of the next decade, neostructuralism moved from the margins to the center of political influence in the region by challenging certain assumptions of the market dogmatism characteristic of orthodox neoliberalism while rebuking simultaneously the core presuppositions of classical structuralism. Neostructrualists sought to "renew ECLAC's conceptual apparatus" by "erasing the stigma" of association with ISI, and "formulat[ing] a new set of alternative foundational ideas and action-oriented propositions seemingly capable of addressing the problems faced by Latin America countries in the era of globalisation."[15] If in the eyes of the most orthodox neoliberal pundits ECLAC of the 1990s remained incompletely redeemed from the legacy of ISI, the institution's postulations on Latin American political economy were warmly embraced by an ever-increasing number of state managers and economic policy elites. Post-Pinochet Chile became the paradigmatic poster child of neostructuralism throughout the 1990s.[16] Neostructuralism was also deeply influential in the "Buenos Aires Consensus" that came out of a June 1999 convention of the Socialist International, and eventually became the model of political economy for Lula's Brazil, Kirchner's Argentina, and Vásquez's Uruguay.

Less well known has been the way in which the key tenets of neostructuralism also extended into the first major multiyear development programs of left governments such as Hugo Chávez in Venezuela and Evo Morales in Bolivia. In the Venezuelan case, Chávez has been famously influenced by neostructuralist economist Osvaldo Sunkel, whose edited volume, *Development from Within: Toward a Neostructuralist Approach for Latin America*, had a profound impact on the future president's outlook as he read it in a jail cell in the 1990s, and Chávez continues to call for the text to be read in schools, ministries, and elsewhere.[17] Neostructuralist principles impacted heavily the country's National Plan of Development for 2001–2007, which called for the necessity of a small "social economy" to complement rather than replace the private sector, the transformation of informal workers into "small managers" through training and micro-credit, and a focus on "endogenous development," among other things.[18]

The areas of conceptual innovation at the heart of neostructuralism revolve around systemic competitiveness, technical progress, proactive labor flexibility, and virtuous circles. In an effort to distinguish itself from orthodox neoliberalism, neostructrualism in Latin America rejects the notion that markets and competition are the exclusive channels for social and economic interaction, and replaces the basic neoclassical notion of comparative advantage with *systemic competitiveness*. By this, neostructuralists essentially mean "that what compete[s] in the world market [are] not *commodities* per se but *entire social systems*."[19] While granting that the market will remain the central organizing force in society, neostructuralists stress that the competitiveness of the entire system depends upon effective and thoroughgoing state intervention in infrastructure (technology, energy, transport), education, finance, labor-management relations, and the general relationships between public and private spheres, in a way that orthodox neoliberal theory cannot grasp.[20] Competitiveness on the international market, for neostructuralists, depends in the long term on "a broad range of structural factors, such as rates of investment, adequate institutions for education, research, and development, which [are] systematically ignored by neoliberal formulations."[21]

In order to achieve systemic competitiveness, according to neostructuralism, a reconfiguration of state theory is necessary. Whereas orthodox neoliberals in the 1970s and 1980s saw the state's basic function as lubricating the dynamism of the market through the protection of property rights, contract enforcement, information collection, and strictly delimited social provision for the destitute, neostructuralism "assigns the state an important auxiliary role in the search for international competitiveness," blending economic policy on various levels, "with political intervention to construct a broad social consensus."[22] The state's role is to stimulate and enhance market-based initiatives, selectively intervene in productive sectors of the economy, and supplement the invisible hand of the market with non-market forms of social, political, and economic coordination. In the area of trade policy, for example, neostructuralists provide a critique of part of orthodox neoliberalism's unidimensional focus on tariff reduction. They ultimately agree that tariffs and nontariff barriers to trade ought to be eliminated in an effort to expand export-led development, but they also call for "the adoption of transitory policies selectively biased in favor of non traditional exports."[23] Latin American neostructuralism sees this sort of modest and temporary state intervention as essential for encouraging a larger share of manufactured and valued-added exports into a country's export profile. A central component of the state's role under this view is to build civil society-state relationships, public-private partnerships, and an overall social, political, and ideological consensus across social classes behind the drive for export-led capitalist growth.

Technical progress refers to the neostructuralist claim from the early 1990s that "genuine" gains in productivity can be achieved through the incorporation of technological advance into the overarching goal of systemic competitiveness. Technological change will foment productivity gains and replace the "spurious" increases in productivity during the era of orthodox neoliberalism, "gained through artificial devaluation and forced reduction in real wages."[24] *Proactive labor flexibility* pivots basically on the notion of more effectively gaining workers' consent and submission to the model of export-led capitalist development. To this end, neostructuralism calls for a change in the character of the Latin American labor movement. Government policies must focus on encouraging the labor movement to become a stakeholder in "systemic competitiveness," and simultaneously to abandon old-fashioned orientations toward class struggle and "conflict-based traditions." Such antiquated forms of labor-state relations will be exchanged for cross-class cooperation, negotiation, and consensus-building.[25]

Neostructuralists certainly agree with orthodox neoliberals on the necessity of maintaining and even expanding labor flexibility, but they emphasize also "the need to provide training and new skills to the labor force so as to facilitate its adaptability in the productive process."[26] The state is supposed to create policies that forge consensus between the public and private sector, and workers' and employers' organizations, in order to advance these aims. Two of the most deleterious aspects of orthodox neoliberal labor flexibility—wage flexibility and subcontracting—will ostensibly be replaced through the implementation of a vague program of so-called functional flexibility.[27]

Systemic competitiveness, technical progress, and proactive labor flexibility come together in the neostructuralist conceptualization of self-reinforcing *virtuous circles*—"a sequence of mutually supportive feedback loops linking international competitiveness, social equity, and political legitimacy."[28] Whereas it was increasingly clear by the early twenty-first century that orthodox neoliberalism was steadily encountering problems of social and political polarization and ideological legitimacy, neostructuralism promised "a synergistic relationship" between "international competitiveness, greater social integration, and increased democratic political stability."[29] Social dialogue and consensus are viewed as necessary for systemic competitiveness, and the way to achieve them, according to neostructuralists, is through democratic, consensus-building institutions and rapid export-led growth. Rising living standards are to work in tandem with consensus-building state institutions to stem the tide of social conflict and political instability, and to help workers and managers see that they "now…share in the common interest of ensuring entrepreneurial success in the never ending race for international competitiveness."[30] Electoral democracy, internationally competitive export capitalism—driven by the market but supplemented by the state—workers' rising living standards, capitalists' profits, social consensus, and political stability are to fuse together in organic unison. For Latin American neostructuralism, capitalist development—properly regulated by the state—is not characterized by conflict-ridden, uneven, zero-sum, and crisis-laden scenarios, but rather by virtuous circles in which everyone wins, eventually.

Hollowing Out Classical Structuralism

Latin American neostructuralism as a paradigm has sanitized ECLAC's classical conceptualizations of Latin American political economy by expunging conflict and power relations from its analytical and policy framework. This accounts, on the one hand, for neostructuralism's broad appeal. Center-left governments have utilized the basic presuppositions of Latin American neostructuralism to distance themselves rhetorically from orthodox neoliberalism, while continuing to promise a high road to capitalist globalization in which a rising tide will lift all boats, and conflict, crisis, and instability will be avoided. On the other hand, the absence of conflict and power relations from Latin American neostructuralist theory has simultaneously exposed it to devastating internal contradictions, as the chasm between its descriptions of Latin American capitalism, and the reality of capitalist development in the region has become increasingly profound and difficult to ignore. Latin American neostructuralism has abandoned the preeminent concern of classical structuralists— "namely a focus on how economic surplus is produced, appropriated, and distributed within a single, world capitalist economy."[31] As a consequence, the school of thought "becomes *analytically impotent in adequately explicating the scope of the qualitative transformations experienced by Latin American capitalism over the last decade.*"[32] It fails to detect transnationalizing tendencies in economic, social, and political structures, the informalization of capital-labor relations, and accelerating financialization. Neostructuralist public policy has actually deepened and extended the processes introduced by orthodox neoliberals in the 1970s and 1980s. By setting aside analytical categories attentive to extant power relations, ostensibly progressive policies aimed at international competitiveness and participatory governance, "led to the *politico-economic consolidation, legitimization, and furtherance of the process of capitalist restructuring initially set in motion by neoliberal ideas and policies.*"[33] This approach, because it excludes history, power relations, and changes in the structure of global capitalism from its analytical lens, cannot fully grasp the changes to Latin American states, class structures, and the dynamics of class formation wrought by thirty years of neoliberalism, and precisely what these changes imply for development theory and practice.

"Looking back today from the ruins of the neoliberal revolution," sociologist Vivek Chibber points out, "it is understandable that there may be a certain nostalgia toward the developmentalist era, and toward that storied class, the national bourgeoisie. The intervening years seem to have left us with a sturdy mythology about the period, one in which states had the power and the vision to navigate a path to autonomous development, in which the business class hitched its wagon to the national project, and labour had a place at the bargaining table."[34] But the political coalitions that made the developmentalist project possible, in fact contributed to the consistent ability of national bourgeoisies to inhibit the projection of state power in the form of economic planning, and the equally consistent subordination, repression, and demobilization of labor. Risks were socialized and profits privatized on an enormous scale, contradictions that eventually contributed to the implosion of ISI. Rather than states disciplining capital by directing domestic private investments into economic sectors with high social returns, capital consistently disciplined the state, directing investments and state subsidies into areas of enormous profits and low social return.[35]

As Chibber points out, "whereas [state] planners saw ISI and industrial policy as two sides of the same coin, for capitalists, ISI generated an incentive to *reject* the discipline of industrial policy. Those institutions intended to further the subsidisation process were supported by capital; but dimensions of state-building aimed at enabling planners to monitor and regulate firms' investment decisions were stoutly resisted. At the surface level, the conflict between the national bourgeoisie and the economic planners was not always apparent. It was common to find industrialists joining the chorus calling for planning, economic management, and the like. But what they meant by this was a process in which public monies were put at their disposal, and at their behest. To them planning meant the socialisation of risk, while leaving the private appropriation of profit intact."[36] Additionally, as a condition for the national bourgeoisie's purported support for the developmentalist project of the nation, state managers participated in the concerted emasculation of labor movements. At the same time, the declining power of labor was often amplified by "labour's own seduction by the rhetoric of national development and planning. Too often, unions reposed an altogether unwarranted confidence in the state's ability to protect their interests, to discipline the capitalist class, and to manage class conflict through an adroit manipulation of plan priorities."[37]

The Political Economy of the Morales Regime

The theoretical and practical shift across much of Latin America, from neoliberal orthodoxy to a reconstituted neoliberalism under the guise of neostructuralism, has played itself out in the Bolivian context as well, albeit with important details specific to the country. The same unwarranted faith in the state's capacity to discipline capital, and the same processes of socializing risk while privatizing profit have become entrenched in the ideological makeup of the Morales government. It should be recalled that as far back as the campaign for the December 2005 elections, when Álvaro Garcia Linera was first selected as Morales's vice-presidential candidate, the former became the spokesperson for "realistic," economic moderation, while the latter continued to deploy a rhetoric in sync with the radical lineage of his party's early history. García Linera's line was, unfortunately, more in tune with the actual development plan the MAS structured for the campaign, and subsequently instituted once elected.

Previous to the election of 2005, García Linera began, of course, by positing the impossibility of socialism in Bolivia for at least half a century, and perhaps a full one. In lieu of a socialist project, the MAS promoted something the vice president called Andean-Amazonian capitalism. This model, in keeping with the developmentalist nostalgia criticized by Chibber above, claimed that a stronger capitalist state could drive a petty-bourgeoisie into a future national bourgeoisie of a size and significance unprecedented in Bolivian history. The new national bourgeoisie would be of indigenous heritage—Andean-Amazonian—as a consequence of the "democratic-cultural" reforms of indigenous liberation, as conceived by the MAS as a process separate from any fundamental socioeconomic transformation of the class structures of

Bolivian society. Parallel to the enduring theoretical postulations of the Stalinist Bolivian Communist Party of the 1930s, García Linera envisioned this intermediary stage of prolonged, capitalist industrialization as a necessary transition between today's mode of production and the socialism that might be possible in a century's time. The vice president soon after refined these formulations in his conceptualization of "Evismo." Indigenous, democratic, and cultural change, in this view, did not imply radical economic transformation of the inherited neoliberal model nor any revolutionary change in political structures of domination and oppression. Instead, modifications to the existing political institutions of the state, arrived at through negotiation with the elite of the eastern lowlands, would be sufficient to ensure an expansion of indigenous cultural rights and the sort of decolonizing, democratic revolution envisioned by the MAS under Morales.

One of the ways the MAS sought ideologically to overcome the apparent contradiction of promoting simultaneously democratic indigenous revolution and neoliberal continuities in various political and economic power structures, was to separate the anticolonial indigenous revolution against racist oppression from the socialist revolution to end class exploitation. Whereas many participants in the social movements of the insurrectionary period between 2000 and 2005 believed that the racist oppression and class exploitation of the majority of indigenous workers and peasants were organically linked, and therefore had to be overthrown simultaneously in a combined liberation struggle, the MAS advocated indigenous cultural revolution immediately, with socialist transformation a mere possibility in the distant future.

In its approach to the state, the early days of the MAS development project closely mirrored the neostructuralist perspective. For neostructuralists, acting on Weberian theoretical foundations, the capitalist state is essentially a benign set of institutions that can act on a more or less rational basis (inside the bounds of capitalist rationality). In this view, the class relations of capitalism and the repressive role of the state in reproducing these relations are obscured, replaced by an ostensibly non-ideological, rational set of institutions acting in the general interests of society. The state disciplines labor as necessary in order to increase the surplus accrued by capital, which, in turn, allows for further reinvestment and accumulation. So long as capitalist competition is the operative framework, private investors require institutions that supply a ready reserve of relatively cheap, flexible, and disciplined labor.[38] The necessary characteristics of state institutions are, again, stability, adaptability, coherence, coordination, and the ability to implement and enforce market rules.

Historical materialists, on the other hand, see the state as maintaining capitalist order and regulating the social contradictions inherent to capitalism, through violence when necessary. The state does this in the interest of the ruling class, economically and politically, in order to reproduce an inherently unstable and conflict-ridden social environment of class exploitation and struggle, which arises out of the irredeemably contradictory economic interests of the popular versus ruling social classes. Economic exploitation and state repression are built-in, constituent parts of the system of capitalism, not merely conjunctural, or unseemly but temporary episodes of late development in the Global South.

As was noted in earlier chapters, during the first several months of the MAS administration the state played its role of reproducing the conditions for accumulation through an array of policies that guaranteed healthy profits for private investors. The broad parameters of neoliberal financial policy inherited by the Morales government was also perpetuated, symbolized not least by the sanctification of Central Bank independence and repeated commitments to extremely low levels of inflation. Through fiscal austerity guarantees and Central Bank independence, the Morales regime set aside from the outset any possibility of enacting economic policies privileging specific popular classes in a new development model. Instead, under the cloak of technical economic policy neutrality, the continuation of neoliberalism ensured that the largest capitalists would continue to enjoy significant profits while the state would reproduce the labor force in their interests. Most other macroeconomic policies, including legislation on the labor market, corresponded with such a conclusion during the first year of the MAS administration.

The Plan de Desarrollo Nacional 2006–2010 (National Development Plan, PDN), released on June 16, 2006, parallels closely the neostructuralism advocated in ECLAC documents since the early 1990s. The development model contained in the plan is predicated on the continuation of extractive capitalism, rooted in the export of primary natural resource commodities—hydrocarbons and minerals—under the principal control of imperialist capital, but with substantial rents going to the state through royalties and taxation. Moderate reforms were introduced in the hydrocarbons sector, as well as in relations to the International Monetary Fund, in the wake of the plan, and these undoubtedly violated the precepts of market fundamentalism. At the same time, the reforms are very much in keeping with the new social engineering approach of neostructuralism, designed to maintain the basic foundations of neoliberalism in a context of its profound crisis of legitimacy as a development model in Latin America.

If our analysis were based exclusively on the record of the first year of the MAS administration, it could plausibly be said that our drawing hard conclusions regarding continuity and change under Morales would be premature. However, an examination of the political economy of the Morales government over the next three years (2007–2010) reveals the deepening and consolidation of the initial trend toward a reconstituted neoliberalism. This is a tendency, not a law, and the course of Bolivian political economy is now, as always, subject to the vicissitudes of domestic and regional class struggles, formations, and alliances, as well as the machinations of global capitalism and the geopolitics of great powers and their attendant implications for Bolivia. Nonetheless, the observable and structural trend toward the consolidation of reconstituted neoliberalism in the first term of the Morales government ought to be recognized and analyzed seriously.

Composition of Bolivia's Economic Structure

The first issue to point out is that prior to the worldwide economic crisis, the fallout from which began to hit Bolivia in late 2008 and early

2009, Bolivia's economy under Morales grew very quickly. As Table 6.1 indicates, after relatively slow growth in the early 2000s, the country rode the region's commodity boom of recent years and registered rates of gross domestic product (GDP) growth between 4 and 5 percent in 2004, 2005, 2006, and 2007. This trend peaked at 6.1 percent in 2008, before dropping to an expected 3.5 percent in 2009, the highest projected rate of growth that year of any country in the hemisphere. Since Morales came to office in January 2006, then, average GDP growth has been 4.8 percent. Between 2003 and 2008, Latin America and the Caribbean as a whole grew consistently at above 3 percent, reaching 5.7 percent in 2007.[39] This period was the region's highest rate of sustained economic expansion in four decades.[40]

TABLE 6.1: BOLIVIA GROSS DOMESTIC PRODUCT (GDP), 2000–2009

Year	2000	2001	2002	2003	2004	2005	2006	2007	2008	2009*
GDP	2.5	1.7	2.5	2.7	4.2	4.4	4.8	4.6	6.1	3.5

Figures for 2009 are preliminary.
Source: Derived from ECLAC, Preliminary Overview of the Economies of Latin America and the Caribbean 2009 (Santiago: ECLAC, 2010) 140.

The basic composition of Bolivia's economic structure has not changed profoundly in the last several years (see Table 6.2). Drivers of GDP growth between 2004 and 2008 included firm demand and high prices in the international market for hydrocarbons and minerals, as well as a modest uptick in private consumption.[41] Oil and gas extraction rose from 4.5 to 6.9 percent of GDP between 1999 and 2007.[42] In subsequent years, the hydrocarbons sector has fallen modestly as a percentage of GDP, but remains a massively important source of government revenue. Since 2004 total government revenue expanded by almost 20 percent, mostly as a consequence of the new tax regime in hydrocarbons established by Morales in 2006. Between 2004 and 2008, government revenue from hydrocarbons accelerated dramatically. The state's take increased by roughly $3.5 billion over these years. Hydrocarbon revenue as a percentage of GDP went from 5.6 to 25.7 between 2004 and the fourth quarter of 2008, after which it fell slightly to 21.1 percent by the second quarter of 2009.[43] Natural-gas exports accounted for 41.3 percent of Bolivia's total exports in 2007, with Brazil being the country's largest export market by far. A twenty-year supply agreement was also signed with neighboring Argentina in 2006. Construction of an important gas pipeline to Argentina, which would expand the volume of Bolivian gas exports significantly, is also currently under construction, although Argentina is increasingly investing in its own gas fields as a way of reducing dependence on Bolivian supply.[44] Mining, too, experienced a resurgence beginning in 2005. Indeed, mineral extraction increased from 3.5 percent of GDP in 2005 to 5.1 percent GDP in 2009.[45] Taken together, mining and hydrocarbons accounted for 12.1 percent of GDP, up from 11 percent in 2004, as can be seen in Table 6.2. In the first half of 2009, Bolivia's GDP grew by 3.2 percent, with metallic and non-metallic mineral extraction outpacing all other sectors at 14.4 percent growth. This is mainly attributable to the intensification of production at the San Cristóbal mine. Despite being the leading sector, however, metallic and non-metallic mineral mining was still down relative to its 63 percent growth over the same period in 2008. Meanwhile, crude oil and natural gas contracted by 13.1 percent during the first half of 2009, mainly as a consequence of the sharp decline in demand from Brazil.[46]

TABLE 6.2: ECONOMIC STRUCTURE—
GROSS DOMESTIC PRODUCT BY SECTOR (% OF GDP)

Year	2003	2004	2005	2006	2007
Agriculture	16.4	15.9	15.9	15.8	15.0
Industry	33.7	34.6	35.1	35.8	36.4
Mining/Hydrocarbons	10.4	11.0	11.8	11.9	12.1
Construction	3.0	2.9	3.0	3.1	3.3
Electricity, Gas, Water	2.2	2.2	2.2	2.2	2.1
Manufacturing	18.1	18.4	18.1	18.7	18.8
Services	53.3	52.6	52.2	51.7	51.7

Source: EIU, Bolivia: Country Profile 2008
(London: Economist Intelligence Unit, 2008) 17.

Table 6.2 indicates, too, that agriculture—including forestry, game, and fishing—shrunk by close to 1 percent of GDP between 2006 and 2007, while preliminary data shows it shrinking still further to 10.4 percent in 2008, before rallying to 12.3 percent in the first half of 2009.[47] Much of this agricultural activity is rooted in the commercial production of sugarcane, soya, maize, and sunflower, among other oil-bearing seed crops (all of which witnessed a rising world demand until recently), in the department of Santa Cruz.[48]

Manufacturing, as can be seen in Table 6.2, has stayed relatively even as a contribution to GDP, hitting a peak of 18.8 percent in 2007. This sector is dominated by the production of nondurable consumer goods, with products "such as food, beverages, tobacco, detergents, textiles, leather goods and shoes," constituting close to one-half of all manufacturing. The rest is largely taken up by "artisan crafts, jewelry and intermediate goods, such as processed soya, refined metals, timber products and petroleum refining."[49] Textiles and clothing manufacturers, many located in the city of El Alto, had benefited from the U.S.-Andean Trade-Promotion and Drug-Eradication Act (ATPDEA), which was originally established for the 2002–2006 period, but was subsequently extended on several occasions. The agreement was designed to lower American tariffs for Andean nations that cooperated with the American "war on drugs" in the region. As with all other diplomatic devices in this hoax of a war, the instruments of regulation and control built into the agreement were constructed such that the U.S. state could retain and extend its geopolitical control over the region under the guise of fighting the production and trade of narcotics. In order to register its displeasure with what it took to be dangerous radicalizing possibilities in Morales's populism, and to pressure the Bolivian government into a bilateral free trade agreement with the United States on American terms, the Bush government took action through the ATPDEA in 2008. On October 23 that year, Secretary of State Condoleezza Rice, speaking at a drug war gathering in Puerto Vallarta, Mexico, announced the temporary suspension of the ATPDEA with Bolivia, citing the Morales government's insufficient efforts at drug eradication. The expectation was that twenty thousand jobs and $150 million a year would be lost, and the Morales government would soon be brought into line.[50]

Instead, observing that George W. Bush's ratings were slumping badly, and that the Republicans were therefore soon on their way out of office, Bolivia decided to expel Philip Goldberg, the U.S. ambassador to Bolivia, from the country in 2008. The Morales government suggested that Goldberg's ties to right-wing domestic forces bent on Morales's overthrow were the reason for the expulsion. The United States, in turn, expelled Gustavo Guzmán, Bolivia's ambassador to the United States. The bilateral relationship did not change under Barack Obama, however, as many in the Morales government had expected it would. Rather, in 2009, the U.S. government, now under the control of the Democrats, definitively suspended the ATPDEA with Bolivia. Thomas Shannon, until late 2009 Obama's assistant secretary of state for western hemisphere affairs, met with Bolivian officials in May 2009, ostensibly to reestablish bilateral relations, but to no avail. According to David Choquehuanca, Bolivia's foreign minister, "We want cooperation to be state to state. This is one of the themes that we have put on the table. We do not want aid arriving from the United States to be administered by them [inside Bolivia] without Bolivia having the right to access the information as to how these funds are spent."[51] Apparently, this was too much to ask of the Obama administration, and formal relations between the countries remain strained, with no ATPDEA revival in sight.

The actual impact of U.S. trade and diplomatic hostility has been less than expected, however, principally due to Bolivia's export diversification in recent years. Between 2000 and 2009, exports to the United States, Canada, and Europe have fallen from 56 to 17 percent of GDP, while exports to Latin America rose to almost two-thirds total exports in 2008, from 41.5 percent in 1999.[52] Brazil became the country's largest export market, rising to 16 from 0.5 percent between 1999 and 2008, with South Korea now second, at 4.3 percent. While the diversification of exports helped the Bolivian economy weather the hostility from Washington and the worst of the world crisis in the United States and Europe, it is still true that ATPDEA exports accounted for 3.2 percent of Bolivia's total export value in 2008, and its loss therefore remains significant, particularly for the manufacturing sector.

TABLE 6.3: BOLIVIA—EXPORTS TO THE FOUR LARGEST
INTERNATIONAL MARKETS (% GDP), 1999–2008

Country	1999	2000	2001	2002	2003	2004	2005	2006	2007	2008
Brazil	0.5	1.9	3.5	4.2	6.1	8.1	11.6	13.5	13.2	16.0
S. Korea	0.0	0.0	0.0	0.0	0.2	0.6	0.6	0.4	1.5	4.3
Argentina	0.6	0.3	0.3	0.3	0.5	1.4	2.7	3.2	3.2	2.6
United States	2.7	2.3	1.9	2.2	2.6	3.8	4.0	3.1	3.1	2.5

Source: Derived from Mark Weisbrot, Rebecca Ray, and Jake Johnston, Bolivia: The
Economy During the Morales Administration *(Washington, D.C.: Center for Economic
and Policy Research, December 2009) 26.*

Austere Continuities

The Morales government has continued to be remarkably austere in its
fiscal policy. In contradistinction to the budget deficits of the
2000–2005 period, Morales registered significant fiscal surpluses between 2006 and 2008, accruing at the same time massive increases in
international reserves.[53] The right-wing opposition has nonetheless
made a consistent uproar about inflation levels at different times, with
the obvious political aim of conjuring up public fear of a return to the
hyperinflationary crisis of the early 1980s. The mainstream media has
done its part to stoke the fire in this regard. It is true that inflation rose
from just under 5 percent at the close of 2006 to 14.1 percent in March
2008. It is also true, however, that the bulk of this trend can be traced to
external shocks in food and energy price increases on the international
market. Once these two factors are removed, core inflation hit a high of
only 9.2 percent in December 2008, and subsequently fell back to 2.4
percent by November 2009.[54] Moving into 2009, overall cumulative inflation hit 0.2 percent by October 2009 or 0.8 percent in annualized
terms. These figures were among the lowest in all of Latin America and
signified 11 and 13 percent point drops, respectively, compared with

rates in the same periods in 2008.[55] The drop is traceable to declines in international commodity prices, especially food, and an increase in supply domestically as a consequence of improved weather patterns.

Public investment, mainly in infrastructure, accelerated from 6.3 percent of GDP in 2005 to 10.5 percent in 2009. This is a priority for the government, given that transportation costs are estimated to be roughly twenty times as high as in neighboring Brazil.[56] The railways run to only 3,700 kilometers, divided into two unconnected networks, some sections of which are no longer in use, owing to neglect and disrepair. Road building has been privileged by the Morales government. This predilection for road building mirrors previous governments' priorities, with the percentage of roads with paved surfaces rising to 33 percent in 2005 from 20 percent in 2000. Two major highway arteries are now under construction, linking Santa Cruz to the Brazilian border city of Puerto Suárez, in one case, and La Paz to the Brazilian border city of Guayaramerin, in the other.[57]

Social Spending and Fiscal Stimulus

Social spending, particularly for a government transitioning toward "communitarian socialism" has been remarkably low. Adjusted for inflation, social spending in real terms rose by only 6.3 percent between 2005 and 2008, and *declined* as a percentage of GDP from 12.4 to 11.2 over the same period.[58] One report, published in December 2009 by a group of extremely sympathetic social democratic economists, put it mildly: "Given the size and needs of Bolivia's poor population…and the increased resources that the government has accumulated in the recent years, it would seem that social spending for poverty alleviation and basic needs such as food, health care, and education should be increased."[59] Some relatively new initiatives in social spending—essentially cash transfers based on hydrocarbon revenues—may begin to partially reverse this trend. These include US$29 per month, per young child, provided to families through the Bono Juancito Pinto program initiated in 2006. So long as children attend school, the cash transfer is distributed as

TABLE 6.4: BOLIVIA—POVERTY AND LIVING STANDARDS, 1997–2007 (PERCENTAGES OF TOTAL POPULATION)

	1997	1998	1999	2000	2001	2002	2003/2004*	2005	2006	2007
Poverty	-	-	63.5	66.4	63.1	63.3	-	59.6	59.9	60.1
Extreme Poverty	-	-	40.7	45.2	38.8	39.5	-	36.7	37.7	37.7
Household Amenities:										
No more than three people per bedroom	42.5	51.6	67.4	67.4	68.0	59.7	60.2	60.6	69.5	71.5
Electricity	67.3	71.3	70.9	70.0	69.3	64.0	66.5	68.3	76.2	80.2
Access to running water†	82.6	85.4	81.5	84.5	84.7	82.3	83.3	85.1	84.3	86.0
Sewage Systems	38.3	43.1	42.6	42.2	41.4	40.7	40.4	45.9	41.9	50.8

Source: Derived from Mark Weisbrot, Rebecca Ray, and Jake Johnston, Bolivia: The Economy During the Morales Administration, Washington, DC: Center for Economic and Policy Research, December 2009, 16.

*Data for 2003–2004 correspond to the Encuesta Continua de Hogares survey that took place between November 2003 and November 2004.

† We classify as having running water those homes with piped or well water (based inside or outside the home, individually, or community-based). We classify as not having access to running water households that access water via rivers, lakes, and trucks. We classify as having sewage systems households with septic tanks or sewage system connections. We classify as not having sewage systems households with outhouses or with no bathroom facilities.

an incentive for children to complete primary school up to grade six. Additionally, there is Renta Dignidad, an initiative kicked off in 2008 that provides roughly $344 per month to low-income citizens over sixty years of age. And, finally, Bono Juana Azurduy (or Bono Madre Niño Niña) was established in May 2009. It provides modest cash transfers to uninsured mothers in an effort to increase the likelihood of their seeking medical care before and after pregnancy. "New mothers receive 50 bolivianos each for four pre-natal medical visits, 120 bolivianos for the childbirth, and 125 bolivianos for each medical appointment until the child's second birthday. Mothers must show that they have the required medical visits in order to receive the funds."[60] The extent of the coverage for Bono Juancito Pinto and Renta Dignidad is outlined in Table 6.6.

TABLE 6.6: BOLIVIA—COVERAGE FOR BONO JUANCITO PINTO
AND RENTA DIGNIDAD, 2006–2008

Year	Number of Beneficiaries		Percent of Population Covered	
	Juancito Pinto	Renta Dignidad	Juancito Pinto	Renta Dignidad
2006	1,085,360	487,832	61.8%	76.9%
2007	1,323,999	493,437	75.1%	75.4%
2008	1,681,135	687,962	95.9%	101.8%

Source: Derived from Weisbrot, Ray, and Johnston, Bolivia: The Economy, 16.

Note: Relevant populations are students enrolled in primary school, for Bono Juancito Pinto, and residents over age sixty, for Renta Dignidad. Enrollment is available through 2007; for 2008, enrollment is estimated as the average of the prior five years. Population estimates are from projections made by Instituto Nacional de Estadística based on the 2001 census, and may result in coverage rates over 100 percent.

In response to the impact of the worldwide crisis on Bolivia, the Morales government introduced a sharp fiscal stimulus between the end of 2007 and 2009, leading to a shift from a surplus of 5 percent of GDP in the first quarter of 2008 to a deficit of 0.7 percent of GDP in the first quarter of 2009. This signified a substantial turn of almost 6 percentage points of GDP.[61] Between the first half of 2008 and the first half of 2009, exports declined by US$853 million, or 27.3 percent, as a result of declining hydrocarbon prices, lower demand in Brazil, and trade sanctions from the United States. Remittances from Bolivian laborers working abroad, meanwhile, dropped by 7.4 percent, or US$39.4 million, over the same period.[62] In this context, the stimulus package was "probably the most important policy move that helped Bolivia avoid the worst effects of the downturn, relative to most of the rest of the region," analysts have pointed out. "It is worth noting that this would not have been possible without the control that the government gained over its natural gas production and revenues."[63]

Social Consequences of Reconstituted Neoliberalism

Figures on poverty and living standards do not indicate a break with neoliberal social policy, much less the start of a revolutionary transition toward communitarian socialism. Drawing on data from Bolivia's National Institute of Statistics, Table 6.4 charts poverty and extreme poverty trends up to 2007, the latest available figures. Note that since 2005 there has been only marginal change in the poverty rate, and that this change has been slightly upward, from 59.9 percent of the population in 2005 to 60.1 percent in 2007.[64] Levels of extreme poverty increase from 36.7 to 37.7 percent over the same two-year period. At the same time, other categories relevant to living standards highlighted in Table 6.4, such as household density, and access to electricity, running water, and sewage systems, all show modest improvements between 2005 and 2007. It is possible that poverty levels have improved since 2007, and it should also be noted that these figures do not take into account improvements in the social wage of workers and peasants—i.e., any improvements in social services for the poor.[65] But the record on poverty nonetheless shows that there is little to celebrate.

Inequality, likewise, remains a huge barrier to achieving social justice in the Bolivian context. Between 2005 and 2007 income inequality, as measured by the Gini Coefficient, declined from 60.2 to 56.3.[66] This hardly represents a revolutionary transfer of wealth, or even effective structural reform, as is perhaps more clearly demonstrated in the figures for the distribution of Bolivian national income, depicted in Table 6.5. Here we see that the poorest 10 percent of the Bolivian population received 0.3 percent of national income in 1999, and still received only

0.4 percent by 2007, the last available figure. Meanwhile, the richest 10 percent of the population took home 43.9 percent of national income in 1999 and precisely the same percentage in 2007. If we broaden our perspective, to compare the bottom and top fifths of the social pyramid, we reach similar conclusions. The poorest 20 percent of society took in a mere 1.3 percent of national income in 1999 and, in 2007, a still paltry 2 percent. The richest 20 percent of the population pocketed 61.2 percent of national income in 1999 and 60.9 in 2007. In other words, there has been almost no change on either end of the scale in terms of the redistribution of income, never mind the redistribution of assets. Abolishing such obscene concentrations of wealth—which are among the worst in Latin America, which is, in turn, the most unequal region of the world—ought to be a fundamental priority for the Morales government. Thus far, it has not been.[67]

TABLE 6.5: DISTRIBUTION OF BOLIVIAN NATIONAL INCOME— URBAN AND RURAL AREAS, 1999–2007

Geographic Area	Year	Quintile 1 (poorest)		Quintile 5 (richest)	
		Decile 1	Decile 2	Decile 9	Decile 10
National	1999	0.3	1.0	17.3	43.9
	2007	0.4	1.6	17.0	43.9
Urban	1999	1.3	2.6	16.7	38.9
	2007	1.5	2.6	16.6	38.9
Rural	1999	0.4	0.8	17.3	48.8
	2007	0.2	1.2	18.7	45.4

Source: Derived from ECLAC, Preliminary Overview of the Economies of Latin America and the Caribbean 2009 *(Santiago: ECLAC, 2010) 67.*

Post-Neoliberal Turns?

There are many who continue to believe that the process of reform has run more deeply than I have suggested. The above sections illustrate that such claims of deep structural transformation do not correspond with the empirical record. Nonetheless, the radical trajectory of the government in its first term is frequently proclaimed, and the current moment, after Morales's decisive victory in the December 2009 elections, is seen as beckoning still further progress in the revolutionary transformation of the country's state, society, and economy. "This revolutionary movement," Frederico Fuentes suggests, for example, "with indigenous and peasant organizations in the forefront, has pushed the traditional Bolivian elite from power through a combination of electoral battles and mass insurrections. It has begun the struggle to create a new 'plurinational' Bolivia—based on inclusion and equality for Bolivia's 36 indigenous nations." Even outside narrow cultural conceptions of indigenous liberation, change is said to have occurred in the economy as well. "The Morales government has reclaimed state control over gas and mineral reserves and nationalised 13 companies involved in gas, mining, telecommunications, railways and electricity," Fuentes argues, drawing on official figures. "This increased state intervention means the public sector has increased from 12% of gross domestic product in 2005 to 32% today." For Fuentes, and many other like-minded observers, "this government is the product of a new anti-imperialism whose roots lie in previous nationalist movements. It surpasses previous nationalist experiments because, for the first time, it is not military officers or the urban middle classes leading the project, but indigenous and peasant sectors."[68]

The perspective advanced by Fuentes is similar to that proposed by Pablo Stefanoni in various interventions, albeit with the important caveat that Stefanoni is increasingly critical of the MAS project as a whole. For Stefanoni, the current process of change under Morales evokes a certain popular nationalism similar to that of the post-revolutionary 1950s, although with a novel indigenous nucleus to the project's social base and ideological statements.[69] "The MAS, although it denies it," Stefanoni suggests, "has resumed the policies and rituals of 1952," with the "indigenous military marches, the nationalization of natural resources, and the multiclass alliance of the 'people,' military nationalists, and 'patriotic' capitalists."[70] But both Fuentes and Stefanoni are confusing the rhetorical commitments of the government to state-led industrialization with actual substantive movement toward that end, as well as superficial rhetorical similarities to the 1952 revolution with the much more limited extent of reforms actually introduced in the Morales era compared to those enacted throughout the earlier epoch. Stefanoni is correct to point out that, today, it is increasingly apparent that the MAS has re-created the legacy of nationalist populism in a new melange fit for the twenty-first century. The government has indeed incorporated some of the language of indigenous liberation developed by the earlier popular struggles but has separated its indigenous focus from the material reality facing indigenous people, and has not proposed economic reform anywhere near the levels of the mid-twentieth-century, nationalist-populist epoch in Bolivia. A glance at the late 1960s, for example, demonstrates that levels of state employment were massively higher than they were after four years of the MAS administration, and the state's proportion of total investment in the country in the late 1960s was 52 percent, by conservative estimates, as compared to the maximum claims of 32 percent today, with ultimate official goals of only 36 percent state participation in GDP.[71]

Fuentes refers to thirteen nationalized companies. If we focus for a moment simply on mining, we start to recognize that a more incisive and careful dissection of the realities on the ground is important. First, the two nationalizations—of the Huanuni mine and the Vinto mining smelter—were a consequence of concerted struggles from below, by the mine workers and community allies, which forced the Bolivian government to act. They can hardly be seen as part of the government's overarching agenda. Second, important as these struggles were, it remains true that the overwhelming majority of active mines in Bolivia are owned and operated by transnational mining capital, principally Indian, Korean, Japanese, Canadian, American, and Swiss capital at the moment, with the possibility of French and Russian involvement soon, through lithium development.[72]

The revolution of 1952 achieved the nationalization of the mines, the breaking up of the haciendas through wide-scale agrarian reform, and the abolition of the hated *pongueaje*, a system through which indigenous rural laborers had been obliged to provide personal service to the landowner, his family, and his overseers in exchange for the ability to sow small sections of land on the hacienda. The labor movement, led by the miners, demanded the full-scale socialization of property relations and the institutionalization of workers' control in the mines and elsewhere during the opening years of the revolutionary process. However, after the initial period in which the Movimiento Nacionalista Revolucionario (Revolutionary Nationalist Movement, MNR) was forced to enact major reforms due to pressure from popular movements, the MNR quickly turned on the workers with the assistance of U.S. imperialism. In alliance with coopted peasant organizations—placated by the recent land reforms—the MNR began reversing the gains of the revolution and rebuilding the army as a means of repressing the miners. In 1956, an IMF-backed economic stabilization program was introduced, and by the arrival of the 1964 right-wing military coup the state had developed an elaborate system of divide-and-rule tactics to deal with rural and urban popular sectors, repressing the most radical and integrating those who could be integrated through co-optation and the divvying up of selective benefits from the state's purse.

Leading into the second term of the Morales government, there remains the possibility of a renewal of an old social pact between fractions of the eastern bourgeois bloc and imperialist forces in their various guises, and the state bureaucracy occupied by the MAS.[73] Such an outcome would require sufficient levels of reform to achieve the temporary quiescence of the masses, while at the same time avoiding a level of reform that would lead to reaction from the "honest," "responsible," and "patriotic" fractions of the bourgeoisie, and a new cycle of crisis and instability. Morales, as an indigenous president and ex-cocalero leader, may continue to have sufficient political capital—legitimacy within the popular classes and indigenous organizations—to facilitate such an outcome. Because such a conclusion would continue to avoid confronting the fundamental class strongholds in the urban and rural economies of transnational capital and their domestic allies, it could lay the basis for fundamental counter-reform over the long term. These reactionary forces—currently ideologically and politically fragmented—would, over time, be able to reorganize politically and socially. We should remember that the far more radical reforms initiated by the MNR following the 1952 Revolution were nonetheless overturned by the far right in a military coup in 1964, in part because the revolution never evolved from left-populist to genuinely socialist and indigenous-liberationist.

Such a trajectory is made more plausible by various recent indications of government intentions. The nostalgia for an honest, patriotic bourgeoisie that might be disciplined by the state ran through García Linera's thinking the night before the December 2009 elections. Expecting a huge majority of votes, journalists asked him how he would respond to those who suggest that the new mandate will lead to a radicalization of the process. "We are going to do what we have said," indicated García Linera. "There is no hidden agenda." Asked if he would move to expropriate the huge tracts of land held by the agro-bourgeoisie in Santa Cruz, he responded by defending the sanctity of private property, as enshrined in the new constitution. "We will never go against a Constitution that we have put together ourselves, and there are parameters [in the Constitution] about land: a maximum size, respect for private property, and that the social functions of the land must be fulfilled." What about the apparent rapprochement with the business elite of Santa Cruz who until that moment had seemed so hostile? "These meetings," between the government and the eastern bourgeois bloc, "are not new. What is new," suggested García Linera, "is that they are publicly acknowledging them. The business class had three blocs: a rabidly oppositional bloc that conspired [against the government] and was defeated; a nucleus that agrees with our policies but will not say so publicly; and a sector that shifts allegiances depending on the political winds. This last section is now inclined to accept the calls from the government to get to work. We will not accept corporate elite acting as though they were a political party. If they understand this, the state is firmly committed to supporting these productive sectors. I believe they have understood."[74]

At the same time, a second exit to the post-December 2009 conjuncture might be that the country polarizes once again in dramatic ways, that social movements obtain some autonomy, at least from the less radical wings of the MAS, and that the left-indigenous forces of the country are once again pitted in open confrontation against the social forces of the right. In such a process, reforms might become increasingly broad, and revolutionary possibilities increasingly plausible once again. Such a virtuous circle of momentum might inspire the masses to take the situation into their own hands, to take over large landholdings in the countryside and workplaces and communities in the cities. As I have suggested, however, the second possibility must be the product of the self-activity and self-organization of the popular classes themselves, as the leadership of the governing party will not initiate such action on its own, and, indeed, will resist it until it becomes impossible to resist. We have shown how this was true in the political economy of the first year of the Morales government, and in the economic structure, fiscal policy, spending patterns, and inequality and poverty outcomes over the next three years (2007–2010). Let us turn now to two final areas that demonstrate the case for understanding the current MAS government as committed to reconstituted neoliberalism.

The Urban Working Class: Proactive Labor Flexibility

It will be recalled that one of the more important theoretical and practical innovations of Latin American neostructuralism has been the concept of *proactive labor flexibility*—that is, the necessity of the state to attempt to construct a consensus among workers to submit to the imperatives of export-led capitalist development. Labor movements must be co-opted and re-engineered, such that they abandon class struggle and conflict with the ruling class, and embrace cross-class cooperation and labor-state stability within the parameters of the given capitalist order. This, it is thought, will improve the "systemic competitiveness" of any given Latin American country within a rigidly hierarchical and fiercely competitive world system of capitalism. The concrete implementation of this innovation in labor markets has manifested itself in a particular way in the Bolivian context. Through a variety of cash transfers mentioned above, the state has begun to introduce a modest redistribution of wealth through state revenue garnered from, and dependent upon, fluctuating natural resource rents. This has become the principal axis through which wealth redistribution is even considered, while the role of decent work and full employment in achieving these ends much more satisfactorily has been essentially ignored.[75] After a serious assessment of the available indicators in the urban world of work is conducted, it is difficult to maintain that

Morales government policies represent a post-neoliberal turn in the economic model of development, much less a revolutionary process of socioeconomic transformation.

Bolivia is an extreme instantiation of the general rule that capitalism
cannot meet the social needs of the majority of humanity. As was indicated above, between 2006 and 2008, the country grew at a reasonably
fast rate as a result, principally, of high prices for primary mineral materials and hydrocarbon exports. And, yet, the social effect of this growth
was neutralized for the majority of the population by increases in the
prices of foodstuffs and other basic necessities. The consumption power
of the poorest working-class and peasant sectors consequently declined.
The growth of GDP, furthermore, did not result in new employment for
workers, as indicated by the unemployment rate of over 10 percent in
June 2008, *before* the impact of the global crisis had really taken hold in
Bolivia. What is more, of those people who are employed, only 60 percent are able to cover the costs of a basic food basket. Many Bolivians
have been forced to emigrate over the last two decades—to Spain, Argentina, the United States, and elsewhere—in search of work. They sent significant levels of remittances home up until 2008. These undoubtedly assisted impoverished families back in Bolivia, but also had the structural
effect of disintegrating family and community networks, as well as reinforcing the super-exploitation of Bolivian labor abroad.[76]

The entire developmental apparatus in Bolivia is utterly fragile, in-
timately tied as it is to the often extreme volatility of international
prices for primary materials. The majority of Bolivians are increasingly
dependent upon the stability of high prices, which are maintained or
undermined globally by the indiscriminate logic and domination of
capital over real human social needs. If the global crisis extends into a
prolonged world slump, as it seems it will, the already terrible human
development scenario in the country is likely to be worsened by growth
in unemployment, reductions in remittances, the return of migrant
workers, further declines in exports, and ongoing diminution in prices
for Bolivia's primary materials, among other factors.[77] All this is unfolding in a context in which the government postulates an alliance
with transnational mining and oil companies as "partners" rather than

"bosses." What has become increasingly clear, however, is that the transnationals are demanding that the state continue to fulfill its historic role as facilitator of the accumulation of capital and exploitation of the Bolivian workforce.[78] The ghosts of neoliberalism lurk in the shadows of persistent class realities, barely concealed behind the vehement official messages promising deliverance from that evil.

Flexibilization of the World of Work and Precarious Labor Continues

One strategy frequently employed by business in its efforts to reduce labor costs has been the flexibilization of job contracts, such that, in Bolivia, job instability and uncertainty have become an ugly norm.[79] Table 6.6 indicates some of these trends and their implications for 2008. Taken together, of the employed workers in the five major cities across the country, only 51 percent were in permanent positions, whereas 28 percent were laboring at jobs with fixed-term contracts, and close to 21 percent were casual laborers. As is evident in Table 6.7, the character of job contracts has a major impact on the income of workers. In the case of El Alto, 61 percent of workers have fixed-term or casual employment.

Contractual flexibility allows employers to reduce the number of employees quickly in response to variations in demand. Calixto Chipana—when he was still a leader of the Federation of Factory Workers in Cochabamba, prior to becoming minister of labor in Morales's cabinet[80]—summarized the situation succinctly: "The capitalist is always going to prefer the casual over the secure worker, because the casual worker is pressured psychologically, materially, and more than anything, by necessity. And, maybe, he or she has the hope of landing a permanent job. Therefore, the casual worker has to work many times as hard. He or she has to demonstrate that they are competent, in order to stay and obtain the permanent position."[81]

The increase in casual or temporary forms of contracts has been a central ingredient in the successes employers have engineered over the last few decades, helping to meet the objectives of decreasing variable production costs, while increasing rates of profit and the exploitation of labor. Increasing job instability and increasing exploitation means that the surplus value extracted from temporary or casual workers is especially high, particularly when one adds the components of intensified work processes and extension of work days. The added political bonus for capital has been the augmented fragmentation of the working class and concomitant competition between workers. The associational power of workers through union organization and their ability to struggle to improve working conditions has declined as a consequence of the flexibilization and increasing precariousness of the world of work.[82]

TABLE 6.6: EMPLOYMENT STABILITY AND MONTHLY SALARY BY CITY, 2008

Type of Contract	Average Monthly Salary (bolivianos)	Percentage of Workers
Total	1,400	100
Permanent	1,732	51.3
Fixed Term	1,190	28
Casual	861	20.7
La Paz	1,477	100
Permanent	1,824	59.3
Fixed Term	1,228	20.9
Casual	701	19.8
Santa Cruz	1,629	100
Permanent	1,932	55.8
Fixed Term	1,401	24.1
Casual	1,065	24.7
Cochabamba	1,219	100
Permanent	1,472	45.7
Fixed Term	1,189	29.5
Casual	789	24.7
El Alto	995	100
Permanent	1,258	37.6
Fixed Term	925	42.4
Casual	655	20.1
Potosí	1,384	100
Permanent	1,565	55.4

Fixed Term	1,326	23.3
Casual	979	21.3

Source: *Silvia Escóbar de Pabón*, Situación de los ingresos laborales en tiempos de cambio *(La Paz: CEDLA, 2009) 52.*

Table 6.7 illustrates patterns of precarious and non-precarious labor across the major cities of the country. Based on an extensive poll carried out by CEDLA economists and sociologists in 2008, the table represents an operationalization of three variables that characterize precarious and non-precarious labor: (1) stability of employment; (2) the magnitude of salaries and income; and (3) social security coverage over the long term. Stability in employment was defined along the lines of different types of job contracts. Stable work was identified with permanent employment, whereas precarious work was identified with temporary or casual labor, or labor for which payment was made for the specific task completed. Stable salary and income was identified as two people in a household earning at least 50 percent of the Canasta Básica Familiar, Basic Family Basket, of recognized necessities. Long-term social security was identified as access to a pension. From these bases, it was concluded that non-precarious labor meets all the conditions of stability, precarious labor signifies a deficit in some of these conditions, and extremely precarious labor is associated with a deficit along all three axes.[83]

TABLE 6.7: PRECARIOUS WORK BY CITY, 2008

Work Type	Total	La Paz	Santa Cruz	Cochabamba	El Alto	Potosí
Non-Precarious	17.1	20.0	20.5	16.2	9.8	16.0
Precarious	24.0	25.6	28.0	20.0	18.4	27.9
Extremely Pecarious	58.9	54.4	51.5	63.8	71.7	56.1

Source: *Escóbar de Pabón,* Situación del Empleo, *76.*

It is evident that, well into the third year of the Morales government, the precariousness of working conditions is starkly reminiscent of erstwhile regimes. Less than one fifth of the working population in the major cities has non-precarious employment, with 24 percent in precarious work, and almost 60 percent in extremely precarious situations. The working classes of El Alto and Cochabamba are experiencing the worst structural conditions of the major cities, with 90 percent of working *alteños* and 84 percent of working cochabambinos stuck in precarious or extremely precarious jobs.

Absent from Table 6.7, but addressed in the larger study of the results, are the gendered dimensions of precarious work in Bolivia's major cities. Overall, 88 percent of working Bolivian women in the major cities have precarious or extremely precarious jobs, the latter category accounting for 70 percent of women's jobs. For men, the respective figures are 79 and 50 percent. So, the major gendered distinction here is in the category of extreme precariousness, where women do much more poorly. In the worst case of El Alto, 81 percent of working women have extremely precarious jobs, compared to 64 percent for men.

In addition to assisting the intensification of work, precarious labor conditions have helped facilitate the extension of working hours. Table 6.8 indicates that the average hours worked per day by salaried workers exceeds the established legal norm of eight hours. Illegal extension of hours worked is a generalized phenomenon. For men, who constitute two-thirds of salaried workers, their work day is, on average, 1.6 hours longer than the eight-hour norm each day. The figure rises to two hours longer each day in the city of El Alto.

TABLE 6.8: AVERAGE WORKING DAY BY CITY ACCORDING TO SEX, 2008

City	Total	Men	Women
Total	9.0	9.6	8.2
La Paz	8.6	9.4	7.8
Santa Cruz	8.9	9.4	8.1
Cochabamba	8.8	9.3	8.2
El Alto	9.6	10.3	8.7
Potosí	8.3	8.6	7.8

Source: Escóbar de Pabón, Situación del Empleo,. *46.*

Battles over Work and Wages

Against this panorama, uncritical leftist MAS sympathizers are likely to point to a series of tentative presidential decrees that have been introduced in the last few years and which purport to increase wages in a variety of ways. These wage initiatives by the Morales government and their attendant contestation through class struggles from below need to be understood against almost two and a half decades of labor flexibilization and neoliberal economic policies—i.e., it is necessary to make up significant lost ground for labor.[84] Studies conducted by economists and sociologists from the Centro de estudios para el desarrollo laboral y agrario (Center for Labor and Agrarian Development Studies) indicate that while the nominal increase in the national minimum salary was 10 percent annually between 2006 and 2010, in real terms the increase amounted to less than 2 percent per annum. Moreover, while there was indeed this small increase in real salaries over the Morales period, it is necessary to highlight three caveats. First, the rate of exploitation of workers—the intensity of work and the correspondent level of surplus value extracted from workers—had increased by almost 5 percent annually over the same period. Second, the share of national income taken home by workers, having dropped consistently over the 2000s, continued to do so under Morales, from 30.1 to 24.6 percent in 2006, to 24.7 percent in 2007, and to 23.7 percent in 2008. Third, the new national minimum salary announced on May 1, 2010, amounts to only 46 percent of a family's basic food basket.[85] In other words, the new minimum levels continued to guarantee poverty wages.

In addition to the various wage decrees issued by the president between 2006 and 2010, a number of proposed changes to the General Labor Law were made public by the government in early 2010. Most significant were proposals around a new Código del Trabajo, or Labor Code, and a new Ley de la Servidora y Servidor Público, or Public Service Law. The proposed modifications to the General Labor Law envisioned in the new Labor Code proposal have been contested by a number of different unions. The changes, critics suggest, would exclude from protection agricultural workers and those employed in urban micro-enterprises. In terms of the public service initiative, critics argue that, if enacted, the reforms would open the door to imposing fidelity to the government as a condition for maintaining employment in the public service. They would also allow for potentially greater restrictions on the right to strike and to unionize in the public sector, as well as facilitate more forceful penalization of other protest measures of civil disobedience commonly practiced by the labor movement in Bolivia. A final concern being raised by unions has to do with what they suggest would be the increased ability of the state to finance unions and therefore restrict their independence, i.e., the "statization" of formerly militant, independent trade unions.[86]

These proposed changes to labor law, and the generalized work patterns of precariousness, flexibilization, and inadequate wages adjustments, have intensified class struggles from below in the last two years, but particularly since the global economic crisis began to have an impact in the Bolivian context in late 2008. Two exemplary set of conflicts will act as reference points here for developing a clearer picture of trends developing across different parts of the country. They should also be understood as potential signs of the sort of resistance that is likely to emerge in coming months and years. Despite vehement denial by uncritical government loyalists, the appearance of incipient social struggles to the left of the government, defending the rights and aspirations of the popular classes and indigenous majority against concrete realities of reconstituted neoliberalism, encourages the view that the Morales government could very well come under increasing pressure from independent, increasingly radical popular class forces in the near future.

The Colquiri Mine Conflict

A string of incidents constitute the first case study in the Colquiri Mining District in 2008 and 2009. As multinational mining companies operating in Bolivia began to feel the effects of the crisis in their profit margins by the end of 2008, their response was an immediate effort to transfer the costs of the crisis onto their workers. This was orchestrated through reductions in company plans for investment, and, most critically, through concerted campaigns at reducing labor costs. In the zinc and tin mine in Colquiri, run by Sinchi Wayra—a subsidiary of the Swiss giant, Glencore—there were layoffs, modifications of the work system (including extensions in work time to twelve hours per day and twenty-one days a month, leaving only seven days of rest), and a compression of salaries by 15 percent. Many workers were also pressured into "voluntary" retirement, through obligatory collective vacations and arbitrary changes in work schedules, among other aggressive employer tactics. In short, there was an intensification of work (increase in the rate of exploitation), an extension of work (through an increase in hours), firing of workers (especially hard hit were those casually employed in the mines), a reduction of subcontracting to informal workers, and forced retirement measures.[87]

Cecilio González, secretary of housing for the Federación Sindical de Trabajadores Mineros de Bolivia (Federation of Bolivian Mine Workers, FSTMB), and union representative for the Colquiri miners, pointed to the super-profits made by Glencore at the mine over the course of 2008 to argue that the company could continue to produce over 2009 without laying off workers: "In 2008, prices per pound of tin and zinc were US$12.24 and US$1.13, respectively. With those prices these business owners took home extraordinary profits. We believe that the company has the capacity to maintain operations, whereas they now want us to believe that with current prices of US$10.00 for tin and US$0.50 for zinc they are in crisis. As a sector, the workers of Colquiri have documented that this is not the case, that this company continues to have the capacity to produce, "[without taking out its recent losses on the workers.]"[88]

By the end of 2008 the workers at the mine initiated their struggle, declaring themselves in a state of emergency, in opposition to the measures imposed by Glencore. On January 14, 2009, union leaders met with company representatives and the ministers of mining and metallurgy and labor. The eventual settlement, pushed by the MAS government in alliance with the company, was particularly harsh on workers. It established a freeze on salary increases for 2009, which, in effect, meant a reduction in light of accumulated inflation. The conflict took a more complicated turn, however, when in February the government launched Supreme Decree 0016, establishing a new national minimum wage and nominal salary increase of 12 percent in the private sector. The decree was supposed to invalidate all existing salary agreements with which it was in contradiction, including the agreement arrived at in the Colquiri mine. This would have meant, of course, an end to the wage freeze in the mine. Instead of carrying out the 12 percent hike in wages in the mine, however, Glencore failed even to live up to the more limited obligations of the agreement between union leaders, the Ministry of Labor, and the Ministry of Mining and Metallurgy, arrived at in January. In light of the company's violations of these terms, Alberto Echazú, the minister of mining and metallurgy, would only say that it was a "complicated situation." The government's "partnership" alliance with transnational mining capital had placed it in an especially weak position to counter Glencore's pressures in the Colquiri mining district. The miners were ultimately unwilling to accept government complacency, and declared a new state of emergency in early March 2009. They noted the failure of the company even to fulfill the terms of the January accord, much less comply with Decree 0016. The conflict is ongoing, with an increasing number of dissident union leaders and rank-and-file miners calling for the expropriation of the mine and the immediate imposition of worker and community control if the company continues its intransigence.[89]

Working-Class Strikes, Government Intransigence, May 2010

The second example of emerging class struggles from below took place in May 2010. A series of relatively small but nonetheless important sectoral strikes were carried out, and the first call for a general strike was made by the Bolivian Workers' Central (COB) since Morales first came to office in 2006.[90] The strikes were led by miners, factory workers, urban teachers, and health care workers. Low-ranking members of the police force and their families also expressed collective discontent early in the month. The only sector to win measurable gains in the course of the struggle turned out to be the miners, and the call for a general strike call did not mature into mass working-class pressure on the government to deepen reforms. This has led to casual dismissal of the significance of workers' actions taken in May by some on the international left. The dominant account in the mainstream Bolivian press is comparable.[91] A more reasonable assessment might be that these conflicts potentially mark the beginning of growing conflicts from below with the MAS government over the contradictions of the development model it is pursuing and the government's failure to meet pressing social needs of the majority of the population. The events of May also illustrate, however, the ideological and political aggressiveness with which the Morales government is prepared to encounter popular sectors that take a position to the left of its official stance. This is only one piece of many in the puzzle of structural and political obstacles standing in the way of building working-class and peasant independence from the MAS government as a means of applying real pressure for serious confrontation with capital and imperialism, and the beginning of authentic structural reform to the country's political economy.

The conflicts in question began in the week leading up to May Day 2010, always a major event for workers in Bolivia, and also frequently an occasion for the Morales government to announce various social reforms, such as the "nationalization" of hydrocarbons in 2006, or the nationalization of various electrical companies in 2010. The Morales government announced toward the end of April that, this year, the nominal increase in the national minimum wage, against which increases in other sectors' wages and benefits are considered, would be only 5 percent (as compared to 12 percent a year earlier), and only 3 percent in the case of the police and the armed forces (after bigger increases the previous year). The official justification for this position rested on three pillars: (i) that, under the MAS government, nominal and real wage increases had already occurred every year since 2006; (ii) that any increase over 5 percent would cause inflation to rise above prudent levels, even provoke hyperinflation; and (iii) that any such excessive increase would, by extension, cause a ripple effect throughout the market, and threaten more generalized macroeconomic disequilibrium. "The raise of 5 percent is what in reality the economy of the country can bear," announced Oscar Coca, minister of the presidency.

"It's a figure that corresponds with the real capacity of the economy. This is not really about what the government is able to provide, but what the productive capacity of the country can bear."[92]

Unions in various sectors responded immediately by pointing to the above mentioned statistical data compiled by CEDLA, showing only extremely modest real salary increases after four years of the Morales government, increases that are indeed canceled out once heightening in the rate of exploitation is taken into account. On May 1, the first scattered mobilizations were initiated. The Confederación General de Trabajadores Fabriles de Bolivia (General Confederation of Bolivian Factory Workers) called for 12 percent salary increases. The Confederación de Maestros Urbanos de Bolivia (Confederation of Urban Teachers of Bolivia, CMUB) demanded 25 percent, and low-ranking police and armed forces called for 15 percent. Minister of Labour Carmen Trujillo, a former militant in the factory workers' confederation, and Vice President Álvaro García Linera publicly defended the government's position, repeating the line that inflation would grow out of control if minimum wages rose above the limit the government had established. Coca added that the 5 percent position was non-negotiable: "What remains open [for discussion] is explanation and analysis. If the workers had the information, that to increase this salary figure would cause hyperinflation…I am sure they would choose to protect the economy as a whole."[93]

On May 2, the situation intensified in La Paz. According to Martín Ajacapa, a factory worker leader in the capital, the police shot a tear-gas canister through the window of an office building where thirty-five factory workers had initiated a hunger strike in opposition to the 5 percent increase. Enraged, hundreds of factory workers responded by attempting to gain entrance and occupy the offices of the Ministry of Labor, which was situated only a few blocks away. In the process, they attempted to kick down, and then burn down, the front door to the building. In ensuing clashes, two factory workers and one employee of the Ministry of Labor were injured. Police arrested twelve factory workers.[94] Also that day, José Luis Delgado, executive secretary of the Confederación Nacional de Trabajadores de Salud de Bolivia (National

Confederation of Bolivian Health Care Workers, CNTSB), called for the closure of activities in all state-run medical centers, except in the case of medical emergencies. The health care workers' confederation, responding to a call by the COB for a twenty-four-hour initial strike, had joined the teachers and factory workers in their demands for better salary increases.[95] It is notable that the COB made this call because its executive leadership, led by Pedro Montes, had been very tightly aligned with the Morales government since 2006. In Oruro and Potosí, the FSTMB announced that the miners, too, would engage in protests and marches the following day in response to the COB's initiative.

On May 3 and 4, the opening forays of strike and protest activities— small but militant marches, blockades, and hunger strikes—took place in a number of cities. Factory workers and teachers marched through the capital in the hundreds calling for a 12 percent raise. Approximately fifty spouses of low-ranking police staged a hunger strike in La Paz in support of a 25 percent raise for their partners, rather than the 3 percent raise they were being offered by the government. Factory workers in La Paz again tried to occupy the offices of the Ministry of Labor, leading to clashes with the police. Tear gas and Neptunes (agile, tank-like vehicles with powerful, crowd-dispersing water guns) were used against the factory workers. Fifteen workers were arrested, and the minister of government, Sacha Llorenti, ironically an eminent human rights proponent in Bolivia during the regime of Gonzalo Sánchez de Lozada, promised that harsh measures would be taken against the strikers. A female factory worker was struck in the head with a tear-gas canister, falling to the ground and lying in her blood in front of the Ministry of Labor. Workers from the newly renationalized ENTEL phone company joined the sectors demanding bigger pay hikes. Temporary splits in the public face of the government emerged, with MAS senator David Sánchez denouncing Minister of Finance Luis Arce for his public intransigence around the 5 percent figure. Sánchez compared Arce to IMF and World Bank technocrats from years past, arguing that those years of neoliberalism should be left behind. Sánchez recommended that Arce meet with workers in all sectors to discuss the overall situation and to be flexible about the 5 percent raise. Government ranks were quickly closed again, however, presumably with words to Sánchez behind closed doors. Furthermore, the Departmental Workers' Central of Santa Cruz (with a less militant history than other departmental centrals), publicly broke with the national executive of the COB on May 5, and opposed the ongoing strikes and protests around the salary increases, defending instead the 5 percent position.[96]

On May 5, the government launched a concerted ideological and political campaign against the protesting workers, drawing on a deep reservoir of Bolivian nationalist populism. "The president will never take measures against the workers," Morales said of himself, "but there also must be rationality among the workers in the interests of the country." Adding to this nationalist appeal, Morales planted the first seed of conspiracy: "some [labor] sectors appear [to suffer] from infiltration by the right, which is confusing the workers."[97] Meanwhile, key ministers were fanned out across the country to counter the message of the workers. The ministers were armed with stories of inflationary instability and counterrevolutionary infiltration of the unions: Finance Minister Luis Arce embarked to Santa Cruz; Minister of Government Sacha Llorenti to Tarija; Minister of Education Roberto Aguilar to Potosí; Minister of Autonomies Carlos Romero to Oruro; Minister of Justice Nilda Copa to Beni; Governmental Coordinator Wilfredo Chávez to Sucre; Minister of Regular Education Iván Villa to Pando; and presidential spokesperson Iván Canelas to Cochabamba.[98]

The official conspiracy theories concocted by state managers escalated when the COB called, on Thursday, May 6, for a general strike to begin on Monday, May 10, in the event that the government did not respond to the workers' demands for a better salary increase. García Linera intimated that the United States and the domestic right were behind the call for a general strike, which he compared to earlier (authentic) right-wing destabilization campaigns that the Morales government had endured. "Those who have been a part of union struggles know that general strikes have a political content; general strikes are declared to overthrow governments," García Linera argued. He said that right-wing groups since 2006 "have tried coup d'états, assassinations, and now they are attempting [destabilization] from within; the right uses these measures, and I wouldn't doubt that behind this there also could be North American functionaries."[99] Morales, who was in New York at the time, bizarrely told CNN that those union leaders behind the protests were "leaders that come from the dictatorships [of the past], who want to be instruments of neoliberalism, and don't represent all the workers, much less the [popular] indigenous [sectors] or peasants."[100] "They use the language of the left," García Linera assured Bolivians, "but their objective is to strengthen the right, the counterrevolution."[101]

Jaime Solares, former executive secretary of the COB, and now executive secretary of the Departmental Workers' Central of Oruro, responded to the government's denunciations: "No one is demanding...the resignation of the president. We need the demands of the workers to be attended to, and a salary that allows us to live."[102] Ángel Asturizaga, a factory workers' leader, told the press that the workers have "supported [Morales] in the elections, and this is the moment in which he must help the workers. His [5 percent] increase is insufficient for survival."[103] Salustiano Laura, executive secretary of the Departmental Workers' Central of La Paz, angrily responded that "the vice president is the one on the right. If we are mobilizing it's because the salary increase is insufficient."[104] Gloria Ruiz, in defense of the workers' protests, noted that "the struggle of the teachers and factory workers in La Paz appear as a clear workers' alternative from the left, and if there is something centrist populism fears more than anything, it is a mobilized working class."[105]

Organized peasant sectors, however, now led by and large by government loyalists, fell into line with the government's position. The elections to the leadership of the Confederación Sindical Única de Trabajadores Campesinos de Bolivia (Trade Union Confederation of Bolivian Peasant Workers, CSUTCB), for example, was won late in 2009 by Roberto Coarite, a candidate closely identified with the former leader, Isaac Ávalos, now a MAS senator. The CSUTCB, although formally part of the COB, said it would not take part in the strike on May 10. Likewise, the women's peasant union confederation (a part of CSUTCB), the Departmental Workers' Central of Santa Cruz, and the coca growers' federations, all led by masistas, came out against the strike.[106] While thirty-nine of fifty sectors affiliated with the COB supported the call for a general strike, the core social forces involved were the teachers, health care workers, factory workers, and miners.[107] The opening day of the "general strike" was relatively poorly observed, but a march, mainly composed of miners, from Caracollo on route to La Paz (200 kilometers away), began on May 9 with six hundred participants. Hunger strikes and small-scale marches occurred in different parts of the country. The principal cities of struggle were La Paz and Cochabamba. "This is a march for the revindication of our rights," Solares argued, "nobody here is marching against the government; we are mobilizing for a just salary and pension."[108]

Between May 10 and 12 the tide of events quickly turned, as the government managed to split the workers by coming to an agreement with the executive of the COB. This was achieved by providing the miners of the FSTMB with a retirement deal, and isolating, first, the health care workers, factory workers, and teachers from the miners, and then, ultimately, successfully separating the teachers off from all other sectors and attacking them as lone provocateurs and Trotskyist ultra-radicals. On May 12, the executive of the COB, Pedro Montes, who had been closely associated with the MAS since 2006, signed an agreement with the government in Panduro, in the department of Oruro, where the march from Caracollo had stalled for negotiations a couple of days earlier. The government, which is in the process of formulating a new pensions law, remained firm on the 5 percent overall salary increase cap, but pledged to lower the retirement age in various sectors from sixty to fifty-eight, and from fifty-six to fifty-one in the case of miners, in recognition of their lower average lifetimes. Over the next few days, the health care workers would settle with the government as well. Still, more than 150 factory workers across the country continued the sixteenth day of a hunger strike for higher wages, and the teachers continued their resistance. Urban teachers in Chuquisaca, Tarija, and Potosí, in addition to those in La Paz and Oruro, called for an additional forty-eight-hour strike. Factory workers in Riberalta, Beni, occupied the regional office of the Ministry of Labor. The factory workers' and teachers' federations called for a congress of the COB to challenge Pedro

Montes' leadership, accusing him of selling out various sectors by favoring a settlement that was in the interests of the miners exclusively.[109]

From May 12 until the end of significant strike activities on May 22, the government focused its propaganda campaign against the teachers, even while the factory workers remained in resistance as well. The government framed the issue as a moral assault on Bolivian children by lazy, overpaid incompetents. "I salute the patriotic teachers," Morales told the press, those "who don't want to harm the children and continue working." However, a nefarious minority still needed to be dealt with. "In the last few days, a group of teachers with their own interests, and different ideologies, have been trying to harm the children, and the people will see "[it for what it is.]"[110] By May 13, the president was launching his full nationalist-populist ire at the teachers: "I regret that some teachers are enemies of education, and therefore enemies of Bolivia."[111]

There were subsequent clashes in the streets of La Paz and El Alto over the next few days, provoked by the actions of the pro-government, and historically conservative, Federación de Padres de Familia (Parents' Federation, FEDEPAF). In El Alto, FEDEPAF attempted to shut down the march of teachers and factory workers (formerly composed mainly of miners), as it arrived finally from the Caracollo. In La Paz, activists with FEDEPAF tried to violently take over the offices of the teachers' union, and started fights in the streets with teachers that led to several injuries. Slogans from the parent activists included, "We want classes!" and "Lazy teachers get back to work!" Wilma Plata, leader of the urban teachers' federation of La Paz, accused the government of organizing the protests and fomenting "clashes between poor people and other poor people." "The government's objective is to chasten the workers by making an example of the teachers in La Paz," Plata said, "so that no workers in the future will open their mouths and will accept all the deepened and consolidated neoliberal policies "[of this government.]"[112] "Everyone knows that the masistas of La Ceja [the main commercial center in El Alto] want to break up the march, but the government has not been able to because the teacher and factory worker comrades are struggling for a just cause," said Juan Salas, a representative of the FEJUVE-El Alto. "We need leaders in the COB who will struggle for union independence and with the principle of solidarity…because Pedro Montes and his friends have become spokespeople for the government."[113]

At the same time, it was clear that there was dissent among the executive leadership of the COB. Felipe Machaca, general secretary of the COB, was far more combative than Pedro Montes when addressing factory workers and teachers in El Alto on May 16. Here he is eloquently describing the workers' objections: "I have listened to the president and the ministers speak, with much derision, [saying] that the issue of the salary increase is closed. But I would like to see them receive the salary of my factory worker comrades, 1,000 bolivianos [per month], and pay their monthly rent, transport costs, buy bread and water, pay for the lights, stretching their salaries out like gum [to cover all their expenses]…It's easy to talk when you have a free car, a driver, free food, a salary of more than 10,000 bolivianos [per month]; that's living comfortably in a bourgeois, neoliberal style."

Such militant sentiments failed ultimately to tip the balance of social forces in favor of the strikers. By May 23, the strike by the teachers had been quelled. Morales used a combination of conspiracy theory, intimidation (through FEDEPAF particularly), and material threats to divide the teachers, after having isolated them from the rest of the striking sectors. The government pledged to cut teachers' pay for each day they missed on strikes (driving many teachers back to work and preventing others from joining the strike in the first place). The minister of education Roberto Aguilar also repeatedly said the government was planning to push forward student vacations so that the strike would be made ineffectual. Finally, the Morales regime went so far as to suggest that striking teachers would be replaced by scabs, drawn from the ranks of unemployed individuals who had just finished teachers' training, as well as from the ranks of retired teachers. At the time of writing (late May 2010) a "pre-agreement" had been reached between the National Confederation of Teachers and the Government, which promised small peripheral benefits but no change on the 5 percent salary. Sixteen teachers' local federations opposed the national confederation's deal with the government, and three others refused to participate in the negotiations. The only federation promising ongoing resist-

ance, however, was the La Paz urban teachers' federation, from the beginning the most militant core of the strike.[114]

In sum, it would be misguided to conceive of the Colquiri mining
conflict or the May 2010 strikes as a dramatic uptick in working-class
struggle from below. It would be equally remiss to suggest that the
strikes and conflicts simply represent weakly organized social forces
that are likely to disappear from the political horizon in the immediate
future given their resolute failure to affect change in this series of actions. The development model of reconstituted neoliberalism is generating its own deep contradictions, and will inevitably continue to be
conflict-ridden and unstable, with new political struggles, formations,
alliances, and forms of resistance from the left, as well as threats from
the belligerent far right, emerging over time. The events in the Colquiri
mining district, and especially the May 2010 strikes, made visible the
hard edge of the MAS government's current stand toward the working
class. It is now plainly evident, if it was not so earlier, that the government will have to be made to change direction by pressure from below,
if it is to eventually take a distinct path toward greater confrontation
with neoliberalism. It is wholly unlikely that such change will be initiated from above.

Conclusion

There is no reason to believe that in today's context a Latin American
reincarnation of a necessary "progressive stage" of capitalism prior to a
transition to socialism—based on a multiclass coalition with an emphasis on renewing national bourgeois capacities—will end very differently
than the failures of import-substitution industrialization (ISI) in the
past. However compelling the ISI model appears when juxtaposed to
neoliberalism, the myths of the national bourgeoisie ought to be decisively countered both within Marxist theory and socialist praxis. The
tendencies toward nostalgic relapse in the current MAS administration,
and particularly in the writings of the vice president—an orientation
toward multiclass developmentalist coalitions, a renewal of certain ISI
objectives within a reconstituted neoliberalism, and an insufficiently

critical theoretical evaluation of classical structuralism—helps to explain the disappointing failure of the Morales government to break with neoliberalism in any sustained and serious manner. There seems in the Morales government to be an uncritical acceptance of the pessimistic ideas of Heinz Dieterich: "There are no objective conditions for socialism at present. They must be developed in accordance with democratic developmentalism."[115] And to the extent that an authentically socialist project exists today in Latin America, it is only a "politically underdeveloped" and "latent alternative," which "has not yet shown itself capable of becoming more than just the aspiration of small political groupings, movements, and radical intellectuals."[116]

With the possibility of socialism thus set aside for the moment, it is much easier to celebrate a model of development that operates "within a capitalist economy, without aiming to end private ownership of the means of production, the profit motive, or capitalist competition."[117] Bolivia's "Andean-Amazonian capitalism" under Morales, is, at best, a "formulation for an alternative to the present order…based…on strengthening the capacity of the state to capture via the tax system part of the nation's economic surplus and redirect it toward micro and small producers in rural areas and cities."[118] "Though not oriented toward eliminating capitalist competition as some would expect," one supporter of the project asserts, "the newly emerging alternatives [in Venezuela and Bolivia] actively and methodically seek to constrain it within certain boundaries so that society and equity may thrive."[119]

However, today as before, the socialist alternative is not a neostructuralist, or even Keynesian, program that seeks merely to allay the worst manifestations of market trends. It is, rather, "a platform to overcome the exploitation and inequality inherent in capitalism," as the Argentine economist Claudio Katz has recently argued. "It seeks to abolish poverty and unemployment, eradicate environmental disasters, and put an end to the nightmares of war and the financial cataclysms that enrich a miniscule percentage of millionaires at the expense of millions of individuals."[120] The comparatively low level of productive forces and material resources available to most Latin American countries has led some to argue that a progressive stage of capitalism is required prior to a transition to socialism, as the quotation from Heinz Dieterich attests. "But," as Katz reminds us, "it is evident that the impediments to developing a competitive capitalist system in countries such as Bolivia are at least as great as the obstacles to initiating socialist transformations. One need merely imagine the concessions that the large foreign corporations would demand for participation in their project, and the conflicts that these commitments would generate with the popular majorities."[121] Such a transition will never last in an isolated peripheral country, or even bloc of such countries, in competition with the imperialist powers that have so long asserted control over the world market. The socialist endeavor in Latin America therefore urgently demands building toward a "continuous sequence of processes that undermine global capitalism," eventually on a world scale.

If we conceptualize neoliberalism not as a set of ahistorical ideas and policy prescriptions associated with the Washington Consensus, but rather as a "historical, class-based ideology that proposes all social, political, and ecological problems can be resolved through more direct free-market exposure, which has become an increasingly structural aspect of capitalism."[122] Neoliberal ideology is certainly undergirded by a purist theory of free-market economic fundamentals, but this is best understood as a flexible tool kit used to justify the class project of restoring capitalist class power.[123] The extent to which actually existing state policy has adhered to these fundamentals has varied quite widely among various Latin American countries since the 1980s, but it is nonetheless legitimate to talk of a pattern of neoliberal transformation that restructured the entire region, apart from Cuba (which went through its own distinct special period of the 1990s). As it has been suggested in this chapter, the neoliberal project in Latin America and elsewhere has been a failure in terms of stimulating economic growth, but has had wild success in terms of the restoration of capitalist class power and the accelerated redistribution of wealth from the popular classes to a tiny elite. Nonetheless, its implementation has precipitated increasingly glaring social contradictions, and this has led to a popular rejection of neoliberalism in many parts of the world, with Latin America at the leading edge of this resistance. In Latin America, even the parties of the far right must rhetorically commit to overcoming the model if they are to stand any reasonable chance in electoral competitions.[124] Neostructuralism, therefore, is best understood as a tactical response of the ruling classes to adjust to the social contradictions generated by the implementation of neoliberalism in the region while preserving the underlying class project and the successes it has enjoyed. Neostructuralism's discursive innovations operate *within* the parameters of actually existing neoliberalism. Understanding this transition at the level of ideas in such a manner, we are better able to appreciate the extent to which deep continuities in the overarching structures of neoliberal political economy in most of the region persist, and the true weight of the challenges still facing the left.

This chapter has tried to show, in concrete terms, how neostructualism in Boliva has taken shape as reconstituted neoliberalism during the first four years of the Morales government. The development model that unfolded in Bolivia between 2006 and 2010, it was argued, is best understood in the context of the wider debates that erupted across much of the Global South since the mid-1990s in the context of neoliberalism's emergent legitimacy crisis. A new, ostensibly anti-neoliberal consensus has taken shape, one that seeks to facilitate the power of the market through an array of market-enhancing institutions and selective state interventions. While the new consensus, and its particular Bolivian manifestation under Morales, represents a modest push beyond neoliberal orthodoxies, it nonetheless continues to conceal the inherent components of class conflict, alienation, dispossession, and state coercion inherent in the capitalist system. Whatever the pretenses of transnational "partners," as opposed to "bosses," the capitalist state's principal role of facilitating the conditions for the ongoing accumulation of capital has not been interrupted by the Morales government's new development program.

The first year of the MAS administration witnessed many continuities in political-economic policy and structure in comparison to past regimes. These trends were deepened and consolidated on a number of different levels over the next three years (2007–2010), as was indicated empirically on several scales. These observable tendencies toward reconstituted neoliberalism are real and ought to be recognized and acknowledged, even if it is similarly important not to treat them as laws. They are relatively contingent structural processes subject to potential change under altered dynamics of domestic and regional class struggle, imperialism, and global capitalism in the near- to medium-term future.

It should also be clear that, prior to the 2008–2009 stimulus spending spurred by the reverberations of the global crisis in Bolivia, the first term of the Morales government is best understood, in economic terms, as one of high growth and low spending. Government revenue increased sharply with high prices for natural gas internationally and a reformed tax regime, but little of that money was redirected into social spending or job creation. The social consequences of reconstituted neoliberal austerity have included almost no change in levels of poverty and inequality during the years under Morales for which data is available. The neostructuralist innovation of proactive labor flexibility, that most egregious of euphemisms, has found its full expression in the Bolivian worker's precariousness. Flexibility has been reproduced systematically. Such patterns have begun to generate conflict, however, as popular classes begin to confront the chasm between government promises and their lived material realities.

Seven

Conclusion

Bolivian popular movements have been at the cutting edge of anti-neoliberal resitance in Latin America in recent years. Latin America, in turn, has been the region of the world most militantly opposed to the social depravities of neoliberalism. Radical left-indigenous movements rose up in an insurrectionary cycle with a breadth and intensity unparalleled in the Western hemisphere in the first five years of the current century. The popular upheavals of the Water War against privatization in 2000 turned the tide against the previous fifteen years of right-wing assault. This was followed by the ousting of two neoliberal presidents in the Gas Wars of 2003 and 2005, through mass extra-parlimentary insurrections—Gonzalo Sánchez de Lozada and Carlos Mesa, respectively, were tossed out over the course of these street battles. All this laid the basis for Evo Morales's successful bid to become the country's first indigenous president, as leader of the MAS party, in the December 2005 elections. He then consolidated this position four years later, with 64 percent of the popular vote in December 2009, on a 90 percent voter turnout.

This book has sought to provide an analytical framework for understanding the insurrectionary cycle between 2000 and 2005 and, most importantly, its relationship with the political-economic trajectory of the MAS government during its first four years in office

(2006–2010). I have tried consistently to separate image from reality, rebellion from reform, with empirical and historical clarity, and in fundamental solidarity with the aims of anti-imperialism, socialist, and indigenous-liberationist transformation in the country, the hemisphere, and, indeed, throughout the world eventually.

What became clear as the historical narrative unfolded was that the left-indigenous insurrectionary period between 2000 and 2005 did indeed amount to a revolutionary epoch, even if its main protagonists have not yet achieved a social revolution. As politics shifted from the streets to the electoral terrain after the May–June 2005 revolts and the lead-up to the December 2005 elections, we witnessed the common turn toward a dampening of revolutionary possibilities and social movements demobilized as a moderate political party came into office. Those elections catalogued the demise of traditional neoliberal parties in Bolivia and popular rejection of their political and economic legacies. Unfortunately, given its changing class composition, ideology, and strategy over the few years leading up to those elections, the party the masses elected into the state apparatus had moderated dramatically since its origins.

The election of Evo Morales signified an historic blow against informal apartheid race relations in the country, and was rightfully celebrated domestically and internationally as a major democratic step forward for the country. But it was also true, and harder for many to come to terms with, that the MAS had long since abandoned the combined liberation struggle from simultaneous liberation from class exploitation and racial oppression of the indigenous majority. Rather, the party had shifted ideologically and programatically toward a crude model of stages, where a much thinner, cultural decolonization of race relations was promised immediately, while socialism was deferred to a distant future. It should perhaps have been less surprising than it was for many that the first year of the Morales government saw only modest breaks with the inherited neoliberal orthodoxies—circumscribed essentially to foreign relations with Cuba and Venezuela and the IMF, and domestic policy in the hydrocarbons sector. At the same time, while popular movements had struggled for a revolutionary Constitutent Assembly to refound the country, the actual assembly established by the government in 2006 was a poor substitute, indeed more remiscent of the proceedings of the existing liberal congress than a participatory and revolutionary rupture with the status quo.

If the first year of the Morales administration was characterized by steady movement away from rebellion and toward reform, the next three years (2007–2010) consolidated that turn in the form of reconstituted neoliberalism. Nontheless, ideological and intellectual confusion as to what the Morales regime represented persisted internationally and within Bolivia on a number of levels. Conservatives sought the overthrow of Morales in order to restore what they took to be a lost neoliberalism. Some liberal currents, meanwhile, saw Morales as a necessary dam against potential destabilization by more radical left-indigenous sectors, although they remained concerned with circumventing any deepening of the modest reforms introduced by the Morales regime. An eclectic loyalist left, meanwhile, continued to see in Morales a beacon of transformative hope, an embodiment of their aspirations. A critical left, finally, vowed to defend the government against imperialism and the domestic right, but saw the need for rebuilding independent working-class and peasant politics among the indigenous popular sectors if sufficient pressure was to ever be mounted to force the Morales government into sincerely breaking with the neoliberal structures of the past.

The tendency of the political economy over the entire four years of Morales's first term was toward a reconstituted neoliberalism, one that abandoned features of neoliberal orthodoxy, but retained its core faith in the capitalist market as the principal engine of growth and industrialization. From an economic standpoint, this period was essentially one of high rates of export-led growth—mainly based in a hydrocarbons and mining mineral boom—and low rates of spending. Government revenue spiked, but international reserves were accumulated at record levels, while social spending decreased as a proportion of GDP. Budget surpluses were tightly guarded, as were inflation rates. Rates of poverty and levels of social inequality showed little alteration. Precarious and flexible labor conditions have persisted. Indeed, they have even been encouraged in many ways, including the denunciation of workers as "counterrevolutionary" when they attempt to organize independently against these trends and for other improvements in their living standards and working conditions.

The arguments advanced above clearly run against the standard accounts of the Morales government from both the right and the left. Left critics of my position might reasonably ask whether I am not being too hard on the Morales government given the structural impediments of global capitalism and imperialist threats. In the opening chapter I discussed at some length the dynamics of contemporary capitalist imperialism and the unusually wide window for change in contemporary Bolivia under current conditions. This, I hope, constitutes at least an opening response to the first objection. Others might suggest that our priority—especially as activists based in the Global North—must be to defend Morales uncritically because his government represents a resolutely anti-imperialist power in a hostile world, which can only be a good thing. I would like to conclude the book by responding to the second possible objection by way of a cursory glance at the World People's Conference on Climate Change and the Rights of Mother Earth, held in Cochabamba in April 2010.

It was undoubtedly an historic step forward for ecosocialist internationalism to have tens of thousands of activists—mainly from the Global South, and particularly from Latin America—gather in Cochabamba with the premise that the capitalist system is the principal enemy of nature. There are also extraordinarily good reasons to celebrate Morales's vigorous denunciations of the hypocrisy and arrogance of leaders of the key imperialist countries at the Copenhagen climate talks in late 2009. He spoke to the aspirations of the thousands resisting in the streets, facing repression and lengthy prison sentences for civil disobedience in the name of preventing the regularized destruction of the earth's ecosystems. We can celebrate this gathering as an initial step forward against imperialism and for building the incipient networks for an authentically anticapitalist, ecologically sane, and internationalist socialism. At the same time, we must not shy away from the contradictions of what is happening domestically in Bolivia, many facets of which I have traced at length in the preceding pages. We must avoid simply putting our faith in the benevolent leadership of state leaders who pledge a commitment to "twenty-first-century socialism" in international forums.

At the same time that Morales speaks about anticapitalist ecological politics to the international media, his domestic policies reinforce a complex and reconstituted neoliberalism, based on the export of primary raw materials, such as hydrocarbons and mining minerals. In the lead-up to the Cochabamba conference, peasants and workers in western Bolivia waged a pitched battle against a Japanese multinational mining corporation at the San Cristóbal mine. In the month after the international activists went home, striking miners, teachers, health care workers, and factory workers were insulted as counterrevolutionaries by Morales government officials, including Morales himself, along with vice president Álvaro García Linera. The contradictions of Morales's moves to endlessly extract and industrialize raw materials with the "partnership" of transnational mining and petroleum capital—leading inevitably to the exploitation of workers and the dispossession of indigenous peasants located on and around natural resource deposits—calls into question a simple relationship between Morales and ecosocialist struggle internationally. Major social struggles are likely to emerge in the near future as debates in Bolivia unfold as to if and how the development of massive lithium deposits will proceed in the country. Taking a position of uncritical loyalty to the MAS government will likely put many well-intentioned progressives on the wrong side of indigenous peasant and proletarian struggles for justice in many instances.[1] Likewise, in Ecuador, indigenous popular movements have often been pitted against the extractive industrial policies of "twenty-first-century socialist president" Rafael Correa.

This book has offered, among other things, a response to the dominant view of Evo Morales's development project in Bolivia on the international left, a view steeped in romanticization. Predictably, the debates occurring inside the country are much more richly grounded in the real contradictions there than what too often passes for analysis outside the country.

From my perspective, the first priority of activists in the Global

North should indeed be to oppose imperialist meddling anywhere. This means, concretely, opposition under any circumstances to imperialist-backed destabilization campaigns against Morales. But the political situation is too complicated to end our discussion at that stage. Our first allegiance ought to be with the exploited and oppressed themselves, rather than any leaders or governments who purport to speak in their name in an uncomplicated way. For example, we should have been with the Bolivian workers when they were demanding decent wages in May 2010, and we should have opposed Morales on that question. We should stand in solidarity with the peasants and workers who take on the mining multinationals, such as the opposition to Japanese capitalists in the San Cristóbal mine, not with the Morales government on these questions. And, of course, we could proceed with many more examples.

Second, we should be clear that the Morales government is not the only force in Bolivia fighting imperialism, nor does the government consistently take anti-imperial positions. Should anti-imperialists automatically defend Morales, for instance, even when he aligns with transnational mining and petroleum capital against the interests of indigenous peasant communities? To do so is not serious left politics, it seems to me. In such instances, Morales is in fact channeling imperial economic power and guaranteeing a legal environment for their ongoing exploitative practices. This is happening against the interests of the popular classes and against the interests of ecologically sustainable development that meets authentic human needs. Morales does so, it has been recognized, at the same time as he hosts the Cochabamba climate conference, which was an important gathering in terms of building ecological consciousness and organization on an international scale. Our politics must be sufficiently mature and nuanced to understand the importance of defending the best possibilities of initiatives such as the Cochabamba gathering, while condemning the gap between rhetoric and reality when it comes to building communitarian socialism inside Bolivia. The peasants, workers, and community members who recently took on the mining companies through direct actions at the San Cristóbal mine are at the forefront of anti-imperialism in Bolivia, and they deserve our solidarity, even when their actions run directly against the Morales administration. Such adherence to principle, as well as to nuanced, and non-dogmatic revolutionary politics, does not align us with imperial capital and imperial states, which would rather see Morales pushed out of office. We will resist them, too, at every turn.

The hope for Bolivia's future remains with the overwhelmingly indigenous rural and urban popular classes, organizing and struggling independently for themselves, against combined capitalist exploitation and racial oppression, with visions of simultaneous indigenous liberation and socialist emancipation, as we witnessed on a grand scale between 2000 and 2005.

Notes

Introduction

1. See the website of Bolivia's National Electoral Court for all election results, http://www.cne.org.bo/.
2. Instituto Nacional de Estatística, *Anuario estadístico* (La Paz: Instituto Nacional de Estatística, 2001).
3. There have of course been indigenous movements dating back to anticolonial insurrections against the Spanish before Bolivia was even a republic. The most recent revival of indigenous struggle, however, dates back to the 1970s.
4. Bolivia is divided into nine departments, or states. In local parlance they have been separated traditionally into those of the *altiplano*, or high plateau (La Paz, Oruro, and Potosí), the valleys (Cochabamba, Chuquisaca, and Tarija), and the eastern lowlands (Pando, Beni, and Santa Cruz). In the current period the term *media luna* (half moon) has gained political currency as a way of describing Pando, Beni, Santa Cruz, and Tarija. These departments are home to the growing right-wing autonomist movement in the country. The media luna departments are also frequently called the "eastern lowlands" today despite Tarija's traditional positioning in the "valley" departments and Pando's location in the northwest of the country.
5. IMF, Bolivia: Country Report No. 06/270 (Washington, D.C.: International Monetary Fund, July 2006). Available online at: http://www.imf.org/external/pubs/ft/scr/2006/cr06270.pdf.
6. Salvador Romero Ballivián, *El Tablero Reordenado: Análisis de la Eleccion Presidencial de 2005* (La Paz: Corte Nacional Electoral, 2005), 41.
7. See the website of Bolivia's National Electoral Court for all election results, http://www.cne.org.bo/.

8. ECLAC, *Preliminary Overview of the Economies of Latin America and the Caribbean 2009* (Santiago: ECLAC, 2010), 140. Figures for 2009 are preliminary.

9. For example, while the Constituent Assembly process of 2006 is discussed in the first part of the book, I do not engage in an elaborate discussion of the new Constitution, which was approved in a popular referendum in June 2009. This emphatically does not imply that such an investigation is unimportant, but simply that it is beyond the scope of this book.

One: Domestic Class Structure, Latin American Trends, and Capitalist Imperialism

1. See, for example, Bill Dunn and Hugo Radice, eds., *100 Years of Permanent Revolution: Results and Prospects* (London and Ann Arbor, MI: Pluto Press, 2006) and the special section of *Cambridge Review of International Affairs* 22, no. 2 (2009), which takes up these themes.

2. *Human Development Report 2005* (New York: United Nations Human Development Program, 2005), 234.

3. Mike Davis, *Planet of Slums* (London: Verso, 2006).

4. UNDP, *Human Development Report 2005*, 234.

5. However, mining accounted for 13.9 percent of export earnings and continued to sustain entire communities in the altiplano, reflecting a political importance in excess of its economic weight (which is also rising).

6. *Bolivia: Country Profile 2006* (London: Economist Intelligence Unit, 2006), 15, 16, 20.

7. See David Camfield, "Re-Orienting Class Analysis: Working Classes as Historical Formations," *Science and Society* 68, no. 4 (Winter 2004): 421–46; E. P. Thompson, *The Making of the English Working Class* (New York: Vintage Books, 1963); and Ellen Meiksins Wood, *Democracy Against Capitalism: Renewing Historical Materialism* (Cambridge: Cambridge University Press, 1995) on classes as social-historical processes and relationships; quotation from James D. Cockcroft, *Mexico's Hope: An Encounter with Politics and History* (New York: Monthly Review Press, 1998), 194.

8. Cockcroft, *Mexico's Hope*, 196.

9. Lorgio Orellana Aillón, "Oligarquía capitalista, régimen de acumulación y crisis política en Bolivia," *Nómadas*, 25 (October 2006): 261–72.

10. Beginning in the mid-nineteenth century, Bolivian capitalism had as its basis silver mining enclaves. This shifted to tin mining at the close of the nineteenth century and beginning of the twentieth. Later in the twentieth century Bolivia witnessed the growth of rubber, nuts, and soybean industries. The close of that century brought with it a shift to hydrocarbons as the new engine of accumulation, still based on the export of primary materials.

There has been, therefore, a general continuity in the centrality of primary commodity exports in Bolivia's capitalist development.

11. Orellana Aillón, "Oligarquía capitalista, régimen," 265.

12. Catherine M. Conaghan, James M. Malloy, and Luis A. Abugattas, "Business and the 'Boys': The Politics of Neoliberalism in the Central Andes," *Latin American Research Review* 25, no. 2 (1990): 24.

13. Cocaine was also extremely important to the creation of a powerful regional bourgeoisie in the eastern lowlands beginning in the late 1970s, with activities of the narco-bourgeoisie bleeding into the enterprises of the legal bourgeoisie. This important topic cannot be addressed here.

14. Orellana Aillón, "Oligarquía capitalista, régimen," 265.

15. Ibid., 265.

16. Benjamin Kohl and Linda Farthing, *Impasse in Bolivia: Neoliberal Hegemony and Popular Resistance* (London and New York: Zed Books, 2006), 109.

17. Conaghan, Malloy, and Abugattas, "Business and 'Boys,'" 9.

18. Representatives of finance and mining worked with advisors from international financial institutions and state technocrats, many of whom had been trained in the neoliberal economic departments of American ivy league universities. Undoubtedly the most important foreign advisor was Jeffrey Sachs, at the time a professor of economics at Harvard.

19. Conaghan, Malloy, and Abugattas, "Business and 'Boys,'" 14–15.

20. Harry Sanabria, "Consolidating States, Restructuring Economies, and Confronting Workers and Peasants: The Antinomies of Bolivian Neoliberalism," *Comparative Studies in Society and History* 41, no. 3 (1999): 538.

21. Orellana Aillón, "Oligarquía capitalista, régimen," 265.

22. See Guillermo Lora, *A History of the Bolivian Labour Movement, 1848–1971* (Cambridge: Cambridge University Press, 1977); Steven S. Volk, "Class, Union, Party: The Development of a Revolutionary Movement in Bolivia (1905–1952), Part II: From the Chaco War to 1952," *Science and Society* 39, no. 2 (Summer 1975): 180–198; and Steven S. Volk, "Class, Union, Party: The Development of a Revolutionary Movement in Bolivia (1905–1952), Part I: Historical Background," *Science and Society* 39, no. 1 (Spring 1975): 26–43.

23. See June Nash, *We Eat the Mines and the Mines Eat Us* (New York: Columbia University Press, 1993 [1982]) on the tin miners.

24. Thomas Kruse, "Transición política y recomposición sindical: Reflexiones desde Bolivia," in Marco Antonio Calderón Mólgora, Willem Assies, and Ton Salmon, eds., *Ciudadanía, cultura política y reforma del Estado en América Latina,* (Michoacán: El Colegio de Michoacán and IFE, 2002), 225.

25. Carlos Arze Vargas, *Crisis del sindicalismo boliviano: Consideraciones sobre sus determinantes materiales y su ideología* (La Paz: CEDLA, 2000), 70.

26. For a discussion of accumulation by dispossession, see David Harvey, *The New Imperialism* (Oxford: Oxford University Press, 2003).

27. Kruse, 'Transición política y recomposición," 228.
28. Ibid., 229–30.
29. Arze Vargas, *Crisis del sindicalismo boliviano*, 45.
30. Ibid., 30.
31. Ibid., 31.
32. María Lorena Cook, *The Politics of Labor Reform in Latin America: Between Flexibility and Rights* (University Park, PA: Pennsylvania State University Press, 2007), 181.
33. Arze Vargas, *Crisis del sindicalismo boliviano*, 32.
34. Ibid., 34.
35. Oscar Olivera with Tom Lewis, *¡Cochabamba! Water War in Bolivia* (Cambridge, MA: South End Press, 2004), 20–21. See Susan Spronk, *The Politics of Third World Water Privatization: Neoliberal Reform and Popular Resistance in Cochabamba and El Alto, Bolivia*, Ph.D. thesis, Toronto: York University, 2007, and Susan Spronk, "Roots of Resistance to Urban Water Privatization in Bolivia: The 'New Working Class,' the Crisis of Neoliberalism, and Public Services," *International Labor and Working-Class History* 71, no. 1 (2007): 8–28 on the rationale behind defining the Bolivian working class in these terms.
36. Olivera and Lewis, *¡Cochabamba! Water War*, 123.
37. Ibid., 124.
38. Arze Vargas, *Crisis del sindicalismo boliviano*, 27.
39. Olivera and Lewis, *¡Cochabamba! Water War*, 123.
40. See Kruse, "Transición política y recomposición."
41. Kenneth M. Roberts, *Deepening Democracy? The Modern Left and Social Movements in Chile and Peru* (Stanford, CA: Stanford University Press, 1998), 62.
42. See Alan Sears, "The End of 20th Century Socialism?," *New Socialist* 61 (2007): 5–9, on the infrastructure of dissent.
43. Walter Chávez and Álvaro García Linera, "Rebelión Camba: Del dieselazo a la lucha por la autonomía," *El Juguete Rabioso*, January 2005, 65.
44. Wes Enzinna, "All We Want Is the Earth: Agrarian Reform in Bolivia," in Leo Panitch and Colin Leys, eds., *Socialist Register 2008: Global Flashpoints, Reactions to Imperialism and Neoliberalism*, (New York: Monthly Review Press, 2007), 217.
45. Carlos Romero Bonifaz, "Los territorios indígenas: Avances y dificultades teóricas y prácticas," *Barataria* 1, no. 3 (2005): 40.
46. Forrest Hylton and Sinclair Thomson, *Revolutionary Horizons: Past and Present in Bolivian Politics* (London: Verso, 2007), 59.
47. Susan Eckstein, "Transformation of a 'Revolution from Below': Bolivia and International Capital," *Comparative Studies in Society and History* 25, no. 1 (1983): 108.
48. James Dunkerley, *Rebellion in the Veins: Political Struggle in Bolivia, 1952–1982* (London: Verso, 1984), 67.
49. Enrique Ormachea Saavedra, *¿Revolución agraria o consolidación de la vía*

terrateniente? El gobierno del MAS y las políticas de tierras (La Paz: CEDLA, 2007), 29–32.

50. Ibid., 33.
51. Ibid., 33–34.
52. Ibid., 34.
53. Pablo Pacheco Balanza and Enrique Ormachea Saavedra, *Campesinos, patrones y obreros agrícolas: Una aproximación a las tendencias del empleo y los ingresos rurales en Bolivia* (La Paz: CEDLA, 2000), 9.
54. Ibid., 19.
55. Ibid., 31–32.
56. Ormachea Saavedra, *¿Revolución agraria o consolidación*, 27–28.
57. Ibid., 28.
58. See Roberto Fernández Terán, *FMI, Banco Mundial y Estado neocolonial: poder supranacional en Bolivia* (La Paz: Plural editores, 2003).
59. James Petras and Henry Veltmeyer, *Globalization Unmasked: Imperialism in the 21st Century* (London: Zed Books, 2001), 139–44.
60. William I. Robinson, *Promoting Polyarchy: Globalization, US Intervention, and Hegemony* (Cambridge: Cambridge University Press, 1996), 2. It should be noted that the brutal occupations of Afghanistan and Iraq clearly illustrate that open coercion is completely operable under the banner of democracy promotion.
61. William I. Robinson, "Global Crisis and Latin America," *Bulletin of Latin American Research* 23, no. 2 (2004): 146.
62. Reed Lindsay, "Exporting Gas and Importing Democracy in Bolivia," *NACLA Report on the Americas*, 39, no. 3 (November–December 2005), 6.
63. Ibid.
64. Ibid., 7–9.
65. On the base in Paraguay see Ben Dangl, "U.S. Military in Paraguay Prepares to 'Spread Democracy,'" *Upside Down World*, September 14, 2005, available at: http://upsidedownworld.org/main/paraguay-archives-44/47-us-military-in-paraguay-prepares-to-qspread-democracyq, and "What Is the U.S. Doing in Paraguay?," *Upside Down World*, August 1, 2005, available at: http://upsidedownworld.org/US-in-Paraguay.htm.
66. The two most ardent anomalies are Colombia and Mexico under the far-right administrations of Álvaro Uribe and Felipe Calderón, respectively.
67. Claudio Katz, "Estrategias socialistas en América Latina," La Haine.org, January 1, 2007, available at: http://lahaine.org/b2-img/katzestr.pdf.
68. Ellen Meiksins Wood, *Empire of Capital* (London: Verso, 2003), 153.
69. Mark Weisbrot and Luis Sandoval, *Bolivia's Challenges* (Washington, D.C.: Center for Economic Policy Research, 2006), 16.
70. Ibid., 11.
71. Nestor Ikeda, "IDB Forgives Debt of 5 Nations," *Los Angeles Times*, March 17, 2007. It should be noted that Table V does not take into account the IDB

debt cancelation because although it was reported that approximately $1 billion in debt was being canceled, the exact figure was still undetermined at the time of writing.

72. Weisbrot and Sandoval, *Bolivia's Challenges*, 7.

73. Ibid., 10–11.

74. Mark Weisbrot, "Political and Economic Changes in Latin America Likely to Continue," ZNet, March 20, 2007, http://www.zcommunications.org/political -and-economic-changes-in-latin-america-likely-to-continue-by-mark-weisbrot?toggle_layout=yes.

75. Weisbrot and Sandoval, *Distribution of Bolivia's*, 11.

76. "Sister-talk: The World Bank and IMF," *Economist*, March 3, 2007, 81.

77. Weisbrot, "Political and Economic Changes."

78. Weisbrot and Sandoval, *Distribution of Bolivia's*, 15.

79. *The Shifting Weight of U.S. Funds in Bolivia* (Cochabamba: Andean Information Network/Red Andina de Información, 2007).

80. Susanne Soederberg, *Global Governance in Question: Empire, Class and the New Common Sense in Managing North-South Relations* (London and Ann Arbor, MI: Pluto Press, 2006), 15.

81. Ibid., 130.

82. Weisbrot and Sandoval, *Distribution of Bolivia's*, 18.

83. "El BCB sugiere que haya un aumento salarial moderado," *La Razón*, April 13, 2006; "El gobierno insiste con las movilizaciones," *La Razón*, September 26, 2006; "El trop técnico para el aumento salarial es 20%," *La Razón*, April 30, 2006.

84. "Bolivia, Venezuela y Cuba firmarán el TCP el día 29," *La Prensa*, April 2006; "El Alba llegó a Bolivia antes de que Morales lo firmara," *La Prensa*, May 2006; "Evo asegura recursos de Venezuela y Cuba," *La Prensa*, April 2006.

85. Miguel Lora, "Evo, Fidel y Hugo Chávez: el Alba y el TCP para integrar la patria latinoamericana," *El Juguete Rabioso*, May 14, 2006.

86. "La Operación Milagro se extendió al Chapare," *La Prensa*, May 2006.

87. Katz, "Estrategias socialistas en América Latina."

88. Ibid.

Two: Revolutionary Epoch, Combined Liberation, and the December 2005 Elections

1. Leon Trotsky, "Results and Prospects," in *The Permanent Revolution and Results and Prospects* (New York: Pathfinder Press, 1969 [1906]), 62.

2. Adolfo Gilly, "Bolivia: A Twenty-First Century Revolution," *Socialism and Democracy* 19, no. 3 (2005): 52.

3. Ibid., 54.

4. Forrest Hylton and Sinclair Thomson, "The Chequered Rainbow," *New Left Review* 2, no. 35 (2005): 42, emphasis added.

5. Ibid., 64.

6. James Dunkerley, "Evo Morales, the 'Two Bolivias' and the Third Bolivian Revolution," *Journal of Latin American Studies* 39, no. 1 (2007): 149.

7. Ibid., 150.

8. Álvaro García Linera, "State Crisis and Popular Power," *New Left Review* 2, no. 37 (2006): 82.

9. Theda Skocpol, *States and Social Revolutions: A Comparative Analysis of France, Russia and China* (Cambridge: Cambridge University Press, 1979), 4–5.

10. See Robert Albro, "The Water Is Ours, *Carajo!* Deep Citizenship in Bolivia's Water War," in *Social Movements: A Reader*, ed., June C. Nash (Malden, MA: Basic Blackwell, 2005); Raquel Gutiérrez, Álvaro García Linera, Raúl Prada, and Luis Tapia, eds., *Tiempos de rebelión* (La Paz: Muela del Diablo, 2001); Raquel Gutiérrez, Álvaro García Linera, Raúl Prada, and Luis Tapia, eds., *Democratizaciones plebeyas* (La Paz: Muela del Diablo, 2002); Olivera and Lewis, *¡Cochabamba! Water War;* and Thomas Perreault, "From the *Guerra Del Agua* to the *Guerra Del Gas:* Resource Governance, Neoliberalism and Popular Protest in Bolivia," *Antipode* 38, no. 1 (2006): 150–172.

11. See John Crabtree, *Patterns of Protest: Politics and Social Movements in Bolivia* (London: Latin America Bureau, 2005); Álvaro García Linera, Marxa Chávez León, and Patricia Costas Monje, *Sociología de los movimientos sociales en Bolivia: Estructuras de movilización, repertorios culturales y acción política* (La Paz: Oxfam and Diakonia, 2005); Forrest Hylton, Felix Patzi, Sergio Serulnikov, and Sinclair Thomson, eds., *Ya es otro tiempo el presente: cuatro momentos de insurgencia indígena* (La Paz: Muela del Diablo, 2005); Benjamin Kohl, "Challenges to Neoliberal Hegemony in Bolivia," *Antipode* 38, no. 2 (2006): 304–26; and Jeffery R. Webber, "Searching for Revolutionary Democracy: Left-Indigenous Struggles in Bolivia," *Monthly Review* 57, no. 4 (2005): 34–48.

12. See Álvaro García Linera, "El Alto insurrecto: rebelión en la ciudad más joven de Bolivia," *El Juguete Rabioso*, October 14, 2003; Álvaro García Linera, Raúl Prada, and Luis Tapia, eds., *Memorias de octubre* (La Paz: La Comuna/Muela del Diablo, 2004); Álvaro García Linera, Luis Tapia, Oscar Verga, and Raúl Prada, eds., *Horizontes y límites del estado y el poder* (La Paz: La Comuna/Muela del Diablo, 2005); Luis A. Gómez, *El Alto de pie: Una insurrección aymara en Bolivia* (La Paz: HdP, La Comuna, Indymedia, Qollasuyu Ivi Iyambae Bolivia, 2004); Forrest Hylton and Sinclair Thomson, "The Roots of Rebellion: Insurgent Bolivia," *NACLA Report on the Americas* 38, no. 3 (2004): 15–19; Hylton and Thomson, "The Chequered Rainbow," 43; Kohl and Farthing, *Impasse in Bolivia;* Pablo Mamani Ramírez, *El rugir de las multitudes: La fuerza de los levantamientos indígenas en Bolivia/Qullasuyu* (La Paz: Aruwiyiri, 2004); Raúl Prada Alcoreza, *Largo octubre* (La Paz:

Plural, 2004); and Raúl Zibechi, *Dispersar el poder: Los movimientos como poderes antiestatales* (La Paz: Textos rebeldes, 2006).

13. Pablo Stefanoni and Hervé Do Alto, *Evo Morales de la coca al Palacio: Una oportunidad para la izquierda indígena* (La Paz: Malatesta, 2006), 17.

14. Salvador Romero Ballivián, *El Tablero Reordenado: Análisis de la Elección Presidencial de 2005*, (La Paz: Corte Nacional Electoral, 2006), 49–50.

15. Ibid., 52–53.

16. Ibid., 50–54.

17. Forrest Hylton, "The Landslide in Bolivia," *New Left Review* II, 37 (January–February), 2006, 69.

18. Romero Ballivián, *El Tablero Reordenado*, 56.

19. Stefanoni and Do Alto, *Evo Morales de la coca al Palacio*, 101. I have often been told by right-wing, middle- and upper-class mestizo Bolivians of Morales's alleged weaknesses in reading, writing, and arithmetic. It was assumed in these conversations that I would draw the obvious conclusion: Evo's not "presidential" material.

20. Stefanoni and Do Alto, *Evo Morales de la coca al Palacio*, 100.

21. See Shirley Orozco Ramírez, "Historia del Movimiento al Socialismo (MAS): Trayectoria política e ideológica," *Barataria* 1, (2005): 17; Pablo Stefanoni, "MAS-IPSP: la emergencia del nacionalismo plebeyo," *Observatorio Social de América Latina* 4 (2003): 57–68; Lesley Gill, *The School of the Americas: Military Training and Political Violence in the Americas* (Durham and London: Duke University Press, 2004), 163–78.

22. Stefanoni and Do Alto, *Evo Morales de la coca al Palacio*, 39; James Petras, "Latin America: The Resurgence of the Left," *New Left Review* 1, no. 223 (1997): 26–29.

23. Orozco Ramírez, "Historia del Movimiento al Socialismo," 17–19; and Sanabria, "Consolidating States, Restructuring Economies."

24. Stefanoni and Do Alto, *Evo Morales de la coca al Palacio*, 51.

25. Orozco Ramírez, "Historia del Movimiento al Socialismo," 20–21.

26. Stefanoni and Do Alto, *Evo Morales de la coca al Palacio*, 57.

27. In attendance were the Central Sindical de Trabajadores Campesinos de Bolivia (CSUTCB), the Confederación de Colonizadores (CSCB), the Central Indígena del Oriente Boliviano (CIDOB), and the Federación Nacional de Mujeres Campesinas de Bolivia – Bartolina Sisa (FNMCB-BS), among other indigenous peasant organizations.

28. Orozco Ramírez, "Historia del Movimiento al Socialismo," 17–18.

29. Stefanoni and Do Alto, *Evo Morales de la coca al Palacio*, 61.

30. Donna Lee Van Cott, *From Movements to Parties in Latin America: The Evolution of Ethnic Politics* (Cambridge: Cambridge University Press, 2005), 86.

31. Robert Albro, "The Indigenous in the Plural in Bolivian Oppositional Politics," *Bulletin of Latin American Research* 24, no. 4 (2005): 440–41.

32. Stefanoni and Do Alto, *Evo Morales de la coca al Palacio*, 64–69.

33. Hylton and Thomson, "The Chequered Rainbow," 43.

34. Albro, "The Indigenous in the Plural in Bolivian Oppositional Politics," 444–46.

35. Stefanoni and Do Alto, *Evo Morales de la coca al Palacio*, 53–56.

36. Orozco Ramírez, "Historia del Movimiento al Socialismo," 20.

37. Álvaro García Linera, "Indianismo y marxismo: El desencuentro de dos razones revolucionarias," *Barataria* 1 (2005): 13.

38. Orellana Aillón "Oligarquía capitalista, régimen," 25.

39. Aresenio Álvarez, "El patrimonio de los ministros de Evo," *El Juguete Rabioso*, February 12, 2006.

40. García Linera was born in Cochabamba in 1962, and trained as a mathematician while in university in Mexico. Upon returning to Bolivia he participated in the short-lived Ejército Guerrillero Túpaj Katari (Túpaj Katari Guerrilla Army, EGTK), as a consequence of which he spent five years in jail, between 1992 and 1997. He was never charged and was tortured while imprisoned. Upon his release he became a sociology professor at the main public university in La Paz, a prolific writer on political affairs and social movements, and one of the most important TV personalities of the 2000s, perpetually making the rounds of the evening news programs and talk shows.

41. Álvaro García Linera, "El capitalismo andino-amazónico," *Le Monde Diplomatique*, edición boliviana, January 2006.

42. Fernando Molina, *Evo Morales y el retorno de la izquierda nacionalista: Trayectoria de las ideologías antiliberales a través de la historia contemporánea de Bolivia* (La Paz: Eureka, 2006), 127.

43. Álvaro García Linera, "El Evismo: Lo nacional-popular en acción," *El Juguete Rabioso*, April 2, 2006.

Three: Neoliberal Continuities, the Autonomist Right, and the Political Economy of Indigenous Struggle

1. As discussed in Chapters 1 and 2, the promotion of so-called Andean-Amazonian capitalism is a central item in the government's agenda. The phrase was coined by Vice President Álvaro García Linera.

2. Miguel Zubieta, executive secretary of the Federación Sindical de Trabajadores Mineros de Bolivia (Union Federation of Mine Workers of Bolivia, FSTMB), speaking at a public forum at the Universidad Mayor de San Andrés (UMSA) in La Paz in 2005. I recorded and transcribed his intervention.

3. Álvaro García Linera, personal interview, April 10, 2005, La Paz. The interview took place prior to García Linera becoming vice-presidential candidate, or even a member, of the MAS.

4. See John Saul, *The Next Liberation Struggle: Capitalism, Socialism and De-*

mocracy in Southern Africa (New York: Monthly Review Press, 2005).

5. See Charles R. Hale, "Does Multiculturalism Menace? Governance, Cultural Rights and the Politics of Identity in Guatemala," *Journal of Latin American Studies* 34, no. 3 (2002): 485–524; Charles R. Hale, "Rethinking Indigenous Politics in the Era of the 'Indio Permitido,'" *NACLA Report on the Americas* 38, no. 2 (2004): 16–21; Charles R. Hale, *Más Que un Indio (More Than an Indian): Racial Ambivalence and Neoliberal Multiculturalism in Guatemala* (Santa Fe, NM: SAR Press, 2006); and Nancy Grey Postero, *Now We Are Citizens: Indigenous Politics in Postmulticultural Bolivia* (Stanford, CA: Stanford University Press, 2006).

6. For the most thorough theoretical development of the position with which the MAS can be closely associated, see Álvaro García Linera, *Estado multinacional: una propuesta democrática y pluralista para la extinción de la exclusion de las naciones indias* (La Paz: Malatesta, 2005).

7. See Pablo Stefanoni, "Panorama preelectoral: Entre la utopia y la realpolitik," *Le Monde Diplomatique*, November 2005; Maurice Lemoine, "Bolivia: An Election for Change and Promise," *Le Monde Diplomatique*, November 2005; Atilio Borón, "La encrucijada boliviana," *Rebelión*, December 28, 2005; Hervé Do Alto and Pablo Stefanoni, "La Asamblea Constituyente: entre la utopía y el desencanto," *Viento Sur,* no. 88 (2006).

8. *Legitimando el orden neoliberal: 100 días de Evo Morales* (La Paz: CEDLA 2006), 6.

9. "Entrevista: 'El BCB tiene $US2.200 millones en reservas,'" *La Razón,* May 7, 2006; "Luis Arce Catacora, ministro de Hacienda habla sobre el buen momento por el que pasan las cuentas fiscales del país y sobre sus perspectivas," *La Razón,* May 7, 2006.

10. "Evo garantiza estabilidad y recibe respaldo de la banca," *La Prensa,* May 10, 2006.

11. CEDLA, *Legitimando el orden neoliberal,* 3.

12. *Informe de Política Monetaria* (La Paz: Banco Central de Bolivia, 2006); "El BCB sugiere que haya un aumento salarial moderado," *La Razón,* April 13, 2006.

13. "El trop técnico para el aumento salarial es 20%," *La Razón,* April 30, 2006.

14. "Expectativa por el salario," *La Razón,* May 4, 2006.

15. "A Year of Evo Morales: Economist Intelligence Unit Briefing," Economist Intelligence Unit, February 2, 2007.

16. A basic tenet of neoliberal capitalist regulation maintained its weight in the new administration: that is, according to the monetarist economics that underpins neoliberalism, an increase in salaries augments the supply of money chasing after commodities. Prices therefore increase, threatening an inflationary cycle, which, in turn, places macroeconomic stability at risk. What neoliberal ideology mystifies are the social relations of exploitation embedded in this dynamic. The structural institutional stability underlying neolib-

eral policies is at base founded on the super-exploitaiton of the working class whose demands for salary increases must be perpetually held at bay. See Orellana Aillón, "Oligarquía capitalista, régimen," 18.

17. Ministry of Planning and Development, *Plan Nacional de Desarrollo 2006–2010* (La Paz: Ministerio de Planificación de Desarrollo, 2006).

18. Orellana Aillón, "Oligarquía capitalista, régimen," 31–34.

19. Ibid., 20.

20. Ibid., 34.

21. Susan Spronk, "A Movement Toward or Beyond 'Statism'?" Socialist Project E-Bulletin, no. 47 (March 2007).

22. Given that Bolivia witnessed the most organized and radical urban and rural insurrections in all of Latin America in the early twenty-first century, it was impossible for Morales to capitulate entirely and immediately to the domestic and international social forces aligned behind neoliberalism in the country.

23. See Walter Chávez, "Un recorrido histórico: Las luchas por la autonomía cruceña," *Barataria* 1, no. 3 (2005): 60–65.

24. EIU, *Bolivia: Country Profile 2006*, 28–30.

25. Carlos Villegas Quiroga, *Privatización de la industria petrolera en Bolivia: Trayectoria y efectos tributarios* (La Paz: FOBOMADE/CIDES-UMSA/Diakona/ CEDLA, 2004), 35–39.

26. Derrick Hindery, "Social and Environmental Impacts of World Bank/IMF-Funded Economic Restructuring in Bolivia: An Analysis of Enron and Shell's Hydrocarbon Projects," *Singapore Journal of Tropical Geography* 25, no. 3 (2004): 288–91.

27. Claire McGuigan, *The Benefits of FDI: Is Foreign Investment in Bolivia's Oil and Gas Delivering?* (La Paz: Christian Aid and CEDLA, 2007), 23.

28. Kohl and Farthing, *Impasse in Bolivia*, 120.

29. Hindery, "Social and Environmental," 282.

30. Kohl and Farthing, *Impasse in Bolivia*, 98.

31. McGuigan, *Benefits of FDI*, 35.

32. Ibid., 31.

33. Kohl and Farthing, *Impasse in Bolivia*, 112.

34. McGuigan, *Benefits of FDI*, 38–49.

35. Ibid., 52.

36. EIU, *Bolivia: Country Profile 2006*, 29.

37. "Todas las petroleras firman y aceptan pagar 82% al Estado," *La Razón,* October 29, 2006.

38. Raúl Zibechi, "Evo Morales' First Year," in *America's Program Report* (Washington, D.C.: Americas Program Report: IRC Americas, 2007), 1.

39. Aaron Luoma and Gretchen Gordon, "Turning Gas into Development in Bolivia: Will Evo Morales' Attempt at Re-nationalization Bring Real Change?," *Dollars & Sense,* November–December 2006.

40. "Evo Morales logra $US144 millones adicionales al año por la venta de gas a Brasil," *La Razón*, February 15, 2007.

41. Observatorio Boliviano de Industrias Extractivas (OBIE), "El patrón primario-exportador: Contratos que consolidan la vieja política neoliberal," *El Obervador*, December 2006, 1.

42. Ibid., 2.

43. Ibid.

44. Ibid.

45. "Alcance de los nuevos contratos petroleros," *Bolivia Press*, December 27, 2006.

46. Observatorio Boliviano de Industrials Extractivas (OBIE), "El patrón primario-exportador," 4.

47. Zibechi, "Evo Morales' First Year," 1.

48. Gualberto Choque, executive secretary of the Federación Única Departamental de Campesinos Trabajadores de La Paz, Tupaj Katari (Departmental Federation of Peasant Workers of La Paz – Túpaj Katari, FUDCTLP-TK), speaking at an Emergency Assembly of the Federación de Juntas Vecinales de El Alto (Federation of Neighborhood Councils of El Alto, FEJUVE-El Alto) on May 27, 2005. This was near the apogee of the insurrection of May–June 2005. President Carlos Mesa was forced to resign following the occupation of La Paz by five hundred thousand demonstrators on June 6, 2005. I tape-recorded and transcribed Choque's intervention at the FEJUVE assembly.

49. See José Luis Martínez and Pablo Stefanoni, *Movimientos sociales y asamblea constituyente* (La Paz: Cuadernos de Pulso, 2005); René Orellana H., "Asamblea Constituyente: Inventorio de propuestas campesino-indígenas, sus características y procedimientos," in *Participación Política, Democracia y Movimientos Indígenas en Los Andes*, ed. Rubén Vargas (Lima: Instituto Francés de Estudios Andinos [IFEA], 2005); Pablo Regalsky, "Bolivia indígena y campesina: una larga marcha para liberar sus territorios y un contexto para el gobierno de Evo Morales," *Herramienta*, no. 31 (2006).

50. Raúl Prada, "De la Constituyente a la *Desconstituyente*: Un proceso histórico a punto de frustrarse," *El Juguete Rabioso*, March 19, 2006.

51. Olivera and Lewis, ¡*Cochabamba! Water War in Bolivia*, 136, 137, 139.

52. For insights into how the MAS has in some ways modeled its top-down, controlling relationship with popular movements on the Movimiento Nacionalista Revolucionario (Revolutionary Nationalist Movement, MNR), which in turn modeled itself on the old Partido Institucional Revolucionario (Institutional Revolutionary Party) of Mexico, see, Jeffery R. Webber, "Bolivian Horizons: An Interview with Historian Sinclair Thomson," ZNet, December 13, 2007, http://www.zcommunications.org/bolivian-horizons-an-interview-with-historian-sinclair-thomson-by-jeffery-r-webber.

53. Dunia Mokrani and Raquel Gutiérrez, *The Hidden Politics of Bolivia's Constituent Assembly Process* (Silver City, NM: International Relations Center,

September 2006), 1.

54. See Miguel Lora, "La Asamblea Constituyente no irá más allá de la reforma," *El Juguete Rabioso*, March 19, 2006; Miguel Lora, "Los duelos regionales para la constituyente," *El Juguete Rabioso*, April 23, 2006; "El Alba llegó a Bolivia antes de que Morales lo firmara," *La Prensa*, May 9, 2006; "Las claves para saber qué es y qué hará la Asamblea Constituyente," *La Razón*, April 16, 2006; Pablo Regalsky, "¿Autonomías departamentales? Territorios indígenas originarios campesinos y democracia municipal," *Bolpress*, March 4, 2006.

55. Mokrani and Gutiérrez, *Hidden Politics of Bolivia's*, 2.

56. Ibid., 3.

57. For further information on how these extra-parliamentary maneuverings of the Right unfolded, see Jeffery R. Webber, "Dynamite in the Mines and Bloody Urban Clashes: Contradiction, Conflict and the Limits of Reform in Bolivia's Movement Towards Socialism," *Socialist Studies/Études Socialistes* 4, no. 1 (2008): 79–117.

58. Geographically, the positioning of these four departments resembles the crescent shape of a half moon, beginning in the northwestern tip of the Pando and arching around east before returning to Tarija in the south-center of the country.

59. Kent Eaton, "Backlash in Bolivia: Regional Autonomy as a Reaction against Indigenous Mobilization," *Politics and Society* 35, no. 1 (2007): 73.

60. Ibid.

61. Lora, "La Asamblea Constituyente."

62. Eaton, "Backlash in Bolivia," p. 77.

63. Dunkerley, *Rebellion in the Veins*, 219.

64. Eaton, "Backlash in Bolivia," 74.

65. Lesley Gill, *Peasants, Entrepreneurs and Social Change: Frontier Development and Lowland Bolivia* (Boulder, CO: Westview Press, 1987).

66. Eaton, "Backlash in Bolivia," 77.

67. Ada Vanía Sandóval Arenas, "El problema agrario en el oriente boliviano," *Le Monde Diplomatique*, edición boliviana, January 2005.

68. Chávez and García Linera, "Rebelión, Camba: Del dieselazo" 65.

69. César Rojas Ríos, "La sociedad abidextra," *La Prensa*, January 23, 2005.

70. Personal interview, July 14, 2005, Santa Cruz.

71. Recall that 62 percent of the Bolivian population self-identify as indigenous. In the departments of the media luna, the figures of self-identification are lower than elsewhere in the country: Santa Cruz, 37 percent; Pando, 16 percent; Tarija, 20 percent; Beni, 33 percent. In the other five departments the figures are higher: Chuquisaca, 66 percent; Cochabamba, 74 percent; La Paz, 77 percent; Oruro, 74 percent; and Potosí, 84 percent. See Van Cott, *From Movements to Parties*, 51.

72. Kathleen Lowrey, "*Bolivia Multiétnico y Pluricultural* Ten Years Later: White

Separatism in the Bolivian Lowlands," *Latin American and Caribbean Ethnic Studies* 1, no. 1 (2006): 66.

73. Personal interview, July 11, 2005, Santa Cruz.

74. Eaton, "Backlash in Bolivia," 74.

75. Ibid., 86–89.

76. Romero Bonifaz, "Los territorios indígenas," 44; Miguel Lora, "Hacendados armados en el norte de Santa Cruz," *El Juguete Rabioso*, May 15, 2005. It is important to highlight the presence of paramilitary developments in Bolivia without exaggerating their current stature. The situation in Bolivia is simply not comparable, for example, to the horrors of paramilitary terror in Colombia; see Forrest Hylton, *Evil Hour in Colombia* (London: Verso, 2006), 69.

77. Zibechi, "Evo Morales' First Year," 2.

78. Chávez and García Linera "Rebelión, Camba: Del dieselazo."

79. See Part II.

80. See Jeffery R. Webber, "'Agenda de Octubre' or 'Agenda de Enero'? The Rebellion in Bolivia," *Against the Current*, no. 115 (2005): 13–16.

81. Eaton, "Backlash in Bolivia," 84.

82. Félix Patzi is a preeminent Aymara sociologist and activist who lives in El Alto and teaches at the Universidad Mayor de San Andrés in La Paz. He was Morales's first education minister, but was soon driven from the ministry for proposing a whole series of radical reforms to education policy. This quotation is drawn from a public talk he delivered at the anarchist-feminist group Mujeres Creando's (Women Creating) meeting place and café in La Paz on June 27, 2005. The talk was titled, "La polarización del país: entre el movimiento indígena y la oligarquía cruceña." I recorded and transcribed the lecture. Patzi's public stature later eroded significantly when he was arrested for driving under the influence of alcohol.

83. "Evo instruye aprobar reglas de la Asamblea por mayoría absoluta," *La Razón*, September 24, 2006.

84. Just as the right-wing opposition to the government of Hugo Chávez in Venezuela presented themselves as the defenders of democracy even as they backed a coup attempt in 2002, the right-wing opposition in Bolivia conceals its defense of the narrow interests of a privileged few under the guise of democracy and the rule of law.

85. "La aprobación al Presidente baja al 52%," *La Razón*, September 29, 2006; "Santa Cruz propone 'un pacto de paz' al Gobierno," *La Razón*, September 24, 2006; "UN y MNR rescatan la convocatoria del MAS para dialogar," *La Razón*, September 24, 2006.

86. "Constituyente: el vice se dobla ante la oligarquía," *Econoticias*, September 20, 2006; "El gobierno insiste con las movilizaciones," *La Razón*, September 26, 2006; "El gobierno no ve peligro de un enfrentamiento," *La Razón*, September 23, 2006; "Los campesinos masificarán su vigilia a la Constituyente,"

La Razón, October 2, 2006; "Los sectores anuncian medidas para la defensa del Gobierno," *La Razón*, September 23, 2006.

87. "La aceptación de la Constituyente bajó 24 puntos," *La Razón*, September 29, 2006; "La aprobación al Presidente baja al 52%," *La Razón*, September 29, 2006.

88. ICG, *Bolivia's Reforms: The Danger of New Conflicts* (Bogotá/Brussels: International Crisis Group, 2007). On the role of ICG as ideological apologist for imperialism, see Tom Hazeldine, "The North Atlantic Counsel: Complicity of the International Crisis Group," *New Left Review*, II, 63 (May–June): 17–33.

89. Andean Information Network, *Shifting Weight of U.S. Funds.*

90. A new constitution was eventually approved by popular referrendum in January 2009. It suffers from extensive ambiguities as well as many of the weaknesses that were predictable as early as 2006.

Four: Dynamite in the Mines and Bloody Urban Clashes

1. "Evo se dobla ante EEUU: dos cocaleros muertos y varios heridos," Econoticias, September 26, 2006, www.econoticiasbolivia.com; "Gobierno acusa a cocaleros de narcotraficantes," Econoticias, September 29, 2006, www.econoticiasbolivia.com; "Los cocaleros de Yungas de Vandiola se enfrentan a Morales," *La Patria*, October 5, 2006; "Dirigencia cocalera dice que no inician el enfrentamiento," *La Prensa*, October 2, 2006; "Dos muertos y tres heridos en erradicación de coca ilegal," *La Prensa*, September 30, 2006; "Un enfrentamiento entre policies y cocaleros deja dos muertos," *La Razón*, September 29, 2006.

2. David McNally, *Another World Is Possible: Globalization and Anti-Capitalism*, 2nd ed. (Winnipeg: Arbeiter Ring Publishing, 2006), 375–76.

3. Ibid., 358, 360.

4. CEDLA, "La refundación de COMIBOL se aleja cada vez más: se mantendrán los contratos de riesgo compartido," *Alerta Laboral*, May 2006.

5. Pham-Duy Nguyen and Feiwen Rong, "Commodities Defy Greenspan Recession Odds," *Globe & Mail*, March 13, 2007.

6. "Evo defiende contrato con Jindal para El Mutún," *Los Tiempos*, January 23, 2007.

7. CEDLA, "La entrega del Mutún: ¿quién festejará?," *Alerta Laboral*, September 2006.

8. Dunkerley, *Rebellion in the Veins*; Nash, *We Eat the Mines*; Sanabria, "Consolidating States, Restructuring Economies."

9. Osvaldo Guachalla, "La batalla por Huanuni y el doble discurso del MAS," *Econoticias*, September 21, 2006 http://www.econoticiasbolivia.com/documentos/notadeldia/minelucha3.html.

10. "Evo destituye a Villarroel y censura el egoísmo del cooperativismo minero," *Bolpress*, October 6, 2006 http://www.bolpress.com/art.php?Cod=2006100618.

11. "Mineros y autoridades se reúnen para tartar problema de Huanuni," *La Prensa*. May 10, 2006; "Cooperativistas y asalariados libran una batalla por Huanuni," *La Razón*, May 7, 2006.

12. "Mineros levantan la bandera de nacionalización," *Econoticias*, September 27, 2006 http://www.econoticiasbolivia.com/documentos/notadeldia/minelucha5 .html.

13. "La presión de los desocupados de Huanuni llega hoy a su fin," *La Razón*, September 29, 2006.

14. "Pushing Tin: Indonesian Mining," *Economist*, March 1, 2007 http://www .economist.com/node/8784689.

15. "El conflicto echo raíces desde hace siete meses," *La Razón*, October 6, 2007; "El Defensor logra un pacto de paz y el diálago se abre en Huanuni," *La Razón*. October 6, 2006; "La Guerra del estaño estalló en Huanuni; hay al menos 9 muertos," *La Razón*, October 6, 2006; "Los cooperativistas piden paz y los asalariados anuncian protestas," *La Razón*, October 6, 2006; "Algunos diputados del MAS propnen semi privatizar Huanuni," *Bolpress*, 2006, www.bolpress.com; "Aumentan a 16 los muertos en Huanuni," *Bolpress*, October 6, 2006, http://www.bolpress.com/art.php?Cod=2006100616; "Evo destituye a Villarroel y censura el egoísmo del cooperativismo minero," *Bolpress*, October 6, 2006, http://www.bolpress.com/art.php?Cod=2006100616; "García Linera sigue apagando incendios," *Bolpress*, 2006; "Todovía no hay acuerdo, una tregua para entrar los muertos," *Bolpress*, 2006; Dan Keane, "Morales Fires 2 Mining Officials," Associated Press, October 7, 2006; "Evo echa a su ministro y pacifica Huanuni," *Econoticias*, October 6, 2006, http:// www.econoticiasbolivia.com/documentos/notadeldia/minelucha11.html; "Quieren ahogar en sangre la nacionalización de las minas," *Econoticias*, October 6, 2006, http://www.econoticiasbolivia.com/documentos/notadeldia/ minelucha10.html; "Bolivia's President Fires Mining Officials after Clashes Leave 16 Dead," Associated Press, October 6, 2006.

16. "Vuelve con fuerza la confrontación política," *La Razón*, October 6, 2006.

17. Dan Keane, "Bolivia Hints at Expropriating Mines," Associated Press, October 7, 2006.

18. "Bolivia: Tin Soldiers," *Economist*, February 15, 2007 http://www.economist .com/node/8706221.

19. Jeffery R. Webber, "Bolivia's Nationalization of Gas! Evo Morales' Historic May Day," Counterpunch, May 3, 2006 http://www.counterpunch.org/ webber05032006.html.

20. "Pushing Tin: Indonesian Mining," *Economist*, March 1, 2007 http://www .economist.com/node/8784689.

21. "Bolivia: Tin Soldiers," *Economist*, February 15, 2007 http://www.economist .com/node/8706221.

22. Olivera and Lewis, ¡*Cochabamba! Water War*; Susan Spronk and Jeffery R.

Webber, "Struggles Against Accumulation by Dispossession in Bolivia: The Political Economy of Natural Resource Contention," *Latin American Perspectives* 34, no. 2 (2007): 31–47; Albro, "The Water Is Ours," 249–71; Willem Assies, "Davis versus Goliath in Cochabamba: Water Rights, Neoliberalism, and the Revival of Social Protest in Bolivia," *Latin American Perspectives* 30, no. 3 (2003): 14–36.

23. "Pulseta entre Manfred y Evo genera violencia." *Los Tiempos*, January 14, 2007.

24. Abdiel Arcadio, "El Prefecto de Cochabamba abandona sus funciones y opera desde Santa Cruz," rebelion.org, January 15, 2007, http://www.rebelion .org/noticia.php?id=44812&titular=el-prefecto-de-cochabamba-abandona-sus -funciones-y-opera-desde-santa-cruz-; "Denuncian la formación de las uniones juveniles," *Los Tiempos*, January 14, 2007; "Gobierno y Prefectura se lavan las manos y el diálogo se aleja," *Los Tiempos*, January 12, 2007; "Comité pro Santa Cruz covocó a 10 mil personas en el Plan Tres Mil," *La Prensa*, January 17, 2007; "Los prefectos huyeron de La Paz," *La Prensa*, January 12, 2007; "Evo sugiere ley para revocar el mandato por referéndum," *La Razón*, January 13, 2007.

25. "Evo echa a su ministro y pacifica Huanuni," *Econoticias*, October 6, 2006, http://www.econoticiasbolivia.com/documentos/notadeldia/minelucha11.html.

26. "¿En puertas una guerra civil? La polarización entre izquierda y derecha cobra sus primeros muertos," *Bolpress*, January 12, 2007 http://www.bolpress .com/art.php?Cod=2007011208; "Las masas movilizadas rebasan a las direcciones masistas y a la burocracia sindical," *Bolpress*, January 10, 2007, http:// www.bolpress.com/art.php?Cod=2007011016; "Bolivia: El Pueblo va por la cabeza del prefecto," *Econoticias*, January 13, 2007, http://archivos.bolivia .indymedia.org/es/2007/01/38868.shtml; "Guerra de posiciones, January 11, 2007, http://archivos.bolivia.indymedia.org/es/2007/01/38612.shtml; Miguel Lora Ortuño, "Enseñanzas de las jornadas de Cochabamba," *Bolpress*, January 15, 2007, http://www.bolpress.com/art.php?Cod=2007011512.

27. Rebecca Tarlau, "Protests in Cochabamba: An Eyewitness Account," *Z Magazine*, January 11, 2007, http://www.zcommunications.org/protests-in-cochabamba-by -rebecca-tarlau.

28. "Pulseta entre Manfred y Evo genera violencia," *Los Tiempos*, January 14, 2007.

29. Ibid.

30. "El gobierno respetará a Manfred a cambio del No a la autonomía," *La Razón*, January 11, 2007.

31. Jim Shultz, "Walking the Battle Zone," *Cochabamba Democracy Center Blog*, January 12, 2007, http://www.democracyctr.org/blog/2007/01/walking-battle -zone.html; "La gente llega a enfrentarse a causa del MAS y del Prefecto," *La Razón*, January 11, 2007.

32. "El paro y la marcha," *Los Tiempos*, January 12, 2007; "Hallan a tres personas con armas de fuego," *Los Tiempos*, January 12, 2007; "Marchas derivan en batalla civil," *Los Tiempos*, January 12, 2007; "Policía está a la deriva y prohi-

bida de reprimir," *Los Tiempos*, January 12, 2007.

33. "Cochabamba vivió ayer una jornada de violencia y luto," *La Prensa*, January 12, 2007; "Jornada violenta radicaliza pedido de campesinos," *Los Tiempos*, January 12, 2007; "Sangrienta jornada dejó al menos 200 heridos," *Los Tiempos*, January 12, 2007; "Tragedia en Cochabamba," *Los Tiempos*, January 12, 2007.

34. "El conflicto se extiende a La Paz y Santa Cruz," *La Razón*, January 12, 2007.

35. "El presidente le hablará a Bolivia sobre la situación en Cochabamba," *La Razón*, January 12, 2007.

36. "La prefectura pide al gobierno detener las manifestaciones de los movimientos sociales," *Los Tiempos*, January 12, 2007.

37. "García Linera acusa a Manfred," *La Prensa*, January 12, 2007; "Gobierno y Prefecto se acusan, pese al dolor y luto," *La Razón*, January 12, 2007; "Gobierno y Prefectura se lavan las manos y el diálogo se aleja," *Los Tiempos*, January 12, 2007.

38. "Jornada violenta radicaliza pedido de campesinos," *Los Tiempos*, January 12, 2007.

39. "Tras el cabildo, Cochabamba vivió una jornada de zozobra," *La Razón*, January 13, 2007.

40. "Evo propone revocatoria para prefectos, Presidente y alcaldes," *La Razón*, January 13, 2007; "Evo sugiere ley para revocar el mandato por referéndum," *La Razón*, January 13, 2007; Abdiel Arcadio, "El Prefecto de Cochabamba abandona sus funciones y opera desde Santa Cruz," January 15, 2007, http://www.rebelion.org/noticia.php?id=44812&titular=el-prefecto-de-cochabamba-abandona-sus-funciones-y-opera-desde-santa-cruz-.

41. "Tras el cabildo, Cochabamba vivió una jornada de zozobra," *La Razón*, January 13, 2007.

42. "Los sectores afines al MAS levantan el bloqueo del valle," *La Razón*, January 13, 2007; Pablo Stefanoni, "En Cochabamba la crisis no acabó," *Clarín*, January 15, 2007; "Sectores ceden, pero vigilia sigue," *Los Tiempos*, January 13, 2007.

43. "Memoria de una tragedia que enlutó a Cochabamba," *Los Tiempos*, January 14, 2007; "Persisten los bloqueos en Cochabamba," *Los Tiempos*, January 14, 2007; "Reyes Villa pide garantías y Evo justifica el pedido de renuncia," *Los Tiempos*, January 14, 2007.

44. "Poder Ejecutivo declara ilegal decisión de cabildo popular," *La Jornada*, January 17, 2007; José A. Sánchez, "Gobierno desautoriza decisión," *El Deber*, January 17, 2007.

45. "El cabildo vaciló entre lo legal y el grito de masas," *Los Tiempos*, January 17, 2007. Fernández's position at this time is especially noteworthy because earlier in the conflict he made more radical statements in favor of continued mobilization against Reyes Villa. These distanced him from the leadership of the MAS at the national level. As the conflict wore on, however, it appears party discipline effectively reigned him in to take the official line.

Thanks to Susan Spronk for reminding me of the trajectory of the senator's position in this regard.

46. "Cochabamba cabildo rechaza solución legalista propuesta por el Ejecutivo y arma un gobierno popular," *Bolpress*, January 16, 2007, http://www.bolpress .com/art.php?Cod=2007011615.

47. "Gobierno respalda al prefecto de Cochabamba," Red Erbol, 2007, www.erbol .com.bo.

48. José A. Sánchez, "Gobierno desautoriza decisión," *El Deber*, January 17, 2007.

49. "Sectores del MAS se retiran y el Prefecto delega el mando," *La Razón*, January 17, 2007.

50. "Radicales imponen su 'Prefectura,'" *Los Tiempos*, January 17, 2007. Herradas Lamas was a former comrade of García Linera's in the short-lived organization Ejército Guerrillero Tupaj Katari (Tupaj Katari Guerrilla Army, EGTK) of the late 1980s and early 1990s. Both men, along with other comrades of theirs, were incarcerated for five years for their activities in the EGTK although neither was formally charged, nor did they receive a trial.

51. José A. Sánchez, "Gobierno desautoriza decisión," *El Deber*, January 17, 2007.

52. "Gobierno Departamental Transitorio toma el mando de la Prefectura," Red Erbol, 2007.

53. "Sectores del MAS se retiran y el Prefecto delega el mando,"*La Razón*, January 17, 2007.

54. José A. Sánchez, "Gobierno desautoriza decisión," *El Deber*, January 17, 2007.

55. "Bolivia: Vacío poder en Cochabamba," *Econoticias*, January 18, 2007, http:// colombia.indymedia.org/news/2007/01/55984.php.

56. Laura Gotkowitz, *A Revolution for Our Rights: Indigenous Struggles for Land and Justice in Bolivia, 1800–1952* (London and Durham: Duke University Press, 2007), 164.

57. The Chaco War between Bolivia and Paraguay (1932–1935) left more than 65,000 Bolivians and 36,000 Paraguayans dead. To have a sense of just how massive the scale of death, Bolivia's population at the time was only two million. The frontline Bolivian troops were almost entirely indigenous, the only exceptions being left-wing Bolivian radicals who were drafted and forced into the war.

58. BIF, *Bolivia Information Forum Bulletin*, Special Edition (London: Bolivia Information Forum [BIF], August 2008).

59. For one representative example, see Ángel Guerra, "Bolivia, después de la Victoria," *La Jornada*, August 14, 2008.

60. "Bolivia: Divided We Rule," *Economist*, August 11, 2008, http://www.economist .com/node/11914316.

61. Tom Lewis, "Evo Morales' Hollow Victory," *Socialist Worker*, August 12, 2008.

62. Heinz Dieterich, "Washington y la oligarquía triunfan en Bolivia: referendo ratifica demembramiento del país," *Rebelión*, August 12, 2008.

63. Simon Romero, "Recall Vote Seen as Win in Bolivia," *New York Times*, Au-

gust 11, 2008.

64. "La media luna rompe diálogo y declara paro cívico regional," *La Prensa*, August 15, 2008; "Chuquisaca también para y pide capitalidad para Sucre," *La Prensa*, August 16, 2008.

65. CEJIS, Communiqué (Santa Cruz: Centro de Estudios Jurídicos y Investigaciones Sociales [CEJIS], 2008). This follows on earlier attacks on the offices in November 2007 and the general intimidation and frequent violence meted out against dissidents in the media luna departments.

66. "Evo y la oligarquía cantan Victoria," *Econoticias*, August 11, 2008; Heinz Dieterich, "Washington y la oligarquía."

67. "Evo: Blando con la oligarquía, feroz con los obreros," *Econoticias*, August 7, 2008.

68. Heinz Dieterich, "'Desterrado' Evo Morales en su propia tierra," *Rebelión*, August 7, 2008.

69. Weisbrot and Sandoval, *Distribution of Bolivia's*, 5.

70. Ibid., 6–9.

71. Lewis, "Evo Morales' Hollow Victory."

72. "Evo: Blando con la oligarquía," *Econoticias*.

73. Enrique Ormachea S., "En Santa Cruz la tierra es para quién tiene plata: El MAS y la política agrarian del Banco Munial," *Alerta Laboral*, no. 56, August 2008, 3.

74. George Gray Molina, *Bolivia's Long and Winding Road*, Working Paper (Washington, D.C.: Inter-American Dialogue, July 2008), 12.

75. Tom Lewis, "Evo Morales' Hollow Victory."

76. This section draws from Jeffery R. Webber, "Bolivia: A Coup in the Making? Oligarchs on the March," *CounterPunch*, September 11, 2008, http://www.counterpunch.org/webber09112008.html. The CounterPunch article draws on the September 12, 2008, issues of *La Razón*, *La Prensa*, and *El Deber* (in which all the uncited quotes in the remainder of this chapter appeared).

Five: The Ideological Structures of Reconstituted Neoliberalism

Antonio Gramsci, *Selections from the Prison Notebooks* (New York: International Publishers, 1971), 276; Álvaro García Linera, "Empate catastrófico y punto de bifurcación," *Crítica y emancipación: Revista latinoamericana de Ciencias Sociales* 1, no. 1 (June 2008): 26; APA, "Trabajadores alteños apuestan por una sociedad socialista y comunitaria: Afirman que la Agenda de Octubre no se cumplió," Agencia de Prensa de El Alto, May 22, 2007, http://www.bolpress.com/art.php?Cod=2007052306.

1. "The Explosive Apex of Evo's Power: Bolivia's Presidential Election," *Economist*, December 10, 2009.

2. See Pablo Stefanoni, "Bolivia después de las elecciones: ¿a dónde va el

evismo?," *Nueva Sociedad*, no. 225 (January–February 2010): 4–17; and, on the recall and constitutional referendums, see Pablo Rossell, "El proyecto de Evo Morales más allá de 2010," *Nueva Sociedad*, no. 221 (May–June 2009): 23–32.

3. Atilio A. Borón, "¿Por qué ganó Evo?," *Rebelión*, December 8, 2009.

4. Rosa Rojas, "Arrasa Evo Morales: Gana reelección y el MAS tiene mayoría en el Congreso," *La Jornada*, December 7, 2009.

5. Stefanoni, "Bolivia después de las elecciones," 4–5. For a discussion of the origins and trajectory of the eastern bourgeois bloc, see Jeffery ·R. Webber, "Carlos Mesa, Evo Morales and a Divided Bolivia (2003–2005)," *Latin American Perspectives* 37, no. 3 (May 2010).

6. For the election results, see Corte Nacional Electoral, "Resultados: Elecciones departamentales y municipales 2010," http://www.cne.org.bo/. For the April 2010 departmental elections, the position historically known as "prefect" was changed to "governor."

7. Judy Rebick, "Bolivia Re-invents Democratic Socialism with Indigenous People in the Lead," *rabble*, November 14, 2009, http://www.rabble.ca/blogs/bloggers/judes/2009/11/bolivia-re-invents-democratic-socialism-indigenous-people-lead.

8. Naomi Klein, "Bolivia's Fight for Survival Can Help Save Democracy Too," *Guardian*, April 22, 2010.

9. Borón, "¿Por qué ganó Evo?"

10. Ana Esther Ceceña, "Es el tiempo de crear el sistema del vivir bien y el manantial está en Bolivia," *La Epoca*, December 11, 2009. See also Ángel Guerra Cabrera, "La victoria de Evo y las nuevas amenazas," *La Jornada*, December 11, 2009.

11. Quoted in Hugo Moldiz Mercado, "Evo pide acelerar el camino al socialimso," *La Epoca*, December 10, 2009.

12. For a discussion of the way forward after Copenhagen, see Mike Davis, "Who Will Build the Ark?," *New Left Review* 2, 61 (January–February 2010): 29–46.

13. See Amy Goodman, "Evo Morales Opens Climate Change Conference in Tiquipaya," *Democracy Now!*, April 21, 2010, http://www.democracynow.org/2010/4/21/evo_morales_opens_climate_change_conference.

14. See Jorge G. Casteñeda and Marco A. Morales, eds., *Leftovers: Tales of the Two Latin American Lefts* (New York: Routledge, 2008).

15. "A Passport to Utopia: Bolivia's New Constitution," *Economist*, January 22, 2009; Michael Reid, "Latin Drift: Sorting Latin America's Pragmatists from Its Populists," *Economist*, November 19, 2008; "The Explosive Apex of Evo's Power," *Economist*, December 10, 2009.

16. Diego Ore and Eduardo García, "Bolivia Nationalizes Four Power Companies," *Washington Post*, May 2, 2010.

17. Parts of this discussion concerning intellectual trends in contemporary Bolivia draws on Jeffery R. Webber, "Evo Morales and Bolivia's Movement Towards Socialism: Recent Studies on Bolivian Social Movements and Political

Change," *Latin American Research Review*, 45, no. 3, 2010: 248–60.

18. Only the first two camps will be discussed here, as the book as a whole is an engagement with and, it is hoped, a contribution to the third camp.

19. For a comprehensive review of this literature and my own contribution to the debates, see Jeffery R. Webber, *Red October: Left-Indigenous Struggles in Modern Bolivia* (Leiden: Brill Academic Publishers, 2011).

20. Franz Xavier Barrios Suvelza, "The Weakness of Excess: The Bolivian State in an Unbounded Democracy," in Crabtree and Whitehead, *Unresolved Tensions: Bolivia*, 125.

21. Ibid.

22. Ibid., 133.

23. José Luis Roca, "Regionalism Revisited," in Crabtree and Whitehead, *Unresolved Tensions: Bolivia*, 65–82. On the reactionary demands of the eastern bourgeois bloc, see, among other sources, Weisbrot and Sandoval, *Distribution of Bolivia's*.

24. Roca, "Regionalism Revisited," 78.

25. Roca, "Regionalism Revisited," 76.

26. Alcides Arguedas, *Pueblo Enfermo* (La Paz: Libreria – Editorial "Juventud," n.d.).

27. Roca, "Regionalism Revisited," 78.

28. Ibid., 74.

29. See Frederico Fuentes, "Bolivia: The Real Divide," *Green Left Weekly*, February 23, 2005, http://www.greenleft.org.au/2005/616/35332.

30. Juan Antonio Morales, "Bolivia in a Global Setting: Economic Ties," in Crabtree and Whitehead, *Unresolved Tensions: Bolivia*, 236.

31. Naomi Mapstone, "Morales Keeps Faith with Populism Ahead of Bolivia Poll," *Financial Times*, December 5, 2009.

32. Naomi Mapstone and Andres Schipani, "Bolivia Rejects 'Savage Capitalism,'" *Financial Times*, December 5, 2009; see also Horst Grebe López, "Estado y Mercado en Bolivia: una relación pendular," *Nueva Sociedad*, no. 221, (May–June 2009): 137–150.

33. George Gray Molina, "State-Society Relations in Bolivia: The Strength of Weakness," in Crabtree and Whitehead, *Unresolved Tensions: Bolivia*, 109.

34. Ibid., 120.

35. Ibid., 113.

36. Xavier Albó, "The 'Long Memory' of Ethnicity in Bolivia and Some Contemporary Oscillations," in Crabtree and Whitehead, *Unresolved Tensions: Bolivia*, 16–17.

37. Ibid., 24.

38. Webber, *Red October*.

39. Albó, "'Long Memory' of Ethnicity," 29.

40. The most important are Pablo Stefanoni and Hervé Do Alto, *Evo Morales de la coca al palacio: una oportunidad por la izquierda indígena* (La Paz: Malatesta,

2006); Shirley Orozco Ramírez, "Historia del Movimiento al Socialismo (MAS): Trayectoria política e ideológica," *Barataria* 1, no. 2 (2004): 16–22, 2005; and Pablo Stefanoni, "MAS-IPSP: la emergencia del nacionalismo plebeya," *Observatorio Social de América Latina* 4, no. 12 (2003): 57–68.

41. See Ma. Teresa Zegada, Yuri F. Tórrez, and Gloria Cámara, *Movimientos sociales en tiempos de poder: Articulaciones y campos de conflicto en el gobierno del MAS* (La Paz: Plural Editores, 2008).

42. Jorge Komadina and Céline Geffroy, *El poder del movimiento politico: Estrategia, tramas organizativas e identidad del MAS en Cochabamba (1999–2005)* (Cochabamba: CESU-UMSS, 2008).

43. The influence of new social movement theorists Alberto Melucci, Alain Touraine, Chantal Mouffe, and Ernesto Laclau, for example, resonates throughout the text. Recurring theoretical asides on Michel Foucault in various chapters introduce French poststructuralism, but in their non-integrated form add nothing by way of insight and break up the analytical flow of the material. Explicit sources of American liberal institutionalism are less frequently cited, but the presuppositions of this school of thought underline Komadina and Geffroy's focus on formal Weberian state institutions to the neglect of social class and political economy. From American social movement theory, the authors rely most heavily on the works of Charles Tilly and Sidney Tarrow, whose "political opportunity structure" theses they borrow and merge with the identity and discourse concerns of new social movement theory.

44. Not a single reference is made to the voluminous literature produced by the economists and sociologists working at the La Paz–based Centro de Estudios para el Desarrollo Laboral y Agrario (CEDLA), for example.

45. James Petras and Henry Veltmeyer's *Social Movements and State Power: Argentina, Brazil, Bolivia, and Ecuador* (London: Pluto, 2005) is the main focus in this respect. Ignored are the powerful, if preliminary, analyses of the MAS government by Marxist sociologist Lorgio Orellana Aillón. See his *Nacionalismo, populismo y regimen de acumulacion en Bolivia: hacia una caracterizacion del gobierno de Evo Morales* (La Paz: CEDLA, 2006) and *El Gobierno del MAS no es nacionalista ni revolucionario: Un análisis del Plan Nacional de Desarrollo* (La Paz: CEDLA, 2006).

46. As regards the populist thesis, Komadina and Geffroy focus on brief journal articles by Fernando Mayorga and René Mayorga. For Fernando Mayorga's longer theoretical and historical account of "neopopulism" see *Neopopulismo y democracia: Compadres y padrinos en la política boliviana (1988–1999)* (La Paz: Plural Editores, 2002). For a critique of the MAS from the left, which characterizes the party as "indigenous-ascendant populist," see Jeffery R. Webber, "Dynamite in the Mines and Bloody Urban Clashes: Contradiction, Conflict and the Limits of Reform in Bolivia's Movement Towards Social-

ism," *Socialist Studies/Études Socialistes* 4, no. 1 (2008): 79–117.

47. The peasantry, too, is depicted as a congealed, homogeneous mass, as though there were no class stratification in the countryside.

48. Karin Monasterios, Pablo Stefanoni, and Hervé Do Alto, eds., *Reiventando la nación en Bolivia: Movimientos sociales, Estado y poscolonialidad* (La Paz: Plural Editores, 2008).

49. Pablo Stefanoni, "Bolivia, bajo el signo del nacionalismo indígena: Seis preguntas y seis respuestas sobre el gobierno de Evo Morales," in Monasterios, Stefanoni, and Do Alto, *Reiventando la nación*, 36. Elsewhere, Stefanoni exaggerates the similarities between the state-capitalist developmentalism of the Movimiento Nacionalista Revolucionario (Revolutionary Nationalist Movement, MNR) in the aftermath of the 1952 National Revolution, and the development model currently coming to life under Morales (see Stefanoni, "Bolivia después de las elecciones"). My own view is that Andean-Amazonian capitalism is merely a Bolivian adaptation of the neostructuralist school of economics associated with the thinking of the Economic Commission for Latin America and the Caribbean (ECLAC) since the early 1990s—that is to say, a reconstituted neoliberalism. For a powerful critique of neostructuralism, see Fernando Leiva, *Latin American Neostructuralism: The Contradictions of Post-Neoliberal Development* (Minneapolis, MN: University of Minnesota Press, 2008). For a persuasive Marxist critique of the developmental state capitalism favored by García Linera and Stefanoni alike, see Ben Selwyn, "An Historical Materialist Appraisal of Friedrich List and his Modern-Day Followers," *New Political Economy* 14, no. 2 (2009): 157–80.

50. Stefanoni, "Bolivia después de las elecciones," 16.

51. Personal interview, November 12, 2010, Regina, Canada.

52. Even right-wing candidates in elections attempt to disassociate themselves from the idea of neoliberalism because that socioeconomic model has been so thoroughly discredited in the region.

53. Jim Shultz, "'Evonomics' Gets a Second Term," *NACLA Report on the Americas* 43, no. 1 (January–February 2010): 4–5. On IMF praise, see also, "El FMI aprueba al país y el BID anuncia créditos," *La Razón*, October 27, 2009; "FMI: Bolivia no crecerá al 4 por ciento y requiere mayor inversión," *La Prensa*, October 27, 2009.

54. Economist Intelligence Unit, *Bolivia: Country Profile 2008* (London: Economist Intelligence Unit, 2008), 22.

55. Naomi Mapstone and Andres Schipani, "Bolivia Rejects 'Savage Capitalism,'" *Financial Times*, December 5, 2009.

56. For some background, see Forrest Hylton, "The Landslide in Bolivia," *New Left Review* 2, no. 37 (January–February 2006): 69–72.

57. Luis Tapia, "Constitution and Constitutional Reform in Bolivia," in Crabtree and Whitehead, *Unresolved Tensions: Bolivia*, 161.

58. Ibid., 162.
59. Ibid., 161.
60. Ibid., 160.
61. Ibid., 171.
62. García Linera, "Empate catastrófico y punto de bifurcación."
63. Ibid., 25.
64. Ibid., 25.
65. Due to the fact that none of the traditional neoliberal parties had sufficient electoral support to rule the country on their own, they would negotiate formal pacts between themselves immediately after elections. The most powerful party would assume control of the presidency, while other parties would be divvied out cabinet posts of variable importance, depending upon their strength within the ruling coalition.
66. García Linera, "Empate catastrófico y punto de bifurcación," 26.
67. Ibid., 26.
68. Ibid., 26–27.
69. Ibid., 27.
70. Ibid., 27.
71. Ibid., 28.
72. Ibid., 30–31.

Six: The Economic Structures of Reconstituted Neoliberalism

Simon Romero and Andres Schipani, "In Bolivia, a Force for Change Endures," *New York Times*, December 9, 2009.

1. See, among others, Robert Wade, *Governing the Market*, 2nd ed. (Princeton, NJ: Princeton University Press, 2004); Robert Wade, "Choking the South," *New Left Review* 2, no. 38 (2006): 115–27; Ha-Joon Chang, *Kicking Away the Ladder? Economic Development in Historical Perspective* (New York: Monthly Review Press, 2002); Atul Kohli, *State-Directed Development: Political Power and Industrialization in the Global Periphery* (Cambridge: Cambridge University Press, 2004); Alice Amsden, *Asia's Next Giant: South Korea and Late Industrialization* (New York: Oxford University Press, 1989); Alice Amsden, *Escape from Empire: The Developing World's Journey Through Heaven and Hell* (Cambridge, MA: MIT Press, 2007); Linda Weiss, "Global Governance, National Strategies: How Industrialized States Make Room to Move under the WTO," *Review of International Political Economy* 12, no. 5, (2005): 723–49; World Bank, *World Development Report* (New York: Oxford University Press, 1997); World Bank, *World Development Report* (New York: Oxford University Press, 2004); Inter-American Development Bank, "The Politics of Policies," *Ideas for Development in the Americas (IDEA)*, no. 8 (September–December

2006), Washington, D.C.: Inter-American Development Bank.

2. Ben Selwyn, "An Historical Materialist Appraisal of Friedrich List and His Modern-Day Followers," *New Political Economy* 14, no. 2 (June 2009): 157–80.

3. Greig Charnock, "Why Do Institutions Matter? Global Competitiveness and the Politics of Policies in Latin America," *Capital and Class* 33, no. 2 (Summer 2009): 67.

4. Ibid., 87.

5. Selwyn, "An Historical Materialist Appraisal."

6. Joseph L. Love, "The Rise and Decline of Economic Structuralism in Latin America: New Dimensions," *Latin American Research Review* 40, no. 3 (2005): 101.

7. Ibid., 116–18.

8. John H. Coatsworth, "Structures, Endowments and Institutions in the Economic History of Latin America," *Latin American Research Review* 40, no. 3 (2005): 132–33. Also see Sylvia Maxfield and James Nolt, "Protectionism and the Internationalization of Capital: U.S. Sponsorship of Import Substitution Industrialization in the Philippines, Turkey and Argentina," *International Studies Quarterly* 34, no. 1 (1990): 44–81. According to James Petras and Henry Veltmeyer, "A wave of nationalisation in the 1960s and early 1970s led to state control of the strategic sectors of the economy" across many countries in Latin America. "In some cases imperial firms were generously compensated and many found lucrative new investments. Tariff barriers fostered national industrialisation but did not prevent multinational corporations (TNCs) from setting up branch plants. However, the TNCs generally had to abide with legislation relating to content, employment of nationals, and foreign exchange requirements. The TNCs' direct investments and their repatriation of profits were also restricted, forcing them to resort to subterfuges such as transfer pricing so as to have profits surface in less restrictive economies." Under the national-populist regimes of this period, TNCs were able to "make substantial profits on invested foreign capital and operations. However, in the wake of the Cuban revolution, new and more radical measures were on the agenda of many governments, creating conditions for political reaction. A new class of wealthy business operators and bankers chafed at the labour legislation and the controls placed on their capital, as well as at measures designed to redistribute productive resources such as land. This class turned towards both the armed forces and the TNCs for support in breaking the populist alliance and to secure greater overseas market shares, financing for ventures and access to new technology. Thus was formed the social base for the counter-reform politics and the ascendancy of U.S. imperialism that characterised Latin American capitalism over the next two decades." James Petras and Henry Veltmeyer, *Globalization Unmasked: Imperialism in the 21st Century* (London: Zed, 2001), 76–77. U.S. foreign policy makers were right to be concerned about the possi-

bility of radicalization within various currents of structuralism, as became clear with the migration of various former structuralists to the dependency school in the late 1960s and early 1970s. There is no room here to deal with dependency theory. Suffice it to say that the radical wing of dependency advocated a version of socialist revolution.

9. See David Harvey, *The New Imperialism* (New York: Oxford University Press, 2003); David Harvey, *A Brief History of Neoliberalism* (New York: Oxford University Press, 2005); Gregory Albo, "Neoliberalism and the Discontented," in Leo Panitch and Colin Leys, eds., *Socialist Register 2008: Global Flashpoints, Reactions to Imperialism and Neoliberalism* (New York: Monthly Review Press, 2007); Alfredo Saad-Filho, "From Washington to Post-Washington Consensus: Neoliberal Agendas for Economic Development," in Alfredo Saad-Filho and Deborah Johnston, eds., *Neoliberalism: A Critical Reader* (London: Pluto, 2005); Peter Gowan, *The Global Gamble: Washington's Faustian Bid for World Dominance* (London: Verso, 1999).

10. See, among others, Susanne Soederberg, *The Politics of the New International Financial Architecture: Reimposing Neoliberal Domination in the Global South* (London: Zed Books, 2004); Susanne Soederberg, *Global Governance in Question: Empire, Class and the New Common Sense in Managing North-South Relations* (London: Pluto, 2006); Duncan Green, "A Trip to the Market: The Impact of Neoliberalism in Latin America," in Julia Buxton and Nicola Phillips, eds., *Developments in Latin American Political Economy: States, Markets and Actors* (Manchester: University of Manchester Press, 1999).

11. See John Williamson, "Democracy and the 'Washington Consensus," *World Development* 21, no. 8, (1993): 1329–1336.

12. Greg Grandin, *The Last Colonial Massacre: Latin America in the Cold War* (Chicago: University of Chicago Press, 2005), 14.

13. ECLAC, *Changing Production Patterns with Social Equity* (Santiago: ECLAC, 1990).

14. Marcus Taylor, "The Contradictions and Transformations of Neoliberalism in Latin America: From Structural Adjustment to 'Empowering the Poor,'" in Laura Macdonald and Arne Ruckert eds., *Post-Neoliberalism in the Americas* (New York: Palgrave, 2009), 23.

15. Leiva, *Latin American Neostructuralism*, 1.

16. See Marcus Taylor, *From Pinochet to the Third Way: Neoliberalism and Social Transformation in Chile, 1973–2003* (London: Pluto, 2006).

17. Although these days Chávez also calls for Venezuelans to read Marxists such as István Mészáros, among others.

18. See Osvaldo Sunkel, ed., *Development from Within: Toward a Neostructuralist Approach for Latin America* (Boulder, CO: Westview Press, 1993); Michael Lebowitz, *Build It Now! Socialism for the Twenty-First Century* (New York: Monthly Review Press, 2006), 90–93.

19. Leiva, *Latin American Neostructuralism*, 4.

20. Ibid., 4.

21. Ibid., 6.

22. Ibid., 9–10.

23. Ibid., 15.

24. Ibid., 6.

25. Ibid., 11.

26. Ibid., 11.

27. Ibid., 12.

28. Ibid., 12.

29. Ibid., 12–13.

30. Ibid., 14.

31. Ibid., xxvii.

32. Ibid.

33. Ibid.

34. Vivek Chibber, "Reviving the Developmental State? The Myth of the 'National Bourgeoisie,'" in Leo Panitch and Colin Leys, eds., *The Empire Reloaded: Socialist Register 2005* (New York: Monthly Review Press, 2005), 242.

35. Ibid., 229.

36. Ibid., 233.

37. Ibid., 243.

38. Ben Selwn, "An Historical Materialist Appraisal," 164.

39. ECLAC, *Economic Survey of Latin America and the Caribbean 2007–2008* (Santiago: ECLAC, 2008), 13.

40. ECLAC, *Economic Survey of Latin America and the Caribbean 2008–2009* (Santiago: ECLAC, 2009), 13.

41. EIU, *Bolivia: Country Profile 2008* (London: Economist Intelligence Unit [EIU], 2008), 21.

42. Ibid., 17.

43. Mark Weisbrot, Rebecca Ray, and Jake Johnston, *Bolivia: The Economy During the Morales Administration* (Washington, D.C.: Center for Economic and Policy Research, December 2009), 6 and 12.

44. EIU, *Bolivia: Country Profile 2008*, 22–23.

45. Weisbrot, Ray, and Johnston, *Bolivia: The Economy*, 6.

46. ECLAC, *Preliminary Overview of the Economies of Latin America and the Caribbean 2009* (Santiago: ECLAC, 2009), 92.

47. Ibid., 6.

48. EIU, *Bolivia: Country Profile 2008*, 21.

49. Ibid., 23.

50. "Bolivia: U.S. Suspends a Trade Deal," Associated Press, October 24, 2008.

51. "La relación con EEUU no preocupa al Gobierno," *La Razón*, May 12, 2010; Simon Romero, "Bolivia: President Denounces Obama Over Trade," *New*

York Times, July 2, 2009.

52. Weisbrot, Ray, and Johnston, *Bolivia: The Economy*, 25.
53. Ibid., 13.
54. Ibid., 10.
55. ECLAC, *Preliminary Overview of the Economies*, 92.
56. Weisbrot, Ray, and Johnston, *Bolivia: The Economy*, 25.
57. EIU, *Bolivia: Country Profile 2008*, 14–15.
58. Weisbrot, Ray, and Johnston, *Bolivia: The Economy*, 19.
59. Ibid.
60. Ibid., 15.
61. Ibid., 13.
62. ECLAC, *Preliminary Overview of the Economies*, 92.
63. Weisbrot, Ray, and Johnston, *Bolivia: The Economy*, 13.
64. It ought to be noted here that poverty figures from ECLAC do not correspond with the figures discussed here. The latest ECLAC publications provide national figures for 1999 and 2007, and claim that there has been a downward shift in Bolivian poverty from 60.6 percent poverty to 54 percent poverty between these years. See ECLAC, *Anuario Estadístico de América Latina y el Caribe, 2009* (Santiago: ECLAC, 2009), 65.
65. Again, however, social spending has actually *declined* as a percentage of GDP under Morales, even as it increased in real, inflation-adjusted terms.
66. Weisbrot, Ray, and Johnston, *Bolivia: The Economy*, 18.
67. An analysis of agrarian reform remains beyond the scope of this book, but others have pointed out that in this area, too, reform has been wildly disappointing. See, Enrique Ormachea Saavedra, *Soberanía y seguridad alimentaria en Bolivia: Políticas y estado de situación* (La Paz: CEDLA, 2009).
68. Frederico Fuentes, "Bolivia: Between Mother Earth and an 'Extraction Economy,'" *Bullet*, Socialist Project E-Bulletin, no. 355 (May 17, 2010).
69. Stefanoni, "Bolivia después de las elecciones," 5.
70. Ibid., 14. There is an increasing rupture between the socioeconomic and socio-cultural dimensions of *evismo*, with intensifying class differentiation and stratification *within* the indigenous nucleus of MAS supporters, and one way to maintain the cohesion of the social base in light of these growing contradictions has been the appeal to indigenous populist nationalism. See Pablo Rossell, "El proyecto de Evo Morales más allá de 2010," *Nueva Sociedad*, no. 221 (May–June 2009): 27.
71. James Malloy and Eduardo Gamarra, *Revolution and Reaction: Bolivia, 1964–1985* (Piscataway, NJ: Transaction Books, 1988), 16.
72. Osvaldo Guachalla, "La exacerbación de la política extractivista del M.A.S.: Privatización con fachada nacionalista," *El Observador* 4, no. 8 (January 2010): 14–15.
73. See, for various political developments suggesting an inclination toward this

end, Hervé Do Alto and Pablo Stefanoni, "Las ambivalencias de la democracia corporativa," *Le Monde Diplomatique*, Bolivian edition, May 2010, 4–6.

74. Silvina Heguy and Pablo Stefanoni, "'No hay una agenda oculta: la Constitución respeta la propiedad': Entrevista a García Linera," *Clarín*, December 6, 2009.

75. See Pablo Rossell, "El proyecto de Evo Morales más allá de 2010," *Nueva Sociedad*, no. 221 (May–June 2009): 29.

76. Javier Gómez Aguilar, "Las cifras del desastre," *Alerta Laboral*, no. 58 (April 2009): 2.

77. Ibid.

78. Javier Gómez Aguilar, "Leyes laborales en el congelador, orientación neoliberal en marcha," *Alerta Laboral*, no. 61 (May 2010): 3.

79. Silvia Escóbar de Pabón, *Situación de los ingresos laborales en tiempos de cambio* (La Paz: CEDLA, 2009), 51.

80. Carmen Trujillo replaced Chipana as minister of labor in January 2010, when Morales announced his new cabinet after the December 2009 elections.

81. Quoted in Sivia Escóbar de Pabón, "La flexibilización laboral continúa vigente," *Alerta Laboral*, no. 58 (April 2009): 6.

82. Ibid., 7.

83. Escóbar de Pabón, *Situación del empleo en tiempos de cambio* (La Paz: CEDLA, 2009), 75.

84. See Bruno Rojas Callejas, "Los salarios no alcanzan para 'vivir bien,'" *Alerta Laboral*, no. 58 (April 2009): 3.

85. Arze Vargas, "El aumento salarial."

86. CEDLA, "A favor de capital: La reforma laboral del gobierno atenta contra los trabajadores," *Alerta Laboral*, no. 61 (May 2010): 3; CEDLA, "Neutralización del sindicato y penalización de la huelga: Dos proyectos de reformulación de la LGT," *Alerta Laboral*, no. 61 (May 2010): 4–5; CEDLA, "Tímidos avances y puertas abiertas a la flexibilización," *Alerta Laboral*, no. 61 (May 2010): 6; CEDLA, "El gobierno da un paso atrás: Sectores sociales rechazan la ley del servidor público," *Alerta Laboral*, no. 61 (May 2010): 8.

87. Osvaldo Guachalla, "Crisis minera: Protección al empresario y sobreexplotación," *Alerta Laboral*, no. 58 (April 2009): 4–5.

88. Quoted in ibid.

89. Ibid., 5.

90. It should be noted that the call for a "general strike" is used quite loosely in Bolivian labor movement politics, and for the last twenty-five years it has rarely meant a genuine general strike in practice in the sense commonly understood elsewhere in the world.

91. Frederico Fuentes, "Bolivia: When Fantasy Trumps Reality," *Green Left Weekly*, May 22, 2010; Pablo Stefanoni, "Huelga general indefinida, con pocas perspectivas," *Il Manifesto*, May 10, 2010.

92. "Bolivia: Alza salarial propuesta por Evo genera rechazo y amenazas de

huelga," *La Razón*, May 3, 2010; see also, Carlos Arze Vargas, "El aumento salarial del 'vivir bien,'" Nota de Prensa, CEDLA, May 2010.

93. Confederación General de Trabajadores Fabriles de Bolivia, "Rechazamos el incremento salarial de 5%," Nota de Prensa, April 27, 2010; "Pugna por el 5% se agudiza," *La Razón*, May 1, 2010; "Trabajadores marcha divididas por el rechazo y la simpatía a Evo," *La Razón*, May 2, 2010; "Bolivia: Alza salarial propuesta por Evo genera rechazo y amenazas de huelga," *La Razón*, May 3, 2010; "Policías, militares y COB, en pie de guerra por el incremento," *La Razón*, May 3, 2010.

94. "Policía detiene a 12 trabajadores luego de violento enfrentamiento," *La Razón*, May 3, 2010.

95. "Hospitales sólo atienden emergencia por el paro de la COB," *La Razón*, May 3, 2010; "La COB va al paro dividida," *La Razón*, May 4, 2010.

96. "Fabriles y profesores realizaron su marcha por la ciudad de La Paz," *La Razón*, May 4, 2010; "Empieza una huelga en la policía," *La Razón*, May 4, 2010; "Salarios: Senador del MAS reprocha a ministro Arce y le pide no cerrarse," *La Razón*, May 5, 2010; "El país siente el paro y en La Paz deriva en violencia," *La Razón*, May 5, 2010; "COD de Santa Cruz convoca a una marcha en defensa del incremento del 5%," *La Razón*, May 6, 2010; "El Gobierno de Morales cierra debate sobre salarios pese a las protestas," *La Razón*, May 6, 2010.

96. "Evo reitera el 5% y la COB advierte con cerrar vías," *La Razón*, May 6, 2010.

97. Ibid.

98. "Bolivia: Principal sindical obrera desafía a Evo Morales con huelga general," *La Razón*, May 7, 2010.

99. Ibid.

100. "Gobierno de Morales cree que sindicatos quieren derrocarlo con ayuda de EEUU," *La Razón*, May 7, 2010.

101. "La COB al paro indefinido y el lunes inicia marcha," *La Razón*, May 7, 2010.

102. *La Razón*, "Bolivia: Principal sindical obrera."

103. "García ve a EEUU detrás de protestas contra el 5%," *La Razón*, May 5, 2010.

104. Gloria Ruiz, "¿Por qué García Linera se ensaña con la movilización del magisterio?," *Bolpress*, May 19, 2010.

105. La Razón, "La COB al paro indefinido."

106. La Razón, "Bolivia: Principal sindical obrera"; "Los trabajadores inician divididos la huelga general y la marcha de protesta," *La Razón*, May 10, 2010.

107. "La marcha avanza pese a las nuevas ofertas de Evo," *La Razón*, May 11, 2010; "Bolivia: Evo inicia gestiones con sectores sociales para aplacar conflictos," *La Razón*, May 11, 2010; "Escaso apoyo a la huelga general de la principal central sindical boliviana," *La Razón*, May 10, 2010.

108. "Fabriles rechazan acuerdo COB-Gobierno y anuncian masificar marcha y huelga en todo el país," *La Razón*, May 12, 2010; "Salubristas dejan solos a maestros y fabriles," *La Razón*, May 12, 2010; "Bolivia: Maestros públicos si-

guen protestas pese a acuerdo con el gobierno," *La Razón*, May 12, 2010; "Maestros urbanos exigen nivelación salarial con el magisterio rural," *La Razón*, May 13, 2010; "Evo Morales da por terminada la negociación por mejor incremento salarial," *La Razón*, May 13, 2010; "Gobierno y COB firman acuerdo salarial en medio de protestas," *La Razón*, May 13, 2010; "Dos sectores mantienen su protesta," *La Razón*, May 13, 2010.

109. "Dos sectores mantienen su protesta," *La Razón*, May 13, 2010.

110. "Evo llama 'enemigos de Bolivia' a los maestros," *La Razón*, May 16, 2010.

111. Ibid.

112. "Morales da por cerrado el lío por el alza salarial," *La Razón*, May 14, 2010; "El lunes, el magisterio inicia paro indefinido," *La Razón*, May 15, 2010; "Padres de familia afines al MAS intentaron sede de maestros, hay heridos," *La Razón*, May 19, 2010; "Padres alteños denuncian que son obligados a marchar por fichas," *La Razón*, May 20, 2010; "Marcha de padres de familia colapsa el centro de La Paz," *La Razón*, May 20, 2010; "El paro de los maestros crece y el diálogo tropieza," *La Razón*, May 20, 2010.

113. Quotes from this and the next paragraph are from "Dirigentes alteños: Gobierno no pudo impedir marcha del magisterio," *La Razón*, May 17, 2010.

114. "Padres y maestros se enfrentan en La Paz por huelga en escuelas," *La Razón*, May 19, 2010; "Gobierno y magisterio pactan, pero no tocan temas sensibles," *La Prensa*, May 22, 2010; "Gobierno logra preacuerdo con el magisterio; en 5 regiones lo rechazan," *La Razón*, May 22, 2010; "Los maestros vuelven a clases, pero en La Paz aún hay incertidumbre," *La Razón*, May 23, 2010.

115. Leiva, *Latin American Neostructuralism*, 228.

116. Ibid, 225.

117. Ibid., 228.

118. Ibid.

119. Ibid., 231.

120. Claudio Katz, "Socialist Strategies in Latin America," *Monthly Review* 59, no. 4 (September 2007): 26.

121. Ibid., 28.

122. Thomas Marois, "From Economic Crisis to a 'State' of Crisis? The Emergence of Neoliberalism in Costa Rica," *Historical Materialism* 13, no. 3 (2005): 101–134.

123. See Harvey, *A Brief History of Neoliberalism*.

124. See William I. Robinson, "Transformative Possibilities in Latin America," in Leo Panitch and Colin Leys, eds., *Socialist Register 2008: Global Flashpoints, Reactions to Imperialism and Neoliberalism* (New York: Monthly Review Press, 2007); William I. Robinson, *Latin America and Global Capitalism: A Critical Globalization Perspective* (Baltimore, MD: Johns Hopkins University Press, 2008); Emir Sader, "The Weakest Link? Neoliberalism in Latin America," *New Left Review* 2, no. 52 (2008): 5–31.

Seven: Conclusion

1. For discussion of the Latin American left's relationship to extractive industries, and the lithium debates in Bolivia more particularly, see Eduardo Gudynas, "El Nuevo extractivismo progresista: Tesis sobre un viejo problema bajo nuevas expresiones," *El Observador* 4, no. 8 (January 2010): 1–10; Osvaldo Guachalla, "La exacerbación de la política extractivista del M.A.S.: Privatización con fachada nacionalista," *El Observador* 4, no. 8 (January 2010): 11–16; Rebecca Hollender and Jim Shultz, *Bolivia and Its Lithium: Can the "Gold of the 21st Century" Help Lift a Nation Out of Poverty?* (Cochabamba: Democracy Center, 2010).

Index

Also from Haymarket Books

Class Struggle and Resistance in Africa
Leo Zeilig • This collection of essays and interviews studies class struggle and social empowerment on the African continent. Employing Marxist theory to address the postcolonial problems of several different countries, experts analyze such issues as the renewal of Islamic fundamentalism in Egypt, debt relief, trade union movements, and strike action. Includes interviews with leading African socialists and activists. ISBN: 978-1-931859-68-4

The Dispossessed: Chronicles of the Desterrados of Colombia
Alfredo Molano • Here in their own words are the stories of the *desterrados*, or "dispossessed"—the thousands of Colombians displaced by years of war and state-backed terrorism, funded in part through US aid to the Colombian government. These gripping stories show the human face of those who suffer the effects of the US "Plan Colombia" and the policies of a state that serves the interests of wealthy landlords instead of the poor. ISBN: 978-1-931859-17-2

Fields of Resistance: The Struggle of Florida's Farmworkers for Justice
Silvia Giagnoni • Migrant farmworkers in the United States are routinely forced to live and work in unsafe, often desperate, conditions. In Immokalee, Florida, the tomato capital of the world—which has earned the dubious distinction of being "ground zero for modern slavery"—farmworkers organized themselves into the Coalition of Immokalee Workers, and launched a nationwide boycott campaign that forced McDonald's, Burger King, and Taco Bell to recognize their demands for workers' rights. ISBN: 978-1-60846-093-9

Hopes and Prospects
Noam Chomsky • In this urgent book, Noam Chomsky exploring challenges such as the growing gap between North and South, American exceptionalism (including under President Barack Obama), the fiascos of Iraq and Afghanistan, the US-Israeli assault on Gaza, and the recent financial bailouts, he also sees hope for the future and a way to move forward—in the democratic wave in Latin America and in the global solidarity movements that suggest "real progress toward freedom and justice." ISBN: ISBN: 978-1-931859-96-7

Imperialism, Neoliberalism, and Social Struggles in Latin America
Richard A. Dello Buono and José Bell Lara • The first part of this collection deals with the intensifying regional crisis created by neoliberal policies. In the second part, a sympathetic yet critical evaluation is offered on the diverse development strategies that have been pursued by four leftist governments in power. The final section considers various aspects of the constraints facing the region along with some of the emerging social movements that seek to radically transform Latin America. ISBN: 978-1-60846-040-3

Live Working or Die Fighting: How the Working Class Went Global

Paul Mason • The stories in this book come to life through the voices of remarkable individuals: child laborers in Dickensian England, visionary women on Parisian barricades, gun-toting railway strikers in America's Wild West, and beer-swilling German metalworkers who tried to stop World War I. *Live Working or Die Fighting* celebrates a common history of defiance, idealism, and self-sacrifice, one as alive and active today as it was two hundred years ago. It is a unique and inspirational book. ISBN: 978-1-60846-070-0

Ours to Master and to Own: Workers' Control from the Commune to the Present

Immanuel Ness and Dario Azzellini • From the dawning of the industrial epoch, wage earners have organized themselves into unions, fought bitter strikes, and even gone so far as to challenge the premises of the system by enacting democratic self-management aimed at controlling production. This pathbreaking volume illuminates this underappreciated and under-investigated aspect of working-class resistance. While capitalism would have us believe we need our bosses, this volume reveals the history of workers who dare to disagree. ISBN: 978-1-60846-119-6

The Politics of Combined and Uneven Development: The Theory of Permanent Revolution

Michael Löwy • Löwy's book is the first attempt to analyze, in a systematic way, how the theories of uneven and combined development and of the permanent revolution emerged in the writings of thinkers such as Karl Marx and Leon Trotsky. These theories allow us to understand how "advanced" and "backward" elements fuse, come into tension, and collide—and how the resulting ruptures make it possible for the oppressed and exploited to change the world. ISBN: 978-1-60846-068-7

El Precio del Fuego: Resource Wars and Social Movements in Bolivia (Español)

Benjamin Dangl • "Ben Dangl takes the reader on an unforgettable and inspiring journey through Bolivia and neighboring countries, providing a window on the revolutionary struggles of the poor and dispossessed."—Roxanne Dubar-Ortiz New social movements have emerged in Bolivia over "the price of fire"—access to the basic elements of life for the impoverished majority. ISBN: 978-1-60846-069-4

Sin Patrón: Stories from Argentina's Worker-Run Factories

Edited by lavaca collective, foreword by Naomi Klein and Avi Lewis • In 2001, the economy of Argentina collapsed. Unemployment reached a quarter of the workforce. Out of these terrible conditions was born a new movement of workers who decided to take matters into their own hands. They took over control of their workplaces, restarted production, and democratically decided how they would organize their work. *Sin Patrón* lets the workers themselves tell their inspiring stories. ISBN: 978-1-931859-43-1

About Haymarket Books

Haymarket Books is a nonprofit, progressive book distributor and publisher, a project of the Center for Economic Research and Social Change. We believe that activists need to take ideas, history, and politics into the many struggles for social justice today. Learning the lessons of past victories, as well as defeats, can arm a new generation of fighters for a better world. As Karl Marx said, "The philosophers have merely interpreted the world; the point, however, is to change it."

We take inspiration and courage from our namesakes, the Haymarket Martyrs, who gave their lives fighting for a better world. Their 1886 struggle for the eight-hour day, which gave us May Day, the international workers' holiday, reminds workers around the world that ordinary people can organize and struggle for their own liberation. These struggles continue today across the globe—struggles against oppression, exploitation, hunger, and poverty.

It was August Spies, one of the Martyrs targeted for being an immigrant and an anarchist, who predicted the battles being fought to this day. "If you think that by hanging us you can stamp out the labor movement," Spies told the judge, "then hang us. Here you will tread upon a spark, but here, and there, and behind you, and in front of you, and everywhere, the flames will blaze up. It is a subterranean fire. You cannot put it out. The ground is on fire upon which you stand."

We could not succeed in our publishing efforts without the generous financial support of our readers. Many people contribute to our project through the Haymarket Sustainers program, where donors receive free books in return for their monetary support. If you would like to be a part of this program, please contact us at info@haymarketbooks.org.

Order these titles and more online at www.haymarketbooks.org or call 773-583-7884.

About the Author

Tieneke E. Dykstra

Jeffery R. Webber is a lecturer in the School of Politics and International Relations at Queen Mary, University of London, and the author of *Red October: Left-Indigenous Struggles in Modern Bolivia*. He is member of the editorial boards of *Historical Materialism* and *Latin American Perspectives*. His articles on Latin American politics have appeared in *Third World Quarterly, Bulletin of Latin American Research, Latin American Research Review, Latin American Politics and Society,* and *Monthly Review,* among other journals. Webber's political commentary appears regularly in the *International Socialist Review, Against the Current, New Socialist, CounterPunch, ZNet, MRZine, The Bullet,* and *Upside Down World.* He splits his time between Europe, Canada, and various countries in Latin America, where he conducts field research annually.

Praise for *From Rebellion to Reform in Bolivia*

"Jeffery Webber has become one of the shrewdest chroniclers of political developments in Latin America. In this exciting new book, Webber looks at the history of the political movements in Bolivia over the last decade, and in particular the MAS movement of President Evo Morales. As the left attempts to find escape routes from neoliberalism, there is a need for sober assessments of what is being accomplished. This book does just that for Bolivia, and makes an outstanding contribution to our understanding of the new Andean left."

— **Gregory Albo, coauthor with Sam Gindin and Leo Panitch of *In and Out of Crisis: The Global Financial Meltdown and Left Alternatives***

"*From Rebellion to Reform in Bolivia* offers a critical examination of complex political processes in Bolivia since 2000 and challenges existing views of Evo Morales's government. The analysis is characterized by exceptional rigor and clarity. Amidst widespread romanticism and ideological confusion, this book is a welcomed expression of sincere and realistic critique from the left—an excellent example of constructive solidarity with anti-imperialist, socialist, and indigenous liberationist struggles. Webber offers a comprehensive, nuanced, and provocative account of the economic agenda, political reforms, foreign policy, intellectual currents, and social movement activity under the Morales administration. It is a valuable book for those who want to understand the contradictions within the 'Left tide' in Latin America."

— **Jasmin Hristov, author of *Blood and Capital: The Paramilitarization of Colombia***

"*From Rebellion to Reform in Bolivia* provides a welcome addition to recent literature on Bolivia. Rather than simply celebrate the rise of 'Bolivia's first indigenous president,' Webber observes that while Morales and the MAS have made strides toward advancing indigenous rights, they have done little to challenge the nature of capitalist relations. His argument that Morales has 'reconstituted' rather than replaced neoliberalism will remind readers of the importance of class analysis in any project that aims to bring about fundamental change."

— **Benjamin Kohl, coauthor with Linda Farthing of *Impasse in Bolivia: Neoliberal Hegemony and Popular Resistance***